"十二五"普通高等教育本科规划教材

材料成型及控制工程专业英语教程

范小红 徐勇 主编

化学工业出版社

·北京·

本书精选了材料成型及控制工程专业不同领域的英文课文，主要内容分为三部分，第一部分为铸造方面的内容，包括材料凝固理论、各种铸造成形方法以及计算机在金属铸造中的应用等；第二部分为塑性成型方面的内容，包括锻造工艺、冲压工艺、塑性成型设备以及计算机辅助工艺设计等；第三部分为焊接方面的内容，主要包括焊接的基本原理、各种焊接工艺、焊缝评价及质量控制等。每节课文后都附有专业技术词汇以及思考题，以利于学生阅读和理解课文，记忆和掌握词汇。

本书既可作为高等院校材料成型与控制工程专业的专业英语教学用书，也可作为相关专业科技人员的参考书。

图书在版编目（CIP）数据

材料成型及控制工程专业英语教程/范小红，徐勇主编.
—北京：化学工业出版社，2013.10（2025.7重印）
"十二五"普通高等教育本科规划教材
ISBN 978-7-122-18412-2

Ⅰ.①材⋯ Ⅱ.①范⋯②徐⋯ Ⅲ.①工程材料-成型-英语-教材 Ⅳ.①H31

中国版本图书馆 CIP 数据核字（2013）第 216114 号

责任编辑：杨　菁　彭喜英　　　　文字编辑：林　丹
责任校对：顾淑云　　　　　　　　装帧设计：杨　北

出版发行：化学工业出版社（北京市东城区青年湖南街 13 号　邮政编码 100011）
印　　装：北京科印技术咨询服务有限公司数码印刷分部
787mm×1092mm　1/16　印张 14¾　字数 382 千字　2025 年 7 月北京第 1 版第 3 次印刷

购书咨询：010-64518888　　　　　　　　售后服务：010-64518899
网　　址：http://www.cip.com.cn
凡购买本书，如有缺损质量问题，本社销售中心负责调换。

定　　价：33.00 元　　　　　　　　　　　　　　　　　　　　版权所有　违者必究

前言

随着经济全球化的发展，国内制造业的产品出口份额迅速增加，同时也涌现了大量的合资及外资企业。加上国有大中型企业产品结构的调整，这些企业作为用人单位，对毕业生的外语提出了更高的要求，精通外语专业已成为对大中型企业工程技术人员的基本要求。

为了满足高等院校材料成型及控制工程专业本、专科教学需要，我们编写了本书。其中精选了铸造、塑性成型、焊接等方面的专业英语课文，并在文后对重要词汇进行了注释，提出了思考题；课文的选用依据覆盖面广、代表性强和短而精的原则，重点突出了与上述三个实际生产应用较多的专业方向有关的经典英语课文。对于材料成型及控制工程领域的专业人员来说也可在生产实践中参考本书。

本书由山东建筑大学范小红、徐勇主编，李静、赵忠魁、任国成、林晓娟、项东参与了教材的编写工作。山东建筑大学的许斌教授认真审阅了本书，并提出了许多宝贵意见。

在本书编写过程中，参考了国内外众多专家和同行的研究成果和著作，在此表示感谢。除所列参考文献之外，还参考了网络媒体上的讲义等文献资料，因这些资料来源难以考证，无法指明其准确出处，编者在此一并向其作者表示衷心的感谢。

由于编者水平有限，书中难免出现纰漏之处，恳请广大读者批评指正。

编 者

2013.11

Contents

Part Ⅰ Casting ········ 001
    Unit 1   Casting Advantages and Applications ········ 003
    Unit 2   Nucleation Kinetics ········ 007
    Unit 3   Basic Concepts in Crystal Growth and Solidification ········ 011
    Unit 4   Solidification of Single-Phase Alloys ········ 015
    Unit 5   Solidification of Eutectics ········ 019
    Unit 6   Classification of Processes and Flow Chart of Foundry Operations ········ 023
    Unit 7   Sand Molding ········ 027
    Unit 8   Investment Casting ········ 031
    Unit 9   Permanent Mold Casting ········ 036
    Unit 10 Die Casting ········ 041
    Unit 11 Centrifugal Casting ········ 046
    Unit 12 Modeling of Solidification Heat Transfer ········ 051
    Unit 13 Modeling of Fluid Flow ········ 056
    Unit 14 Modeling of Combined Fluid Flow and Heat/Mass Transfer ········ 061
    Unit 15 Modeling of Microstructural Evolution ········ 066

Part Ⅱ Forming and Forging ········ 071
    Unit 1   Introduction to Forming and Forging Process ········ 073
    Unit 2   Open-Die Forging ········ 077
    Unit 3   Closed-Die Forging in Hammers and Presses ········ 082
    Unit 4   Extrusion ········ 086
    Unit 5   Precision Forging ········ 091
    Unit 6   Hammers and Presses for Forging ········ 096
    Unit 7   Selection of Forging Equipment ········ 101
    Unit 8   Dies and Die Materials for Hot Forging ········ 106
    Unit 9   Forging Process Design ········ 111
    Unit 10 Modeling Techniques Used in Forging Process Design ········ 116
    Unit 11 Blanking ········ 121
    Unit 12 Piercing ········ 126
    Unit 13 Press-Brake Forming ········ 130
    Unit 14 Deep Drawing ········ 135
    Unit 15 Presses and Auxiliary Equipment for Forming of Sheet Metal ········ 140
    Unit 16 CAD/CAM Applications in sheet Forming ········ 145
    Unit 17 Statistical Analysis of Forming Processes ········ 149

Part Ⅲ Welding ········ 155
    Unit 1   Energy Sources Used for Fusion Welding ········ 157
    Unit 2   Heat Flow in Fusion Welding ········ 162

Unit 3	Fluid Flow Phenomena During Welding	166
Unit 4	Fundamentals of Weld Solidification	171
Unit 5	Shielded Metal Arc Welding	175
Unit 6	Gas-Metal Arc Welding	179
Unit 7	Gas-Tungsten Arc Welding	184
Unit 8	Plasma Arc Welding	189
Unit 9	Electron-Beam Welding	193
Unit 10	Plasma-MIG Welding	197
Unit 11	Friction Welding	202
Unit 12	Brazing Processes	207
Unit 13	Soldering Welding	211
Unit 14	Inspection of Welding	215
Unit 15	Repair Welding	220
Unit 16	Characterization and Modeling of the Heat Source	224

References 229

Part I
Casting

Unit 1

Casting Advantages and Applications

● **Introduction**

Metal Casting is unique among metal forming processes for a variety of reasons. Perhaps the most obvious is the array of molding and casting processes available that are capable of producing complex components in any metal, ranging in weight from less than an ounce to single parts weighing several hundred tons. Foundry processes are available and in use that are economically viable for producing a single prototype part, while others achieve their economies in creating millions of the same part. Virtually any metal that can be melted can and is being cast. This article will examine the advantages of the metal casting process, the major applications of cast components, and the technical and market trends that are shaping the foundry industry and the products it produces.

It is estimated that castings are used in 90% or more of all manufactured goods and in all capital goods machinery used in manufacturing. The diversity in the end use of metal castings is a direct result of the many functional advantages and economic benefits that castings offer compared to other metal forming methods. The beneficial characteristics of a cast component are directly attributable to the inherent versatility of the casting process.

● **Functional Advantages**

Beyond the rapidly emerging technologies that are keeping metal casting in the forefront in the metal forming industry, castings possess many inherent advantages that have long been accepted by the design engineer and metal parts user. In terms of component design, casting offers the greatest amount of flexibility of any metal forming process. The casting process is ideal because it permits the formation of streamlined, intricate, integral parts of strength and rigidity obtainable by no other method of fabrication. The shape and size of the part are primary considerations in design, and in this category, the possibilities of metal castings are unsurpassed. The flexibility of cast metal design gives the engineer wide scope in converting his ideas into an engineered part.

The following list of functional advantages of castings and the metal casting process illustrate why castings have been and continue to be the choice of design engineers and materials specifiers.

Rapid Transition to Finished Product. The casting process involves pouring molten metal into a cavity that is close to the final dimensions of the finished component; therefore, it is the most direct and simplest metal forming method available.

Suiting Shape and Size to Function. Metal castings weighing from less than an ounce to hundreds of tons, in almost any shape or degree of complexity, can be produced. If a pattern can be made for the part, it can be cast.

Placement of Metal for Maximum Effectiveness. With the casting process, the optimum amount of metal can be placed in the best location for maximum strength, wear resistance, or the enhancement of other properties of the finished part. This, together with the ability to core out unstressed sections, can result in appreciable weight savings.

Optimal Appearance. Because shape is not restricted to the assembly of preformed pieces, as in welding processes, or governed by the limitations of forging or stamping, the casting process encourages the development of attractive, more readily marketable designs. The smooth, graduated contours and streamlining that are essential to good design appearance usually coincide with the conditions for easiest molten metal flow during casting. They also prevent stress concentrations upon solidification and minimized residual stress in the final casting.

Complex Parts as an Integral Unit. The inherent design freedom of metal casting allows the designer to combine what would otherwise be several parts of a fabrication into a single, intricate casting. This is significant when exact alignment must be held, as in high-speed machinery, machine tool parts, or engine end plates and housings that carry shafts.

Improved Dependability. The use of good casting design principles, together with periodic determination of mechanical properties of test bars cast from the molten metal, ensures a high degree of reproducibility and dependability in metal castings that is not as practical with other production methods. The functional advantages that metal castings offer and that are required by the designer must be balanced with the economic benefits that the customer demands. The growth of metal casting and its current stability are largely the result of the ability of the foundry industry to maintain this balancing act. The design and production advantages described above bring with them a variety of cost savings that other metal working processes cannot offer. These savings stem from four areas:

- The capability to combine a number of individual parts into a single integral casting, reducing overall fabrication costs.
- The design freedom of casting minimizes machining costs and excess metal.
- Patterns used in casting lower in cost compared to other types of tooling.
- Castings require a comparatively short lead time for production.

For these and because it remains the most direct way to produce a required metal shape, metal casting will continue to be a vitally important metal forming technology. The diversity in end use in castings is also evidence of the flexibility and versatility of the metal casting process. Major casting end uses and market trends are discussed below.

● Casting Market Trends and End Uses

The use of metal castings is pervasive throughout the economies of all developed countries, both as components in finished manufactured goods and as finished durable goods. As indicated earlier, castings are used in 90% of all manufactured goods and in all capital goods machinery used in manufacturing. They are also extensively used in transportation, building construction, municipal water and sewer systems, oil and gas pipelines, and a wide variety of other applications.

Industry Structure. In the broadest sense, foundries are categorized into two general groups: ferrous foundries (those that produce the various alloys of cast iron and cast steel) and nonferrous foundries (those that produce aluminum-base, copper-base, zinc-base, magnesium, and other nonferrous castings).

Ferrous castings shipments are usually classified by market category. For example, iron castings are generally categorized as engineered (designed for specific, differentiated customers) and non-engineered (produced in large volumes of interchangeable units, usually consisting of ingot molds, pressure and soil pipe).

The diversity among the various foundries makes it difficult to determine the exact structure of the industry. For example, it is not unusual for a single operating foundry to produce a variety of metals and alloys, both ferrous and nonferrous, in the same plant. Some also use a variety of processes in their operations. Many aluminum foundries, for instance, use both sand and permanent mold processes, and some event produce die castings in the same facility.

Casting End Uses. Metal castings have a great variety of end uses and are therefore largely taken for granted by the consuming public. Castings are often the hidden components of the machines and other equipment used on a daily basis, such as automobiles, lawn mowers, refrigerators, stoves, typewriters, and computers. Only in rare cases does a consumer make a conscious decision to buy a cast product unless it is readily identifiable, as in the case of cast iron or aluminum cookware, cast iron bathtubs, or ornamental products such as cast bronze sculptures.

Designers of industrial equipment and machinery, on the other hand, have long recognized the performance qualities of castings and regularly specify their use. These functional and economic advantages were described earlier. The major markets for cast products are listed in Table 1-1.

Ranked in order of tonnage shipped. In some cases, the total of "Other major markets" is larger as a whole than the individual markets listed.

Table 1-1 Major markets for metal castings

Gray iron	Ingot molds; Motor vehicles; Farm equipment; Engines; Construction machinery; Valves; Soil pipe; Pumps and compressors; Pressure pipe; Other major markets include machine tools, mechanical power transmission equipment, hardware, home appliances, and mining machinery, oil and natural gas pumping and processing equipment
Malleable iron	Motor vehicles; Valves and fittings; Construction machinery; Railroad equipment; Engines; Mining equipment; Hardware; Other major markets include heating and refrigeration, motors and generators, fasteners, ordnance, chains, machine tools, general industrial machinery
Ductile iron	Pressure pipe; Motor vehicles; Farm machinery; Engines; Pumps and compressors; Valves and fittings; Metalworking machinery; Other major markets include textile machinery, wood working and paper machinery, mechanical power and transmission equipment, motors and generators, refrigeration and heating equipment, air conditioning
Steel	Railroad equipment; Construction equipment; Mining machinery; Valves and fittings; General and special industrial machinery Motor vehicles; Metalworking machinery; Other major markets include steel manufacturing, spring goods, industrial material handling equipment, ships and boats, aircraft and aerospace

Aluminum	Auto and light truck; Aircraft and aerospace; Other transportation; Engines; Household appliances; Office machinery; Power tools; Refrigeration; Other major markets include machine tools, construction equipment, mining equipment, farm machinery, electronic and communication equipment, power systems, motors and generators
Magnesium	Power tools; Sporting goods; Anodes; Automotive; Other major markets include office machinery, health care, aircraft and aerospace
Copper-base	Valves and fittings; Plumbing brass goods; Electrical equipment; Pumps and compressors; Power transmission equipment; General machinery; Transportation equipment; Other major markets include chemical processing, utilities, desalination, petroleum refining
Zinc	Automotive; Building hardware; Electrical components; Machinery; Household appliances; Other major markets include scientific instruments, radio and television equipment, audio components, toys, sporting goods

● Vocabulary

molding   n. 模塑；铸造；装饰用的嵌线
casting   n. 铸造；铸件   v. 铸造
foundry   n. 铸造，铸造类；铸造厂
prototype   n. 原型；标准，模范
streamline   vt. 使合理化；使成流线型
    n. 流线；流线型   adj. 流线型的
pouring   v. 倾泻；倾诉（pour 的 ing 形式）
    n. 浇注
cavity   n. 腔；洞，凹处
finished   adj. 完结的，完成的；精巧的
pattern   n. 模式；图案；样品   vt. 模仿；
    以图案装饰   vi. 形成图案
unstressed   adj. 无应力的
preform   vt. 预先形成   n. 粗加工的成品
forging   n. 锻造；锻件   v. 锻造

stamping   v. 冲压   n. 冲压，冲击制品
fabrication   n. 制造，建造；装配；伪造物
weldment   n. 焊件；焊成件；焊接装配
ferrous   adj. 亚铁的；铁的，含铁的
nonferrous   adj. 非铁的；不含铁的
aluminum   n. 铝
copper   n. 铜；铜币   adj. 铜的   vt. 镀
    铜于
zinc   vt. 镀锌于……；涂锌于……   n. 锌
magnesium   n. 镁
shipment   n. 装货；装载的货物
ingot   n. 锭；铸块
bronze   n. 青铜；青铜制品   adj. 青铜色
    的；青铜制   vt. 镀青铜于
residual stress   残余应力

● Questions

1. Please explain the advantages of the metal casting process.
2. Please talk about the applications of metal casting.

Unit 2
Nucleation Kinetics

Nucleation Processes play a key role in the solidification of castings by controlling to a large extent the initial structure type, size scale, and spatial distribution of the product phases. During many solidification processes, the size scale of critical nucleation events is too small and the rate of their occurrence too rapid for accurate observation by direct methods. Nonetheless, nucleation effects in the solidification microstructure exert a strong influence on the grain size and morphology as well as the compositional homogeneity. The final microstructure is also modified by the crystal growth, fluid flow, and structural coarsening processes that are important in the later stages of ingot freezing.

● **Nucleation Phenomena**

Nucleation during solidification is a thermally activated process involving a fluctuational growth in the sizes of clusters of solids. Changes in cluster size are considered to occur by a single atom addition or by removal exchange between the cluster and the surrounding undercooled liquid. At small cluster sizes, the energetics of cluster formation reveal that the interfacial energy is dominant, as can be observed by noting that the ratio of surface area to volume of a sphere is $r/3$. For the smallest sizes, clusters are called embryos; these are more likely to dissolve than grow to macroscopic crystals. In fact, the excess interfacial energy due to the curvature of small clusters is the main contribution to the activation barrier for solid nucleation. This accounts for the kinetic resistance of liquids to crystallization and is manifested in the frequent observation of undercooling effects during solidification.

● **Homogeneous Nucleation**

The principal features of nucleation phenomena and the kinetics of the rate process during solidification can be illustrated in the simplest terms by using the capillarity model to evaluate the kinetic factors. With this approach, it is useful to examine first the case of homogeneous nucleation in which solid formation occurs without the involvement of any extraneous impurity atoms or other surface sites in contact with the melt. As a further simplification, only the case of isotropic interfacial energy is treated, but it should be recognized that anisotropic behavior can yield faceted cluster shapes. The energetics of cluster formation for a spherical geometry can be expressed in terms of a surface and a volume contribution as:

$$\Delta G(r) = 4\pi r^2 \sigma + \frac{4}{3}\pi r^3 \Delta G_v \tag{1-1}$$

where $\Delta G(r)$ is the free energy change to form a cluster of size r and $\Delta G_v = \Delta H_f \Delta T / T_f V_m$. The relationship in Eq (1-1) is characterized in Fig. 1-1, in which the activation barrier for nucleation, ΔG_{cr}, is reached at a critical size r_{cr} (that is, $d\Delta G(r)/dr = 0$), as given by:

$$r_{cr} = \frac{2\sigma}{\Delta G_v} = \frac{2\sigma T_f V_m}{\Delta H_f \Delta T} \qquad (1-2)$$

$$\Delta G_{cr} = \frac{16\pi\sigma^3}{3\Delta G_v^2} = \frac{16\pi\sigma^3 T_f V_m^2}{3\Delta H_f^2 \Delta T^2} \qquad (1-3)$$

At increasing values of undercooling, r_{cr} is reduced ($r_{cr} \propto \Delta T^{-1}$) and G_{cr} is reduced more rapidly ($\Delta G_{cr} \propto \Delta T^{-2}$). A cluster is often considered to reach the stage of a nucleus capable of continued growth with a decreasing free energy when the size r_{cr} is achieved, but in fact stable nucleus growth ensues when the cluster size exceeds r_{cr} by an amount corresponding to ($\Delta G_{cr} - kT$) in Fig. 1-1. The relationship between cluster size and the number of atoms in a cluster, n_{cr}, is expressed by $(n_{cr} V_a) = \frac{4}{3}\pi r_{cr}^3/3$ $(n_{cr} V_a)$, where V_a is the atomic volume.

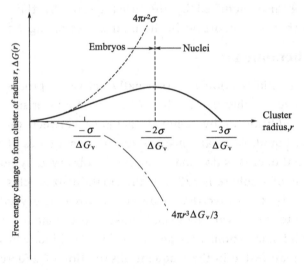

Fig. 1-1 Free energy change for cluster formation as a function of cluster size

● Heterogeneous Nucleation

Homogeneous nucleation is the most difficult kinetic path to crystal formation because of the relatively large activation barrier for nucleus development (ΔG_{cr}). To overcome this barrier, classical theory predicts that large undercooling values are required, but in practice an undercooling of only a few degrees or less is the common observation with most castings. This behavior is accounted for by the operation of heterogeneous nucleation in which foreign bodies such as impurity inclusions, oxide films, or crucible walls act to promote crystallization by lowering ΔG_{cr}. Because only a single nucleation event is required for the freezing of a liquid volume, the likelihood of finding a heterogeneous nucleation site in contact with a bulk liquid is great. Indeed, it has been estimated that even in a sample of high-purity liquid metal there is a nucleant particle concentration of the order of about $10^{12} m^{-3}$. Only by using special sample preparation methods to isolate the melt from internal and external nucleation sites by subdivision into a fine droplet dispersion has it been possible to achieve undercoolings in the range of 0.3 to $0.4T_f$.

The action of heterogeneous nucleation in promoting crystallization can be visualized in terms of the nucleus volume that is substituted by the existing nucleant, as illustrated schematically in Fig. 1-2. For a nucleus that wets a heterogeneous nucleation site with a contact angle θ, the degree of wetting can be assessed in terms of $\cos\theta = (\sigma_{nL} - \sigma_{nS})/\sigma_{LS}$, where the interfacial energies are defined in Fig. 1-2. As θ approaches 0, complete wetting develops; as θ approaches 180°, there is no wetting between the nucleus and the nucleant (which is inert), and the conditions approach homogeneous nucleation.

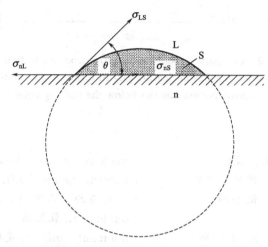

Fig. 1-2 The interfacial energy, σ, relationships among a planar nucleant substrate (n), a spherical sector solid (S), and the liquid (L)

The energetics of heterogeneous nucleation can be described by a modification of Eq (1-1) to account for the different interfaces and the modified cluster volume involved in nucleus formation. In terms of the cluster formation shown in Fig. 1-2, the free energy change during heterogeneous nucleation is expressed by:

$$\Delta G(r)_{het} = V_{SC}\Delta G_v + A_{SL}\sigma_{SL} + A_{nS}\sigma_{nS} - A_{nL}\sigma_{nL} \qquad (1-4)$$

where V_{SC} is the spherical cap volume and A_{SL}, A_{nS}, and A_{nL}, are the solid-liquid, nucleant-solid, and nucleant-liquid interfacial areas, respectively. When the volume and relevant interfacial areas are expressed in terms of the geometry of Fig. 1-2, the evaluation of ΔG_{cr} for heterogeneous nucleation yields:

$$\Delta G_{cr}(het) = \frac{16\pi\sigma_{LS}^3}{3\Delta_v^2}\left[\frac{2 - 3\cos\theta + \cos^3\theta}{4}\right] = \Delta G_{cr}(hom)[f(\theta)] \qquad (1-5)$$

The comparison between heterogeneous and homogeneous nucleation kinetics is illustrated in Fig. 1-3 by a schematic time-temperature transformation diagram. Although only a single transformation curve (that is, C-curve) is shown in Fig. 1-3 for heterogeneous nucleation, in reality there will be as many curves as the number of heterogeneous nucleation sites. Each curve for heterogeneous nucleation will be distinguished by a catalytic potency, that is, $f(\theta)$ and a site density. To attain homogeneous nucleation conditions, it is clear that all heterogeneous nucleation sites must be removed or bypassed kinetically.

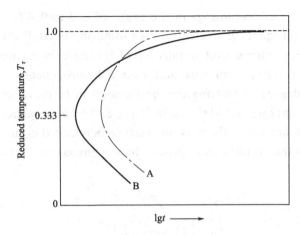

Fig. 1-3 Comparison between heterogeneous nucleation (A) and homogeneous nucleation (B) in terms of the relative transformation kinetics below the melting point

● Vocabulary

nucleation　　n. 成核现象；成核
solidification　　n. 凝固；团结；浓缩
undercooling　　n. 过冷；低冷却
　　vt. 使……过度冷却
supercooling　　n. 过冷　v. 使过冷
fluctuational　　n. 起伏，波动
crystallization　　n. 结晶化；具体化
anisotropic　　adj. 各向异性的；非均质的
homogeneous　　adj. 均匀的；奇次的；同种的

nucleus　　n. 核，核心；原子核
heterogeneous　　adj. 多相的；异种的；不均匀的；由不同成分形成的
oxide　　n. 氧化物
nucleant　　adj. 形成核的
transformation　　n. 转化；转换；改革；变形
catalytic　　adj. 接触反应的；起催化作用的
　　n. 催化剂；刺激因素

● Questions

1. Please tell the principal features of nucleation phenomena.
2. Please tell the difference between heterogeneous and homogeneous nucleation.

Unit 3

Basic Concepts in Crystal Growth and Solidification

Crystal Growth and Solidification in metal castings is largely a function of atomic mobility. Thermal and kinetic factors must be considered when determining whether crystal growth will be inhibited or accelerated. Whether spherical or needle-like in configuration, the metal particles behave differently depending on their location within the composition: in the liquid, at the liquid/solid interface, or in the solid.

● Liquid and Solid State

Atomic Mobility. The solidification of metals results in an enormous and abrupt decrease in atomic mobility. The dynamic viscosity η of pure liquid metals near their melting temperature T_f is comparable to that of water at room temperature, that is, of the order of 10^{-3} Pa·s (10^{-2} P), as shown in both Table 1-2. On the other hand, the following observations can be made:

- In the solid state, metals and alloys have a high tensile strength.
- Pure metals resist stresses of the order of 10^4 Pa (1.5psi) near the melting point.
- The decrease in ductility of commercial alloys several hundred degrees below the solidus temperature is due to the presence of liquid films in the segregated zones.

Table 1-2 Physical properties of pure metals relevant to solidification

Property	Iron (δ)	Copper	Aluminum
Dynamic viscosity η of liquid at $T_f/10^{-3}$ Pa·s	5.03	3.05	1.235
Melting point, T_f/K	1809	1356	933
Enthalpy of fusion per mole/(J/mol)	13.807	13.263	10.711
Enthalpy of fusion per volume/(10^9 J/m³)	1.93	1.62	0.95
Heat capacity C_P of liquid at $T_f/[10^6 J/(K·m^3)]$	5.74	3.96	2.58
Heat capacity C_P of solid at $T_f/[10^6 J/(K·m^3)]$	5.73	3.63	3.0
Thermal conductivity of liquid K_L at $T_f/[W/(m·K)]$	35	166	95
Thermal conductivity of solid K_S at $T_f/[W/(m·K)]$	33	244	210
Thermal diffusivity of liquid α_L at $T_f/(10^{-6} m^2/s)$	6.1	42	37

Heat release. during solidification is large—approximately 270MJ/tonne for steel. The higher the melting point of the metal, the larger the latent heat of fusion (Table 1-2). Therefore, solidification processing is initially a matter of extracting large quantities of heat quickly.

Solidification Shrinkage. Most metals shrink when they solidify. Solidification shrinkage ranges from 3% to 8% for pure metals (Table 1-2). It may result in the formation of voids (microporosity and shrinkage) during solidification. Thermal contraction of the solid during subsequent cooling may increase the risk of shrinkage if care is not exercised in casting of the metal.

Solubility. When the heterogeneous thermodynamic equilibrium between liquid and solid is achieved, most crystalline solid solutions contain a smaller amount of each solute than the related liquid solutions. This difference in composition, combined with slow solid-state diffusion, results in various segregation patterns in cast alloys.

● Solid/Liquid Interface

The first models to describe the solid/liquid interface and its motion at the atomic scale were strongly influenced by the physical models that successfully describe the behavior of the crystal/vapor surfaces. Crystal growth from the vapor can proceed either by two-dimensional nucleation or by lateral motion in steps of atomic height around screw dislocations emerging at the surface. This is because these surfaces are atomically sharp. In this case, the average thermal energy available for the surface atoms to escape from the crystal (that is, RT, where R is the gas constant) is too small compared to the difference in cohesive energy between crystal and vapor (that is, the enthalpy of sublimation per mole ΔH_s). Physicists relate the sharpness of the crystal/vapor surfaces to the high value of the ratio $\Delta H_s/(RT)$.

Interface Equilibrium. The solid/liquid interfacial tension can be considered excess energy associated with any area of the solid/liquid interface. It causes the change in equilibrium melting point, often called Gibbs-Thomson undercooling, when the interface is curved. For pure substances, this curvature undercooling ΔT_k is given by:

$$\Delta T_k = T_f - Tf_k = \Gamma K \tag{1-6}$$

where Tf_k is the equilibrium temperature between liquid and solid across an interface whose curvature is K and where Γ is the Gibbs-Thomson coefficient. The curvature can be expressed as:

$$k = \frac{1}{r_1} + \frac{1}{r_2} \tag{1-7}$$

where r_1 and r_2 are the principal radii of curvature; K is defined such that a positive undercooling is associated with a portion of the solid/liquid interface that is convex toward the liquid.

The Gibbs-Thomson coefficient is given by:

$$\Gamma = \frac{\sigma V_m}{\Delta S_f} \tag{1-8}$$

where V_m is the molar volume of the solid and ΔS_f is the entropy of fusion per mole.

Interface Kinetics. Solidification can be described as a succession of atomic events that occur in series; it includes heterogeneous chemical reactions at the interface. At a diffuse interface, as for pure metals, liquid atoms can become solid atoms at almost every lattice site. The interface then moves more or less continuously, and the growth is said to be continuous. The kinetics of continuous growth have been described by using the rate theory of classical chemistry. This theory leads to the following estimate for the kinetic undercooling

ΔT_k in the case of pure substances:

$$\Delta T_k = Tf_k - T^* = \left(\frac{a}{D_L}\right)\left(\frac{RT_f}{\Delta S_f}\right)v \quad (1\text{-}9)$$

where Tf_k is the equilibrium temperature defined by Eq (1-6), T^* is the actual temperature of the moving interface, D_L is the liquid diffusivity, a is the atomic distance between the crystallographic planes parallel to the interface, and v is the velocity of the interface.

● **Mass and Heat Transport**

Solidification typically involves heat and mass transport phenomena on the micro- and macroscopic levels. Because this Section is devoted to the formation of microstructures in cast metals, this discussion will focus on the problems of microscopic heat and mass transfer near the interface.

From the viewpoint of mass transfer, it is useful to distinguish among the zones of plane front solidification illustrated in Fig. 1-4 (a) and (b).

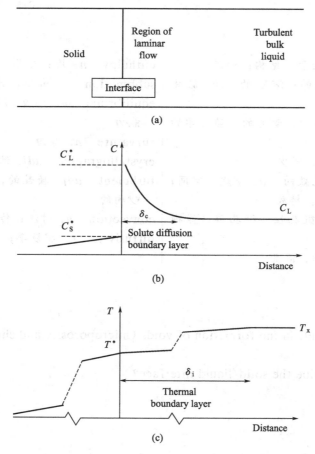

Fig. 1-4 Constrained growth during plane front solidification (a) and schematic profiles of solute concentration (b) and temperature (c)

- The solid, where only diffusion is effective, although it is usually very slow.
- The interface, where heterogeneous chemical reactions occur.
- A boundary layer of thickness δ_i in the liquid, where diffusion is the only mecha-

nism effective for solute i to move perpendicular to the interface.
- The bulk liquid, where convection is also effective.

In the case of plane front solidification, the thickness of the diffusion boundary layer, when controlled by turbulent convection, can be estimated as follows (in SI units):

$$\delta_i = 5.6 \times 10^{-3} L^{0.1} \left(\frac{\eta}{\rho_L}\right)^{0.57} D_{L_i}^{0.33} U^{-0.9} \qquad (1\text{-}10)$$

where L is a characteristic length for the convective flow parallel to the interface, η is the dynamic viscosity of liquid, ρ_L is the density of liquid, and U is the mean liquid velocity parallel to the interface.

From the viewpoint of heat transfer, one can discern three separate zones: the solid, the thermal boundary layer in the liquid, and the bulk liquid. The thickness of the thermal boundary layer δ_t can be calculated as for δ_i by substituting α_L for D_L in Eq (1-10). Because thermal diffusivities α are much larger than chemical diffusion coefficients for metals, the thermal boundary layer is always thicker (by a factor of 10) than the diffusion boundary layer.

● Vocabulary

configuration　*n.* 配置；结构；外形
melting　*adj.* 熔化的；溶解的　*v.* 熔化
　（melt 的 ing 形式）
dynamic　*adj.* 动态的；动力的；动力学的
　n. 动态；动力
shrinkage　*n.* 收缩；减少
void　*adj.* 空的；无效的　*n.* 空虚；空间；
　空隙　*vt.* 使无效；排放
microporosity　*n.* 微孔性；微孔率；显微
　疏松
dislocation　*n.* 转位；混乱

enthalpy　*n.* 焓；热函；热含量
sublimation　*n.* 升华，升华作用；升华物
equilibrium　*n.* 均衡；平静；保持平衡的
　能力
curvature　*n.* 弯曲
crystallographic　*adj.* 结晶的
turbulent　*adj.* 骚乱的，混乱的；狂暴的；
　吵闹的
convection　*n.* 对流；传送
diffusivity　*n.* 扩散率；扩散性

● Questions

1. What can result in the formation of voids (microporosity and shrinkage) during solidification?
2. How to describe the solid/liquid interface?

Unit 4
Solidification of Single-Phase Alloys

The solidification process by which a liquid metal freezes in a mold plays a critical role in determining the properties of the as-cast alloy. Even when the final object is obtained by the mechanical forming of ingots, the solidification structures of ingots often influence the properties of the object.

Two important factors that control solidification microstructures are the composition of the alloy and the heat flow conditions in the mold. These two factors will be described first, and their influence on the microstructure and the accompanying solute segregation profiles will then be discussed in this section.

● Alloy Composition

An alloy consists of a base metal to which other elements are added to give the desired properties. In this discussion, only binary alloys that solidify into a single-phase structure will be considered. When an element is added to the base metal, it significantly alters the solidification process. A pure metal has a specific melting point T_m, while an alloy freezes over a range of temperatures. This freezing range is generally represented by a phase diagram, as shown in Fig. 1-5. The liquidus line represents the temperature at which the liquid alloy begins to freeze, and the freezing process is complete when the solidus temperature is reached, if the solidification occurs close to equilibrium conditions or below the solidus under nonequilibrium conditions.

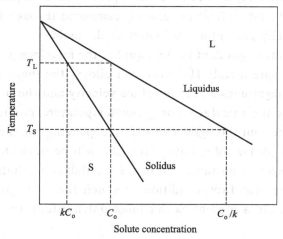

Fig. 1-5 A single-phase region of a phase diagram showing the liquidus and the solidus lines

When an alloy of uniform liquid composition C_o is cooled, it begins to solidify when the temperature of the liquid reaches the liquidus temperature T_L, if nucleation occurs readily. The composition of the solid that forms at T_L will be different from the composition of the liquid, and it is given by the composition on the solidus line at temperature T_L, as shown in Fig. 1-5. The ratio of the solid to liquid composition at a given temperature is called the solute distribution coefficient k. For dilute solutions, the solidus and the liquidus lines are generally assumed to be straight lines in which case k is a constant that does not depend on temperature. Fig. 1-5 shows a phase diagram in which $k < 1$.

The first solid that forms at temperature T_L will have a composition kC_0, which is lower than the liquid composition C_0. Thus, the excess solute rejected by the solid will give rise to a solute-rich liquid layer at the interface. As the alloy is cooled further, the liquid composition increases. This increase in liquid composition, along with the lowering of temperature, gives rise to solute segregation patterns in the solid if the diffusion of solute in the solid is not very rapid.

The buildup of solute in liquid requires diffusion of solute in liquid for further growth. For efficient distribution of the solute in liquid, the interface may change its shape. Thus, the actual solute segregation pattern is dictated by the shape of the interface. In addition to the solute transfer, the interface shape is governed by the effective removal of the latent heat of fusion. This heat flow problem will be described below.

● Heat Flow Conditions

The thermal field in a casting is very important in determining the microstructure of the cast alloy. Two distinctly different heat flow conditions may exist in a mold.

In the first case, the temperature gradients in the liquid and the solid are positive such that the latent heat generated at the interface is dissipated through the solid. Such a temperature field gives rise to directional solidification and results in the columnar zone in a casting.

In the second case, an equiaxed zone exists if the liquid surrounding the solid is undercooled so that a negative temperature gradient is present in the liquid at the solid/liquid interface. In this case, the latent heat of fusion is dissipated through the liquid. Such a thermal condition is generally present at the center of the mold.

A positive temperature gradient in the liquid at the interface gives rise to a planar solid/liquid interface for pure metals. However, for alloys, the shape of the interface is dictated by the relative magnitudes of the interface velocity and the temperature gradients in the solid and liquid at the interface. For given temperature gradients and composition, four different interface morphologies can exist, depending on the velocity. Below some critical velocity v_{cr}, a planar solid/liquid interface will be present. However, above v_{cr}, the planar interface becomes unstable and forms a cellular, a cellular dendritic, or a dendritic interface. For the heat flow condition in which the solid grows in an undercooled melt, a dendritic structure is present. Such equiaxed dendrites form for pure metals as well as for alloys.

● Interface Velocity Below Critical Velocity

Planar interface growth occurs only under directional solidification conditions and, for alloys, only under low growth rate or high-temperature gradient conditions. To describe quantitatively the condition under which a planar interface growth can occur, consider an interface that is moving at a constant velocity v, with heat flowing from the liquid to the solid under temperature gradients G_L and G_S in liquid and solid, respectively, at the interface. Under steady-state growth conditions, the interface temperature corresponds to the solidus temperature T_S in Fig. 1-6. At this temperature, the interface composition in liquid is C_o/k, which is larger (for $k < 1$) than the liquid composition C_o far from the interface so that a solute-rich layer exists in the liquid ahead of the interface (Fig. 1-6). This liquid composition profile gives rise to a variation in the liquidus temperature with distance, as indicated by T_f in Fig. 1-6. If the actual liquid temperature lies below the liquidus profile, a region of supercooled liquid is present ahead of the interface. This supercooled region is indicated in Fig. 1-6.

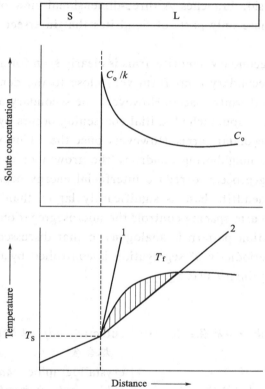

Fig. 1-6 Constitutional supercooling diagram. The solute concentration profile in the liquid gives rise to the variation in the equilibrium freezing temperature T_f of liquid near the interface. The actual temperature in liquid is given by line 1, and the slope of T_f at the interface is given by line 2

● Interface Velocity Exceeding Critical Velocity

Cellular and Cellular Dendritic Structures. Under directional solidification conditions, a cellular or a cellular dendritic interface is observed when the interface velocity exceeds the critical velocity for the planar interface growth. For velocities just above v_{cr}, the cellular structures that form have two important characteristics. First, the length of the cell is small, and it is of the same order of magnitude as the cell spacing. Second, the tip region of the cell is broader, and the cell has a larger tip radius. At higher velocities, a cellular dendritic structure forms in which the length of the cell is much larger than the cell spacing. Also, the cell tip assumes a sharper, nearly parabolic shape, which is similar to the dendrite tip shape so that the term cellular dendritic is used to characterize this structure.

Cellular structures are observed in castings only for heat flow conditions that produce directional solidification and for alloys with very small freezing ranges. Thus, cellular structures are important for very dilute alloys or for alloys that are close to the eutectic composition.

Dendritic Structures. A dendritic structure is formed when the interface velocity is increased beyond the cellular dendritic regime. Dendritic structures are characterized by the formation of side branches. These side branches, as well as the primary dendrite, grow in a preferred crystallographic direction, for example, ⟨100⟩ for cubic metals, so that cubic metals exhibit fourfold side branches. A three-dimensional view of dendrites in metals is difficult to observe because only parts of dendrites that intersect the plane of polish are visible.

The formation of secondary dendrite arms is clearly seen for a dendritic structure in a transparent alloy. The secondary arms form very close to the dendrite tip, and the first few side branches are uniformly spaced. However, the secondary arm spacing increases as the base of the dendrite is approached. Initial coarsening occurs by the competition in the growth process among secondary arms. However, once the diffusion fields of their tips interact with those of the neighboring dendrite, the growth of the secondary arms is reduced, and a coarsening process to reduce interfacial energy begins. The final secondary arm spacing near the dendrite base is significantly larger than that near the dendrite tip. This final secondary arm spacing controls the microsegregation profile in the solidified alloy. This microsegregation pattern is analogous to that discussed for the cellular structure, except that the periodicity of segregation is controlled by the final secondary arm spacing and not by the primary spacing.

● **Vocabulary**

freeze *vi.* 冻结 *vt.* 使……冻住；使……结冰 *n.* 冻结；凝固
ingot *n.* 锭；铸块
as-cast *n.* 毛坯铸件；*adj.* 铸的
liquidus *n.* 液相线；*adj.* 液体的，液态的
nonequilibrium *n.* 非平衡态 *adj.* 不平衡的
columnar *adj.* 柱状的；圆柱的
dendritic *adj.* 树枝状的；树状的
microsegregation *n.* 显微偏析
eutectic *adj.* 共熔的；容易溶解的 *n.* 共熔合金
crystallographic *adj.* 结晶的
cubic *adj.* 立方体的，立方的
intersect *vi.* 相交，交叉 *vt.* 横断，横切；贯穿
coarsen *vt.* 使变粗 *vi.* 变粗糙
interfacial *adj.* 界面的
supercooled *adj.* 过冷的 *v.* 过冷（supercool 的过去分词）

● **Questions**

1. What are the factors that control solidification microstructures in the mold?
2. Which condition can cause planar interface growth?

Unit 5
Solidification of Eutectics

Alloys of eutectic composition make up the bulk of cast metals. The reason for their widespread use can be found in the unique combination of good castability (comparable to that of pure metals), relatively low melting point (minimizing the energy required for production), and interesting behavior as "composite" materials.

● **Eutectic Morphologies**

Eutectic structures are characterized by the simultaneous growth of two or more phases from the liquid. Three or even four phases are sometimes observed growing simultaneously from the melt. However, because most technologically useful eutectic alloys are composed of two phases, only this type will be discussed in this section. Eutectic alloys exhibit a wide variety of microstructures, which can be classified according to two criteria:
- Lamellar or fibrous morphology of the phases.
- Regular or irregular growth.

Lamellar and Fibrous Eutectics. When there are approximately equal volume fractions of the phases (nearly symmetrical phase diagram), eutectic alloys generally have a lamellar structure, for example, Al-Al_2Cu. On the other hand, if one phase is present in a small volume fraction, this phase will in most cases tend to form fibers, for example molybdenum in NiAl-Mo.

In general, the microstructure obtained will usually be fibrous when the volume fraction of the minor phase is lower than 0.25, and it will be lamellar otherwise. This is because of the small separation of the eutectic phases (typically several microns) and the resulting large interfacial area (of the order of $1m^2/cm^3$) that exists between the two solid phases. The system will therefore tend to minimize its interfacial energy by choosing the morphology that leads to the lowest total interface area. For a given spacing (imposed by growth conditions), the interface area is smaller for fibers than for lamellae at volume fractions below 0.25. However, when the minor phase is faceted, a lamellar structure may be formed even at a very low volume fraction, because the interfacial energy is then considerably lower along specific planes, along which the lamellae can be aligned. This is the case in gray cast iron, where the

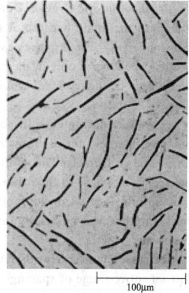

Fig. 1-7 Microstructure of a gray cast iron showing flake graphite

volume fraction of the graphite lamellae is 7.4% (Fig. 1-7).

Regular and Irregular Eutectics. If both phases are nonfaceted (usually when both are metallic), the eutectic will exhibit a regular morphology. The microstructure is then made up of lamellae or fibers having a high degree of regularity and periodicity, particularly in unidirectionally solidified specimens.

On the other hand, if one phase is faceted, the eutectic morphology often becomes irregular. This is because the faceted phase grows preferentially in a direction determined by specific atomic planes. Because the various faceted lamellae have no common crystal orientation, their growth directions are not parallel, and the formation of a regular microstructure becomes impossible. The two eutectic alloys of greatest practical importance—iron-carbon (cast iron) and aluminum-silicon—belong to this category.

Although the examination of metallographic sections of irregular eutectics seems to reveal many dispersed lamellae of the minor phase, these lamellae are generally interconnected in a complex three-dimensional arrangement. In the foundry literature, such eutectic grains are often referred to as eutectic cells.

● Solidification and Scale of Eutectic Structures

Fig. 1-8 shows a schematic eutectic phase diagram. When a liquid L of eutectic composition C_E is frozen, the α and β solid phases solidify simultaneously when the temperature of the melt is below the eutectic temperature T_E. A variety of geometrical arrangements can be produced. For simplicity, the case of a lamellar microstructure is considered in this discussion; the solidification of fibers can be described in terms of similar mechanisms. Because eutectic growth is essentially solute diffusion controlled, there is no fundamental difference between equiaxed and directional solidification. Therefore, the mechanisms described are valid for both cases.

Regular Eutectic Growth. During eutectic solidification, the growing α phase rejects B atoms into the liquid because of their lower solubility with respect to the liquid concentration. Conversely, the β phase rejects A atoms. If the α and β phases grow separately, solute rejection would occur only in the growth direction. This involves long-range diffusion. Therefore, a very large boundary layer would be created in the liquid ahead of the solid/liquid interface.

However, during eutectic solidification, the α and β phases grow side by side in a cooperative manner; the B atoms rejected by the α phase are needed for the growth of the β phase, and conversely. The solute then needs only to diffuse along the solid/liquid interface from one phase to the other. The solute buildup in the liquid ahead of the growing solid/liquid interface is considerably lowered by this sidewise diffusion (diffusion coupling), thus being thermodynamically favorable. This is the fundamental reason for the occurrence of eutectic growth.

Irregular Eutectic Growth. Irregular eutectics grown under given growth conditions exhibit an entire range of spacings because the growth direction of the faceted phase (for example, graphite in cast iron or silicon in aluminum-silicon) is determined by specific atomic orientations and is not necessarily parallel to the heat flux. In this case, growth involves the following mechanism: When two lamellae converge, the growth of one simply ceases

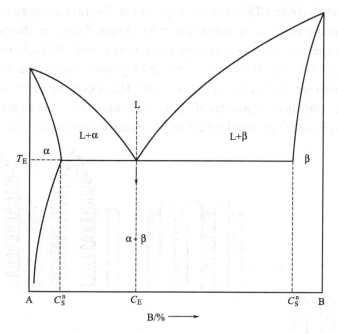

Fig. 1-8 Schematic eutectic phase diagram

when λ becomes smaller than a critical spacing λ_{min} because the local interface energy becomes too large. Thus, the spacing is increased. Conversely, diverging lamellae can grow until another critical spacing, λ_{br}, is reached. When this occurs, one of the lamellae branches into two diverging lamellae, thus reducing the spacing. Growth of an irregular eutectic thus occurs within the range of interlamellar spacings between λ_{min} and λ_{br}.

● Competitive Growth of Dendrites and Eutectics

The solidification of a binary alloy of exactly eutectic composition was examined earlier in this section. In this case, provided the growth is regular, the solid/liquid interface is planar. However, when alloy composition departs from eutectic or when a third alloying element is present, the interface can become unstable for the same reason as in the case of a simple solid/liquid interface. As shown in Fig. 1-9, two types of morphological instability can develop: single-phase and two-phase.

A single-phase instability [Fig. 1-9 (a)] leads to the solidification of one of the phases in the form of primary dendrites plus interdendritic eutectic. This situation is primarily observed in off-eutectic alloys because one phase becomes much more constitutionally undercooled than the other. For example, during the solidification of a hypoeutectic alloy, the α phase is heavily undercooled because the liquidus temperature at that composition is much higher than T_E (Fig. 1-8). The α phase can therefore grow faster (or at higher temperature) than the eutectic.

A two-phase instability [Fig. 1-9 (b)] is characterized by cellular-like growth and leads to the appearance of eutectic colonies. This situation is observed when a third alloying element that partitions similarly at both the α/L and β/L interfaces produces a long-range diffusion boundary layer ahead of the solid/liquid interface, thus making the growing eutectic interface constitutionally undercooled with respect to this element.

Coupled Zone of Eutectics. The eutectic-type phase diagram appears to indicate that microstructures consisting entirely of eutectic can be obtained only at the exact eutectic composition. In fact, experimental observations show that purely eutectic microstructures can be obtained from off-eutectic alloys over a range of growth conditions. On the other hand, dendrites can sometimes be found in alloys with the exact eutectic composition if the growth rate is high. This is of considerable practical importance because the properties of a casting can be significantly changed when single-phase dendrites appear.

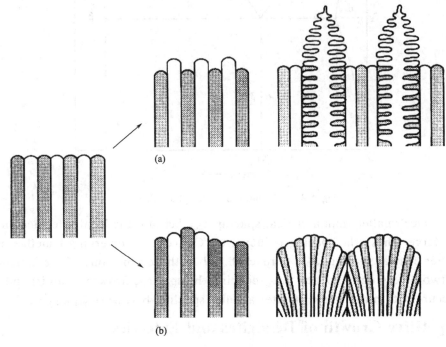

Fig. 1-9 Types of instability of a planar solid/liquid eutectic interface
(a) Single-phase instability leading to the appearance of dendrites of one phase.
(b) Two-phase instability leading to the appearance of eutectic cells or
colonies in the presence of a third alloying element

● Vocabulary

castability   n. 铸造性能；可铸性
lamellar   adj. 薄片状的；薄层状的
fiber   n. 纤维；光纤
graphite   n. 石墨；黑铅   vt. 用石墨涂
（或掺入等）
morphology   n. 形态学，形态论
metallic   adj. 金属的，含金属的

atomic   adj. 原子的，原子能的；微粒子的
metallographic   adj. 金相学的，金相的
equiaxed   adj. 各向等大的
thermodynamic   adj. 热力学的；使用热动力的
interlamellar   adj. 层间的；叶间的
interdendritic   adj. 枝晶间，树枝晶间的

● Questions

1. Please tell the mechanisms of equiaxed and directional solidification.
2. Please tell the mechanism of irregular eutectic growth.

Unit 6

Classification of Processes and Flow Chart of Foundry Operations

    Casting Processes have existed since prehistoric times. Over the years a wide variety of molding and casting methods have been developed, because the only limitation is human ingenuity. These methods will be introduced and classified in this article.

● **Casting Processes**

    Fig. 1-10 shows a simplified flow diagram of the basic operations for producing a sand casting. There are variations from this flow sheet depending on the type of material cast, the complexity of the component shape, and the quality requirements established by the customer. There are also many alternative methods of accomplishing each of these tasks.

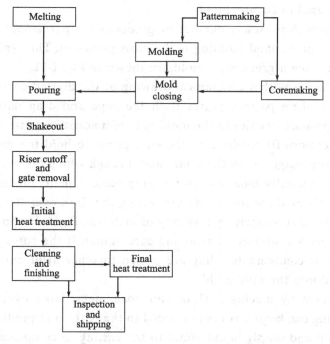

Fig. 1-10 Simplified flow diagram of the basic operations for producing a steel casting

    The right side of Fig. 1-10 begins with the task of patternmaking. A pattern is a specially made model of the component to be produced, used for producing molds.

    Generally, sand is placed around the pattern and, in the case of clay-bonded sand, rammed to the desired hardness. In the case of chemical binders, the mold is chemically hardened after light manual or machine compaction. Molds are usually produced in two halves so that the pattern can be easily removed. When these two halves are reassembled, a cavity remains inside the mold in the shape of the pattern.

Internal passageways within a casting are formed by the use of cores. Cores are parts made of sand and binder that are sufficiently hard and strong to be inserted in a mold. Thus, the cores shape the interior of a casting, which cannot be shaped by the pattern itself. The patternmaker supplies core boxes for the production of precisely dimensioned cores. These core boxes are filled with specially bonded core sand and compacted much like the mold itself. Cores are placed in the drag, or bottom section, of the mold, and the mold is then closed by placing the cope, or top section, over the drag. Mold closing completes the production of the mold, into which the molten metal is then poured.

Casting production begins with melting of the metal (left side, Fig. 1-10). Molten metal is then tapped from the melting furnace into a ladle for pouring into the mold cavity, where it is allowed to solidify within the space defined by the sand mold and cores.

● Classification of Molding and Casting Processes

Foundry processes can be classified based on whether the molds are permanent or expendable. Similarly, subclassifications can be developed from patterns, that is, whether or not the patterns are expendable. A second subclassification can be based on the type of bond used to make the mold. For permanent molding, processes can be classified by the type of mechanism used to fill the mold.

Permanent Pattern Processes. A number of processes use permanent patterns. Of these processes, however, green sand molding is the most prevalent. The typical steps involved in making a casting from a green sand mold are shown in Fig. 1-11.

The sequence begins with a mechanical drawing of the desired part. Patterns are then produced and mounted on pattern plates. Both the cope and drag patterns include core prints, which will produce cavities in the mold to accommodate extensions on either end of the core. These extensions fit solidly into the core prints to hold the core in place during pouring. The gate or passageway in the sand mold through which the molten metal will enter the mold cavity is usually mounted on the drag pattern plate. Locating pins on either end of the pattern plates allow for accurately setting the flask over the plate.

Cores are produced separately by a variety of methods. Fig. 1-11 shows the core boxes, which are rammed with a mixture of sand and core binder. If the cores must be assembled from separately made components, they are pasted together after curing. They are then ready to be inserted into the sand mold.

The mold is made by placing a flask (an open metal box) over the cope pattern plate. Before molding can begin, risers are added to the pattern at predetermined points to control solidification and supply liquid metal to the casting to compensate for the shrinkage that takes place during cooling and solidification. Thus, any shrinkage voids form in the risers, and the casting will be sound. A hole or holes (called sprues) must also be formed in the cope section of the mold to provide a channel through which the molten metal can enter the gating system and the mold cavity.

The cope half of the mold is produced by ramming sand into the flask, which is located on the pattern plate with pins. The flask full of sand is then drawn away from the pattern board, and the riser and sprue pieces removed.

A flask is subsequently placed over the drag pattern plate using the locating pins on

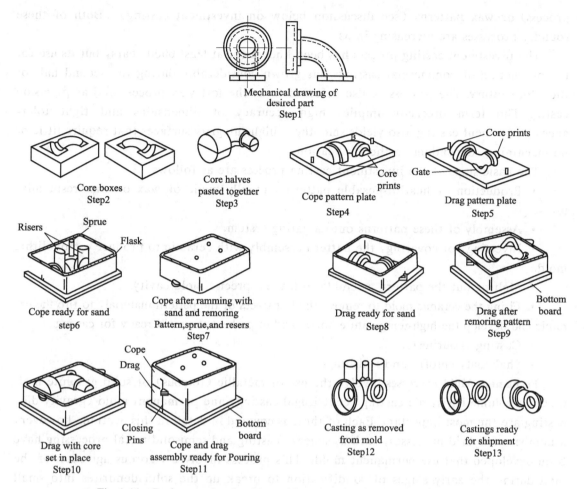

Fig. 1-11 Basic steps involved in making a casting from a green sand mold

the plate. Sand is rammed around the pattern, and a bottom board is placed on top of the flask full of sand. The pattern, flask, and bottom board are then rolled over 180°, and the pattern is withdrawn.

The completed core is set into the core prints in the drag half of the mold and the cope half of the mold is set on top of the drag. Proper alignment of the mold cavity in the cope and drag portions of the mold is ensured by the use of closing pins, which align the two flasks. The flasks can be clamped together, or weights can be placed on top of the cope, to counteract the buoyant force of the liquid metal, which would otherwise tend to float the cope off the drag during pouting.

Metal is then poured into the mold cavity through the sprue and allowed to solidify. The casting is shaken from the sand and appears as shown in Fig. 1-11, with the sprue, gating system, and risers attached. Following shakeout, the flasks, bottom boards, and clamps are cycled back to the molding station while the casting is moved through the production process. When the gates and risers are removed from the casting, they are returned to the furnace to be remelted. After cleaning, finishing, and heat treating, the castings are ready for shipment.

Expendable Pattern Processes use polystyrene patterns (lost foam casting and replicast process) or wax patterns (see discussion below on investment casting). Both of these foundry processes are increasing in use.

The investment casting process has been known for at least 6000 years, but its use for the production of commercial castings has grown considerably during the second half of the 20th century. The process is also referred to as the lost wax process and as precision casting. The term precision implies high accuracy of dimensions and tight tolerances. Investment casting also yields smoother, high-integrity surfaces that require little or no machining, depending on the application.

The basic steps of the investment casting process are as follows:
- Production of heat-disposable patterns, usually made of wax or wax/resin mixtures.
- Assembly of these patterns onto a gating system.
- Investing, or covering, the pattern assembly with ceramic to produce a monolithic mold.
- Melting out the pattern assembly to leave a precise mold cavity.
- Firing the ceramic mold to remove the last traces of the pattern material, to fire the ceramic and develop the high-temperature bond, and to preheat the mold ready for casting.
- Casting (pouring).
- Shakeout, cutoff, and finishing.

Permanent Mold Processes involve the use of metallic (ferrous) or solid graphite molds. On a volume basis, die casting, centrifugal casting, and permanent mold (gravity die) casting are the most important. Each of these is covered in detail in this Section. however, a number of hybrid processes, such as squeeze casting and semisolid metal processing have been developed that use permanent molds. This process involves vigorous agitation of the melt during the early stages of solidification to break up the solid dendrites into small spherulites.

● Vocabulary

patternmaking　*v.* 制模
cavity　*n.* 洞，凹处；腔
furnace　*n.* 火炉，熔炉
pin　*n.* 大头针，针；栓；琐碎物　*vt.* 钉住；压住
flask　*n.* 烧瓶；长颈瓶，细颈瓶
plate　*n.* 金属板；金属牌
sprue　*n.* 注入口，铸口；熔渣
shrinkage　*n.* 收缩；减低
withdrawn　*v.* 取出；撤退

clamp　*vt.* 夹紧，固定住　*n.* 夹钳，螺丝钳
investment　*n.* 投资；投入
shakeout　*n.* 落砂
die　*n.* 冲模，钢模
centrifugal　*adj.* 离心的；远中的　*n.* 离心机；转筒
permanent　*adj.* 永久的，永恒的；不变的
spherulite　*n.* 球粒

● Questions

1. Please give some casting methods introduced in this article.
2. Please tell the basic steps of the investment casting process.

Unit 7
Sand Molding

Sand Molding (Casting) is one of the most versatile of metal-forming processes, providing tremendous freedom of design in terms of size, shape, and product quality.

● Green Sand Molds

The phrase green sand refers to the fact that the medium has been tempered with water for use in the production of molds. As will be described below, the control of a green sand process requires an understanding of the interaction of the various parameters normally measured in a system sand.

● Process Control Requirements

A realistic approach to sand control is to target those system variables with which actual control can be implemented and realized. Put in more simple terms, one must control those system parameters that are directly affected by actions taken on the foundry floor. Clay and water are the primary additives of a system sand. The functions they perform are measured by determining the clay content and the percent of compactability of the prepared sand. Seacoal, cellulose, and starches may also be added to the sand. These organic components of the system sand are normally measured by the percent volatile and/or the total combustible test.

● Sand Systems

Types of Sand. Sand for green sand molding is composed of various ingredients, each with a specific purpose. The most basic of these ingredients is the base sand itself. The most predominant type of base sand is silica sand. It is classified in two categories: naturally bonded and synthetic sand.

The naturally bonded sand (or bank sand, as it is sometimes called) contains clay-base contaminants. These naturally occurring clays are the result of sedimentation deposits produced during the formation of the sand deposit. The use of this type of sand as a green sand molding medium is determined by the type of metal being cast, economics, casting quality, and the degree of consistency demanded by the final product.

Synthetic sand is composed of base sand grains of various grain distributions. Bonding agents are added to these base sands to produce the desired molding characteristics. The major base sand in this category is silica, although zircon, olivine, and chromite are used for special applications.

Controlling Sand Properties. Sand grain structure is a very important characteristic in the selection of a base sand. The selection dictates the ultimate mold permeability and density, and both of these parameters are critical to the production of quality castings.

When molten metal is introduced into a green sand mold, gases and steam are generated as a result of the thermal decomposition of the binder and other additives or contaminants that are present. If the permeability of the mold is not sufficient to allow the escape of the generated gases, mold pressures will increase, impeding the flow of molten metal, or even causing the metal to be blown from the mold. Thus, the selection of a base sand that provides adequate mold porosity is very important.

Because resistance to gas flow increases as the size of the pores (voids) between the sand grains decreases, the minimum porosity required is determined by the volume of the gas generated within the mold cavity. In like turn, the selection of the base sand is determined by the total amount of gas produced within the mold cavity, as well as by surface finish requirements.

The fact that gas is generated within the mold cavity is not always a disadvantage. Pressures within the mold from the generation of gases help prevent metal penetration into the sand. This minimizes burned-on sand grains and resulting problems associated with cleaning and machining the casting. Thus, a balance between mold permeability and gas generation must be maintained. For example, if mold permeability is low because of the fineness of the base sand, the sand additives should be those conducive to the production of a low volume gas. On the other hand, if permeability is high, it is advantageous to select materials that yield higher levels of gas.

● Clays for Green Sand Molding

Green sand additives can be divided into two categories, clays and carbonaceous materials. The major purpose of the clays is to function as a bonding agent to hold together the sand grains during the casting process. The carbonaceous materials aid dimensional stability of the mold, surface finish, and cleanability of the finished casting.

Types of Clay. Clays normally used in green sand molding are of three general types:
- Montmorillonite, or bentonite clays. These are subdivided into two general types: Western, or sodium, bentonite; and Southern, or calcium, bentonite. The two clays differ in their chemical composition as well as in their physical behavior within a system sand.
- Kaolinite, or fireclay as it is normally called.
- Illite, a clay not widely used. The material is derived from the decomposition of certain shale deposits.

The most significant clays used in green sand operations are the bentonites. Western and Southern bentonites differ in chemical makeup and, thus, their physical characteristics also. In general, Western bentonite develops lower green strength and higher hot strength than the same amount of Southern bentonite. Southern bentonite, at the same concentration, produces higher green strength and lower hot strength. This phenomenon is sometimes confused with what is referred to as durability.

Controlling Clay Properties. All clays can be made plastic and will develop adhesive qualities when mixed with the proper amounts of water. All clays can be dried and then made plastic again by the addition of water, provided the drying temperature is not too high. However, if the temperature does become too high, they cannot be replasticized with water. It is this third condition that dictates the durability of the clay in a system sand.

All clays, regardless of type, develop both adhesive and cohesive properties when mixed with water. The amount of adhesive or cohesive property depends on the amount of water added. When the water content is low, the cohesive properties are enhanced and the clays tend to cohere, or stick to themselves, rather than adhere, or stick to the sand grains to be bonded. With high water additions, the converse is true.

● Sand Reclamation

The economics of a foundry operation require sand reclamation to reduce the costs associated with new sand and the costs of landfill use, and to reduce the problems associated with the control of environmentally undesirable contaminants in the discarded sand.

In addition, tangible operational advantages result from sand reclamation. These begin with the ability to select the best sand for the casting process, knowing that most of it will be reclaimed during operation. In addition, the use of reclaimed sand reduces the number of variables that must be controlled, and provides operational consistency over a period of time. Sand grain shape and distribution and binder system bonding are more uniform, thus reducing sand defects. A properly designed sand reclamation system begins with green sand and converts it to a product very similar to new sand.

● Dry Sand Molding

The essential difference between dry sand and green sand molding is that the moisture in the mold sand is removed prior to pouring the metal. Dry sand molding is more applicable to medium and large castings than to small castings. The molds are stronger and more rigid than green sand molds. They can therefore withstand more handling and resist the static pressure of molten metal, which may cause green sand molds to deform or swell. In addition, they may be exposed to the atmosphere for long periods of time without detrimental effect. Such exposure may be necessary for placing and fitting a large number of cores.

Seacoal is the most common carbon material used in green sand; pitch is the most common in dry sand. Other materials in dry sand are gilsonite, cereal (corn flour), molasses, dextrine, glutrin, and resin. These additives thermoset at the baking/drying temperature (150 to 315℃) to produce high dry strength and rigid mold walls. The base sand is normally coarser than in green sand to facilitate natural venting and mold drying.

Dry Sand Molding Methods. As described below, dry sand molds are made by a variety of methods.

Large Sand Compaction Machines of the jolt, roll-over, and draw-type or jolt-only-type compact the sand in conjunction with tucking, hand peening, and air ramming.

Sand Slingers. These machines throw and compact the sand by means of centrifugal force. A variety of sizes are available. Some supplemental hand ramming may be required.

Floor Molding. This molding method uses larger flasks normally requiring the services of an overhead crane. The molds are made by a combination of mechanical equipment (slinger), hand peening, and pneumatic hand-operated rammers. Sand must be placed in the flasks in layers, and care must be taken by the molder to make certain that each layer knits and adheres to the other and is of uniform hardness.

Pit Molding. This method is used for very large castings when flasks are impractical. Pits are normally constructed of concrete walls and sometimes floors to withstand great pressures during pouring. Because the drag part of a pit cannot be rolled over, the sand under the pattern must be rammed or bedded in, or the bottom must be constructed with dry sand cores. A bed of coke, cinders, or other means of venting the pit bottom must be provided. Once the pattern is in place, mold-making procedures are the same as those for floor molding.

Cooling of Castings. Large castings should be cooled slowly in order to prevent internal stresses and/or cracking of the casting. It is sometimes possible to have the molds or cores so rigid that castings will hot tear. The use of inert filler materials placed a safe distance from the casting surface and/or the hollowing out of heavy mold sections will help to prevent such problems.

● Vocabulary

compactability   n. 压实性；紧实性
combustible   adj. 易燃的；燃烧性的   n. 可燃物；易燃物
clay   n. 黏土；泥土；似黏土的东西   vt. 用黏土处理
ingredient   n. 原料；要素；组成部分   adj. 构成组成部分的
synthetic   adj. 综合的；合成的，人造的   n. 合成物
sedimentation   n. 沉降，沉淀
permeability   n. 渗透性；磁导率

porosity   n. 有孔性，多孔性
penetration   n. 渗透；突破；侵入；洞察力
carbonaceous   adj. 碳质的；碳的，含碳的
cleanability   n. 除尘力，除尘度
durability   n. 耐久性；坚固；耐用年限
cohesive   adj. 有结合力的；紧密结合的；有黏着力的
reclaimed sand   再生砂
peening   n. 锤击；轻敲；锤平

● Questions

1. What types of clays are normally used in green sand molding?
2. What is the essential difference between dry sand and green sand molding?

Unit 8

Investment Casting

  In **Investment Casting**, a ceramic slurry is applied around a disposable pattern, usually wax, and allowed to harden to form a disposable casting mold. The term disposable means that the pattern is destroyed during its removal from the mold and that the mold is destroyed to recover the casting.

  There are two distinct processes for making investment casting molds: the solid investment (solid mold) process and the ceramic shell process. The ceramic shell process has become the predominant technique for engineering applications, displacing the solid investment process. The basic steps in the ceramic shell process are illustrated in Fig. 1-12.

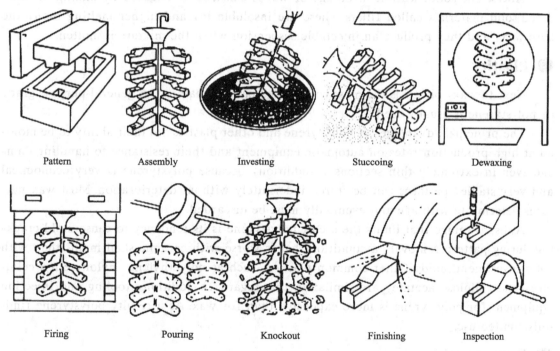

Fig. 1-12 Steps in the investment casting process

● **Pattern Materials**

  Pattern materials for investment casting can be loosely grouped into waxes and plastics. Waxes are more commonly used. Plastic patterns (usually polystyrene) are frequently used in conjunction with relatively thin ceramic shell molds.

● **Waxes**

  Wax is the preferred base material for most investment casting patterns, but blends containing only waxes are seldom used. Waxes are usually modified to improve their properties through the addition of such materials as resins, plastics, fillers, plasticizers, antioxidants, and dyes.

The most widely used waxes for patterns are paraffins and microcrystalline waxes. These two are often used in combination because their properties tend to be complementary. Paraffin waxes are available in closely controlled grades with melting points varying by 2.8°C increments; melting points ranging from 52 to 68°C are the most common. The low cost of these waxes, combined with their ready availability, convenient choice of grades, high lubricity, and low melt viscosity, accounts for their wide usage. However, applications are limited somewhat by their

brittleness and high shrinkage. Grades designated fully refined should be selected for pattern waxes. Microcrystalline waxes tend to be highly plastic and lend toughness to wax blends. Hard, nontacky grades and soft, adhesive grades are available. Microcrystalline waxes are available with higher melting points than the paraffins and are often used in combination with paraffin.

Fillers. The solidification shrinkage of waxes can also be reduced by mixing in powdered solid materials called fillers. These are insoluble in, and higher melting than, the base wax, and they produce an injectable suspension when the mixture is molten.

● Plastics

Next to wax, plastic is the most widely used pattern material. A general-purpose grade of polystyrene is usually used.

The principal advantages of polystyrene and other plastics are their ability to be molded at high production rates on automatic equipment and their resistance to handling damage even in extremely thin sections. In addition, because polystyrene is very economical and very stable, patterns can be stored indefinitely without deterioration. Most wax patterns deteriorate with age and eventually must be discarded.

A disadvantage that limits the use of polystyrene is its tendency to cause mold cracking during pattern removal, a condition that is worse with ceramic shell molds than with solid investment molds. Other common plastics, such as polyethylene, nylon, ethyl cellulose, and cellulose acetate, are similar in this regard. In addition, tooling and injection equipment for polystyrene is more expensive than for wax. As a result, polystyrene finds only limited use.

● Patternmaking

Patterns for investment casting are made by injecting the pattern material into metal molds of the desired shape. Small quantities of patterns can also be produced by machining.

● Injection of Wax Patterns

Wax patterns are generally injected at relatively low temperatures and pressures in split dies using equipment specifically designed for this purpose. Patterns can be injected in the liquid, slushy, pastelike, or solid condition. Injection in the solid condition is often referred to as wax extrusion. Temperatures usually range from about 43 to 77℃, and pressures from about 275kPa to 10. 3MPa. Liquid waxes are injected at higher temperatures and lower pressures; solid waxes, at lower temperatures and higher pressures. In some cases, the same wax can be injected under some, or all, of these conditions, but it is often beneficial to tailor a wax for one particular condition.

Equipment for wax injection ranges from simple and inexpensive to sophisticated and costly. It can be as simple as a pneumatic unit with a closed, heated reservoir tank that is equipped with a thermostat, pressure regulator, heated valve, and nozzle and is connected to the shop air line for pressurization. A small die is held against the nozzle with one hand while the valve is operated with the other. Such machines are limited by available air pressure (usually <690kPa) and are therefore generally used to inject liquid wax. Such equipment is satisfactory for a large variety of small hardware parts that are commonly made as investment castings.

● Injection of Plastic Patterns

Polystyrene patterns are generally injected at temperatures of 177 to 260℃ and pressures of 27. 6 to 138MPa on standard plastic injection machines. These are hydraulic machines with vertical water-cooled platens that carry the die halves, and horizontal injection takes place through the stationary platen. Polystyrene granules are loaded into a hopper, from which they are fed into a plasticizing chamber (barrel). Modern machines have a rotating screw that reciprocates within the heated barrel to prepare a shot of material to the proper consistency and then inject it into the die. Some older machines having plungers instead of screws are still in use.

● Machining of Patterns

When only one or a few patterns are required, as for prototype and experimental work, it is expedient to machine them directly from wax or polystyrene. This avoids the time and expense involved in making pattern tooling. Special waxes have been specifically developed for this application.

● Pattern Tooling For Investment Casting

Investment casting permits various potential tooling options that are made possible by the low melting point, good fluidity, and lack of abrasiveness of waxes. This often represents an important competitive advantage. For a given part configuration, anticipated production requirements, choice of pattern material, and available patternmaking equipment, the selection is based on a consideration of cost, tool life, delivery time, pattern quality, and production efficacy. The methods in use can be grouped into three basic categories: machining, forming against a positive model (using a variety of methods), and casting into a suitable foundry mold.

Machined Tooling. Most production tooling is made by machining. The early investment casting industry favored tooling made from master models, but as parts became larger and more complex and production methods more demanding, machined tooling became dominant. Computer-aided design, electric discharge machining, and computer numerical controlled machine tools are commonly used.

Cast Tooling. Steel and beryllium copper are frequently used for cast tooling. Aluminum and zinc alloys have also been used. Wax can be cast against a master model to produce a pattern, which is then used to make an investment cast cavity. Better as-cast accuracy can be achieved if the model is coated with only a thin layer of wax. This is used to investment cast a steel shell, which is then backed up with cast aluminum. The ceramic mold process can also be used to cast injection cavities.

● Manufacture of Ceramic Shell Molds

Investment shell molds are made by applying a series of ceramic coatings to the pattern clusters. Each coating consists of a fine ceramic layer with coarse ceramic particles embedded in its outer surface. A cluster is first dipped into a ceramic slurry bath. The cluster is then withdrawn from the slurry and manipulated to drain off excess slurry and to produce a uniform layer. The wet layer is immediately stuccoed with relatively coarse ceramic particles either by immersing it into a fluidized bed of the particles or by sprinkling the particles on it from above.

The fine ceramic layer forms the inner face of the mold and reproduces every detail of the pattern, including its smooth surface. It also contains the bonding agent, which provides strength to the structure. The coarse stucco particles serve to arrest further runoff of the slurry, help to prevent it from cracking or pulling away, provide keying (bonding) between individual coating layers, and build up thickness faster.

Each coating is allowed to harden or set before the next one is applied. This is accomplished by drying, chemical gelling, or a combination of these. The operations of coating, stuccoing, and hardening are repeated a number of times until the required mold thickness is achieved. The final coat is usually left unstuccoed in order to avoid the occurrence of loose particles on the mold surface. This final, unstuccoed layer is sometimes referred to as a seal coat.

● Mold Refractories

The most common refractories for ceramic shell molds are siliceous, for example, silica itself, zircon, and various aluminum silicates composed of mullite and (usually) free silica. These three types in various combinations are used for most applications. Alumina has had some use for super-alloy casting, and this application has increased with the growth of directional solidification processes. Alumina is generally considered too expensive and unnecessary for commercial hardware casting. Silica, zircon, aluminum silicates, and alumina find use for both slurry refractories and stuccos.

● Vocabulary

plasticizer *n*. 塑化剂；可塑剂
antioxidant *n*. 抗氧化剂；硬化防止剂；防老化剂
paraffin *n*. 石蜡；硬石蜡 *vt*. 用石蜡处理；涂石蜡于……

microcrystalline *adj*. 微晶的 *n*. 微晶
increment *n*. 增量；增加；增额
lubricity *n*. 润滑能力；不稳定（性）
viscosity *n*. 黏性，黏度
toughness *n*. 韧性；强健；健壮性

deteriorate vi. 恶化，变坏 vt. 恶化
split vt. 分离；使分离；劈开 n. 劈开；裂缝 adj. 劈开的
pneumatic adj. 气动的；充气的
hydraulic adj. 液压的；水力的；水力学的
hopper n. 料斗；漏斗
configuration n. 配置；结构；外形
refractory adj. 难治的；难熔的 n. 耐火物质

● Questions

1. Tell the basic steps in the ceramic shell process.
2. Tell the properties of waxes and plastics for investment casting.

Unit 9
Permanent Mold Casting

In Permanent Mold Casting, sometimes referred to as gravity die casting, a metal mold consisting of two or more parts is repeatedly used for the production of many castings of the same form. The liquid metal enters the mold by gravity. Simple removable cores are usually made of metal, but more complex cores are made of sand or plaster. When sand or plaster cores are used, the process is called semipermanent mold casting. Permanent mold casting is particularly suitable for the high-volume production of castings with fairly uniform wall thickness and limited undercuts or intricate internal coring. The process can also be used to produce complex castings, but production quantities should be high enough to justify the cost of the molds.

Permanent mold casting has the following limitations:
- Not all alloys are suitable for permanent mold casting.
- Because of relatively high tooling costs, the process can be prohibitively expensive for low production quantities.
- Some shapes cannot be made using permanent mold casting, because of parting line location, undercuts, or difficulties in removing the casting from the mold.
- Coatings are required to protect the mold from attack by the molten metal.

● **Casting Methods**

Manually operated permanent molds may consist of a simple book-type mold arrangement Fig. 1-13 (a). For castings with high ribs or walls that require mold retraction without rotation, the manually operated device shown in Fig. 1-13 (b) can be used. With either type of device, the mold halves are separated manually after releasing the eccentric mold clamps.

In Constant-Level Pouring, the mold is placed in a device, and as the metal is poured into the mold, the mold is lowered at a rate consistent with the rate of fill, effectively pouring the metal at one constant level. If the metal source, rather than the mold, is in the device, the metal source is raised and the mold remains stationary. This method virtually ensures lamellar flow and greatly reduces oxide formation.

In Centrifugal Casting, cylindrical or symmetrically shaped castings are poured using the centrifugal force of a spinning mold to force the metal into the mold. The sprue is located at the center of rotation. The force generated by the spinning of the mold helps the metal fill thin casting sections and maintains good contact between the metal and the mold. This provides a higher rate of heat flow and a more rapid solidification rate, resulting in increased mechanical properties. Multiple molds can be used in centrifugal casting, and care should be taken to design gating systems that produce little or no turbulence.

Squeeze Casting is another variation of the permanent mold process. It consists of pouring a specific amount of metal into the lower half of a mold, closing the mold, and then allowing the metal to solidify under pressure. One of the advantages of squeeze casting is the casting yield, because no gating system is required.

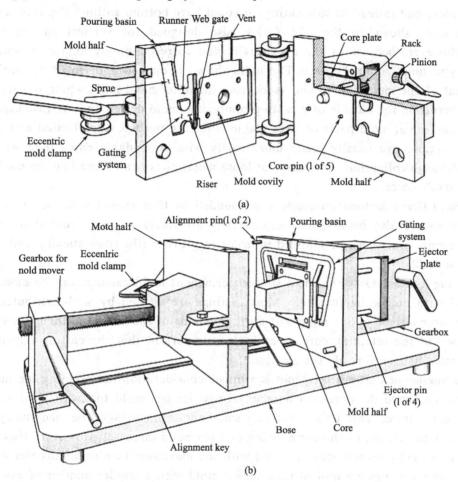

Fig. 1-13 Two types of manually operated permanent mold casting machines.
(a) Simple book-type mold for shallow-cavity castings.
(b) Device with straight-line retraction for deep-cavity molds

● Mold Design

A simple permanent mold is shown in the book-type casting device illustrated in Fig. 1-13. Here the two mold halves are hinged on a pin and aligned. The mold cavity with the mold halves closed determines the shape of the casting. The casting is poured by means of the sprue and runners to the riser, which is provided with a web gate to the mold cavity. The cavity is vented to allow air to escape. The plate-shape cavity shown in Fig. 1-13 required five core pins, which were moved by means of the manually driven gearbox mounted on the back of the right-hand mold half.

In operation, the mold halves are closed and locked. Metal is then poured to fill the gating system and the mold cavity. After the metal has solidified, the mold is opened, leaving the casting on the core pins. The core pins are withdrawn, and the casting is removed manually.

The mold shown in Fig. 1-13 is designed with the parting vertical and in a single plane. This mold could also be designed for horizontal parting or with parting in two or more planes, and instead of side gating, it could have bottom gating [Fig. 1-14(a)].

The mold shown in Fig. 1-14 (b) is also designed for vertical parting and side gating. However, because of the deep cavity and correspondingly long core required, a hinged-type mold cannot be used. The mold shown is opened and closed by straight-line movement of one mold half to and away from the other mold half, which remains fixed.

Undercuts on the outside of a casting complicate mold design and increase casting cost because additional mold parts or expendable cores are needed. Complicated and undercut internal sections are usually made more easily with expendable cores than with metal cores, although collapsible steel cores or loose metal pieces can sometimes be used instead of expendable cores.

Isolated Heavy Sections completely surrounded by thin areas should be avoided. Thin deep ribs should also be avoided because they are likely to cause cold shuts and misruns. Adequate draft must be allowed in order to prevent ribs from sticking and breaking off in the mold.

Casting Ejection. Only the most simple permanent mold castings can be ejected from the mold with no mechanical help. Most castings are ejected by well-distributed ejector pins, or are confined in one mold half during opening of the mold and then ejected by the withdrawal of the retaining core or cores. It is important that the casting remain in the correct mold half until ready for ejection.

The Number of Castings per Mold is a major consideration in designing the mold; the objective is to have the optimum number of cavities per mold that will yield acceptable castings at the lowest cost. Except for very small and thin castings, the machine cycle time increases as the weight of the metal being cast per mold increases. However, these increases are not directly proportional. A mold with the maximum number of cavities will often produce more castings per unit of time than a mold with a smaller number of cavities that was designed to operate on a shorter cycle. This is because there is a minimum solidification time for every casting, regardless of the number of cavities in the mold. The number of rejects sometimes increases as the number of cavities is increased, but this is usually offset by the greater productivity. For relatively simple castings, the cavities can be placed one above the other. This permits maximum use of the face area of the mold. However, for more complex castings, especially those for which there are significant projections in the cavities, it is usually necessary to gate each cavity individually.

Progressive Solidification. Alloys should be cast so that solidification takes place progressively toward the risers, which are generally to one side or on top of the casting. To achieve this solidification pattern, thinner sections of the casting should be away from the gating system, and heavy sections should be adjacent to it. Rib sections and thin walls vent and fill more easily when they are vertical, but filling a vertical mold cavity may promote turbulence in the molten metal, resulting in excessive dross; consequently, the mold should be tilted when being poured.

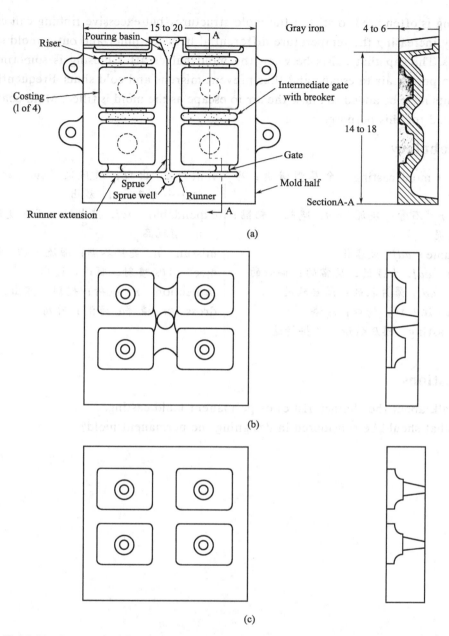

Fig. 1-14 Bottom-gated permanent mold (a) with stacked cavities for four castings. (b) Multicavity mold with low-pressure gating system. (c) Alternate gating system for low-pressure or vacuum casting

In designing a permanent mold, the part is laid out in the desired orientation, and the mold is designed around it, allowing sufficient space for gating, for the seal needed to prevent metal leakage, and for coring and mold inserts. It is common practice to contour the back of the mold so that its exterior conforms roughly with the cavity. This permits a more even temperature distribution and heat dissipation. For castings with heavy sections, the adjacent mold sections are generally heavier. For aluminum castings, a ratio of three or four mold wall thicknesses to one casting wall thickness is often used, but a mold wall this thin cannot always be used in making thin-wall castings without jeopardizing mold stability. Ribbing is often used to stiffen the mold structure, but excessive ribbing can cause distortion by increasing the temperature differential between inner and outer mold surfaces.

Vents. The gap that exists between the mold halves after closing is sometimes large enough to permit air to escape and thus prevent misruns and cold shuts. Frequently, however, vents must be added to allow the air to escape as the mold is filled. Mold coatings can also be used for this purpose.

● **Vocabulary**

permanent mold casting　金属型铸造；冷硬铸造
plaster　*n.* 石膏；灰泥　*vt.* 减轻；粘贴；涂以灰泥
high-volume　*adj.* 大容量
eccentric　*adj.* 古怪的；反常的；偏心的
lamellar　*adj.* 薄片状的；薄层状的
sprue　*n.* 注入口，铸口；熔渣
squeeze casting　模压铸造，压挤铸造

vent　*n.* 出口；通风孔　*vt.* 放出……；给……开孔　*vi.* 放出
expendable　*adj.* 排出的；不重复使用的　*n.* 消耗品
misrun　*n.* 浇铸不满；滞流　*vt.* 滞流
eject　*vt.* 喷射；驱逐，逐出
projection　*n.* 投射；规划；突出；发射
dross　*n.* 渣滓；浮渣；碎屑

● **Questions**

1. Talk about the characteristics of permanent mold casting.
2. What should be considered in designing the permanent mold?

Unit 10
Die Casting

Die Casting is characterized by a source of hydraulic energy that imparts high velocity to molten metal to provide rapid filling of a metal die. The die absorbs the stresses of injection, dissipates the heat contained in the metal, and facilitates the removal of the shaped part in preparation for the next cycle. The hydraulic energy is provided by a system that permits control of actuator position, velocity, and acceleration to optimize flow and force functions on the metal as it fills the cavity and solidifies.

● **Die Casting Processes**

The variety in die casting systems results from trade-offs in metal fluid flow, elimination of gas from the cavity, reactivity between the molten metal and the hydraulic system, and heat loss during injection. The process varieties have many features in common with regard to die mechanical design, thermal control, and actuation. The three primary variations of the die casting process are the hot chamber process, the cold chamber process, and direct injection.

The Hot Chamber Process is the original process invented by H. H. Doehler. It continues to be used for lower-melting materials (zinc, lead, tin, and, more recently, magnesium alloys). Hot chamber die casting places the hydraulic actuator in intimate contact with the molten metal (Fig. 1-15). The hot chamber process minimizes exposure of the molten alloy to turbulence, oxidizing air, and heat loss during the transfer of the hydraulic energy. The prolonged intimate contact between molten metal and system components presents severe materials problems in the production process.

The Cold Chamber Process solves the materials problem by separating the molten metal reservoir from the actuator for most of the process cycle. Cold chamber die casting requires independent metering of the metal (Fig. 1-16) and immediate injection into the die, exposing the hydraulic actuator for only a few seconds. This minimal exposure allows the casting of higher-temperature alloys such as aluminum, copper, and even some ferrous alloys.

Direct Injection extends the technology used for lower-melting polymers to metals by taking the hot chamber intimacy to the die cavity with small nozzles connected to a manifold, thus eliminating the gating and runner system. This process, however, is still under development.

Process Control in die casting to achieve consistent high quality relates to timing, fluid flow, heat flow, and dimensional stability. Some features are chosen in die and part geometry decisions and are therefore fixed; others are defined by the process at the machine and can be adjusted in real time. All are related and therefore must be dealt with in parallel; the best die castings result from an intimate interrelationship between product design and process design.

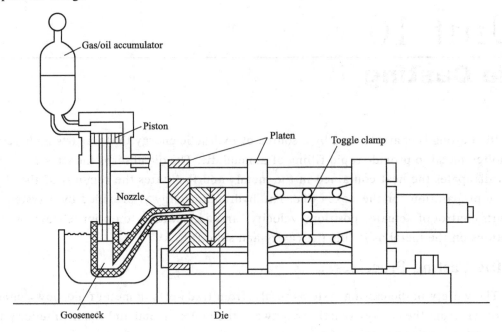

Fig. 1-15 Schematic showing the principal components of a hot chamber die casting machine

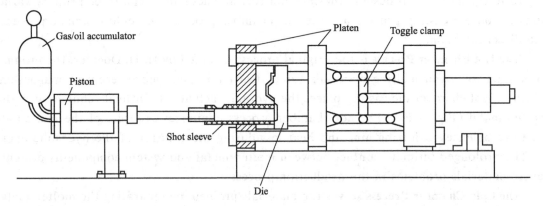

Fig. 1-16 Schematic showing the principal components of a cold chamber die casting machine

● Gating

The first step in the process sequence is the supply of the molten alloy to the casting machine and its injection into the die. The fluid flow is divided into three considerations: metal injection, air venting, and feeding of shrinkage.

● Metal Injection

The distinguishing characteristic of the die casting process is the use of high-velocity injection. The short fill time (of the order of milliseconds) allows the liquid metal to move a great distance despite a high rate of heat loss. The elements of a typical metal gating system are illustrated in Fig. 1-17.

Proper process performance depends on the delivery of molten metal with high quality

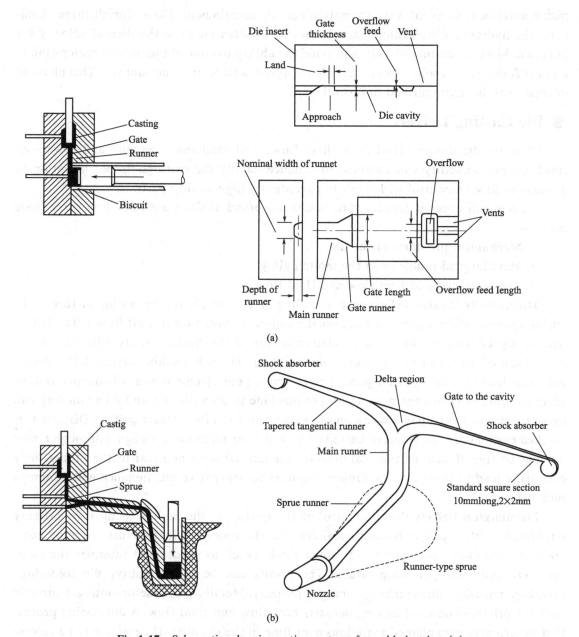

Fig. 1-17 Schematics showing gating systems for cold chamber (a) and hot chamber (b) die casting machines

as defined by temperature, composition, and cleanliness (gas content and suspended solids). The molten alloy is prepared from either primary ingot or secondary alloys. A melting furnace is used to provide the proper temperature and to allow time for chemistry adjustment and degassing.

The Injection Chamber. Three components make up the injection chambers used for the three types of die casting: the shot sleeve, the gooseneck, and the nozzle (Fig. 1-15, Fig. 1-16). The cold chamber shot sleeve (Fig. 1-16) is unique. Initially, it is only partially filled to prevent splashing and to allow for metering error, and it must be filled by slow piston movement to avoid wave formation and air entrainment. Then, for all three chambers, the hydraulic piston rapidly accelerates the molten metal to the desired velocity for injection. Most die casting machines provide the ability to control the piston acceleration in a linear fashion. Parabolic velocity curves are also available on some controls. This phase of injection can be accomplished in several steps.

● Die Casting Defects

Effective die design (fluid flow, heat flow, and mechanical design) and a well-defined process capability will combine to produce quality die castings. Proper attention to die casting process control will result in consistently high quality parts.

Defects will occur if process variation is too broad. Defects are caused by three basic sources:
- Mechanical problems in the die.
- Metallurgical problems in the molten alloy.
- The interaction of heat flow and fluid flow.

Mechanically Induced Defects such as galling or drag marks on the casting surface occur during ejection of the casting and are usually caused by insufficient draft in the die. Galling will be aligned with the direction of relative motion of the casting and its adjacent die segment. Lack of draft can be an error in die building, but it is readily corrected. Die design can cause lack of draft by inadequate specification, poor ejector system alignment, and inadequate slide or core alignment. Improper machine setup with uneven tie bar loading can cause the die to shift upon closing and opening and therefore create galling. Distorted or cracked castings are the result of extreme cases of poor mechanical design. Although a new die may be free of such mechanical defects, the normal wear and tear of the process may eventually lead to these defects. Proper attention to preventive maintenance will minimize such behavior.

Metallurgical Defects. Proper control of the quality of the molten metal is of primary importance with regard to metallurgical defects. The four principal factors are alloy composition, dissolved gas content, entrained solids (such as oxides and intermetallic compounds), and improper temperatures. The results can be poor fluidity, die soldering, shrinkage porosity, hot cracking, and gas porosity. Metallurgical factors interact directly with the primary causes of casting defects: heat flow and fluid flow. A die casting process that experiences unexplained variations over time in the quantity of defects may be receiving poor-quality metal. As with a deterioration in the mechanical behavior of the die, metal quality is one of the first process parameters to be checked.

Interaction of Heat Flow and Fluid Flow. The die casting die is primarily a means of shaping a molten volume of metal and removing enough heat to permit ejection. Improper interaction of fluid and heat flow can lead to poor casting quality. The rapid fill time, the complex part geometries, and the high heat transfer rates of die casting combine to form a complex set of potential causes of defects. Flow/heat defects can be built into the die by poor design of the gating, venting, and thermal die layout. However, once the process is proven and the die is properly maintained, these parameters should not produce variations in the process.

● **Vocabulary**

hydraulic   *adj*. 液压的；水力的；水力学的
filling   *n*. 填充；填料   *v*. 填满；遍及
chamber   *n*. 室，膛   *adj*. 室内的
  vt. 把……关在室内
schematic   *adj*. 图解的；概要的   *n*. 原理图；图解视图
runner system   流道系统；浇道系统；冒口系统

degassing   *n*. 除气；排气   *adj*. 除气的；排气的   *v*. 除气；给……排气
intermetallic   *adj*. 金属间（化合）的   *n*. 金属间化合物
fluidity   *n*. 流动性；流质；易变性
soldering   *n*. 焊接；焊料；焊接处   *adj*. 用于焊接的   *v*. 焊接
layout   *n*. 布局；设计；安排；陈列

● **Questions**

1. What are the elements of a typical metal gating system?
2. What could lead to the die casting defects?

Unit 11

Centrifugal Casting

Horizontal Centrifugal Casting is used to cast pieces having an axis of revolution. The technique uses the centrifugal force generated by a rotating cylindrical mold to throw the molten metal against the mold wall and form the desired shape.

● **Equipment**

A horizontal centrifugal casting machine must be able to perform four operations accurately and with repeatability:
- The mold must rotate at a predetermined speed.
- There must be a means to pour the molten metal into the rotating mold.
- Once the metal is poured, the proper solidification rate must be established in the mold.
- There must be a means of extracting the solidified casting from the mold.

Fig. 1-18 shows a common design for a horizontal centrifugal casting machine. Many variations of this basic design are in use. Details may vary; for example, there are different types of drive systems, carrying rollers, and so on.

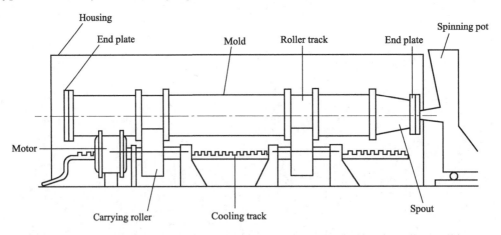

Fig. 1-18 Schematic of a common design for a horizontal centrifugal casting machine

● **Molds**

Molds consist of four parts: the shell, the casting spout, roller tracks, and end heads. The mold assembly is placed on interchangeable carrying rollers that enable the use of different mold diameters and fine adjustments. Molds are cooled by a water spray, which can be divided into several streams for selective cooling.

Different types of molds are generally used according to the geometry and quantity of castings needed and the characteristics of the metal or alloy being cast. Molds can be either expendable (a relatively thin case lined with sand) or permanent.

Expendable Molds lined with sand are widely used in centrifugal casting, especially for producing relatively few castings. A single mold case can be used with different thicknesses of sand linings to produce tubes of various diameters within a limited range.

Green Sand is commonly used as the liner in expendable molds. Various mixtures and binders are used—for example, a mixture of 60% silica sand and 40% calcined and crushed asbestos or sand bound with resin. Phenolic binders are also used with silica sand. One proprietary process uses a mixture of sand, silica flour, bentonite, and water.

Dry Sand Molds can also be employed; in this case, the sand is pressed down around a pattern having the same dimensions as the casting. Hardening is sometimes accomplished with carbon dioxide.

● Casting Techniques

Pouring. Molten metal can be introduced into the mold at one end, at both ends, or through a channel of variable length. Pouring rates vary widely according to the size of the casting being produced and the metal being poured. Pouring rates that are too slow can result in the formation of laps and gas porosity, while excessively high rates slow solidification and are one of the main causes of longitudinal cracking.

Casting Temperatures. The degree of superheat required to produce a casting is a function of the metal or alloy being poured, mold size, and physical properties of the mold material. The following empirical formula has been suggested as a general guideline to determine the degree of superheat needed:

$$L = 2.4 \Delta T + 110 \qquad (1\text{-}11)$$

where L is the length of spiral fluidity (in millimeters) and ΔT is the degree of superheat (in degrees centigrade). The use of Eq (1-11) for ferrous alloys results in casting temperatures that are 50 to 100℃ above the liquidus temperature. In practice, casting temperatures are kept as low as possible without the formation of defects resulting from too low a temperature.

A high casting temperature requires higher speeds of rotation to avoid sliding; low casting temperatures can cause laps and gas porosity. Casting temperature also influences solidification rates and therefore affects the amount of segregation that takes place.

Mold Temperature. Numerous investigators have studied the relationship between initial mold temperature and the structure of the resultant casting. Initial mold temperatures vary over a wide range according to the metal being cast, the mold thickness, and the wall thickness of the tube being cast. Initial mold temperature does not affect the structure of the resultant casting as greatly as the process parameters discussed above do.

Speed of Rotation. Generally, the mold is rotated at a speed that creates a centrifugal force ranging from 75 to 120g (75 to 120 times the force of gravity). Speed of rotation is varied during the casting process; Fig. 1-19 illustrates a typical cycle of rotation. The cycle can be divided into three parts:

• At the time of pouring, the mold is rotating at a speed sufficient to throw the molten metal against the mold wall.

• As the metal reaches the opposite end of the mold, the speed of rotation is increased.

• Speed of rotation is held constant for a time after pouring; the time at constant speed varies with mold type, metal being cast, and required wall thickness.

The ideal speed of rotation causes rapid adhesion of the molten metal to the mold wall with minimal vibration. Such conditions tend to result in a casting with a uniform structure.

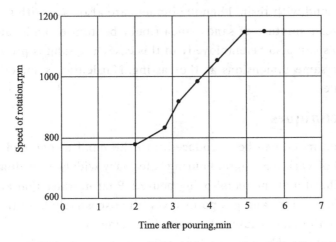

Fig. 1-19 Typical cycle of rotation in horizontal centrifugal casting

As the molten metal enters the mold, a pressure gradient is established across the tube thickness by centrifugal acceleration. This causes alloy constituents of various densities to separate, with lighter particles such as slags and nonmetallic impurities gathering at the inner diameter. The thickness of these impurity bands is usually limited to a few millimeters, and they are easily removable by machining.

Too low a speed of rotation can cause sliding and result in poor surface finish. Too high a speed of rotation can generate vibrations, which can result in circumferential segregation. Very high speeds of rotation may give rise to circumferential stresses high enough to cause radial cleavage or circular cracks when the metal shrinks during solidification.

● Solidification

In horizontal centrifugal casting, heat is removed from the solidifying casting only through the water-cooled mold wall. Solidification begins at the outside diameter of the casting, which is in contact with the mold, and continues inward toward the casting inside diameter. Several parameters influence solidification:

• The mold, including the mold material, its thickness, and initial mold temperature.

• The thickness and thermal conductivity of the mold wash used.

• Casting conditions, including degree of superheat, pouring rate, and speed of rotation.

• Any vibrations present in the casting system.

Thermal Aspects of Solidification. It appears that the mold-related parameters listed above have relatively little influence on solidification. Large variations in mold thickness, however, could become significant.

The parameters with the greatest effect are the degree of superheat in the molten metal and the thickness of the mold wash employed. Both of these process variables affect local solidification conditions and therefore modify the structure of the casting. Fig. 1-20 illustrates the general effects of mold wash thickness and degree of superheat on solidification rates. Charts such as Fig. 1-20 can be used to predict total solidification time. They are especially useful in determining the optimal casting conditions for bimetallic tubes based on the type of bond required.

Process Advantages

Flexibility in Casting Composition. Horizontal centrifugal casting is applicable to nearly all compositions with the exception of high-carbon steels (0.40% to 0.85% C). Carbon segregation can be a problem in this composition range.

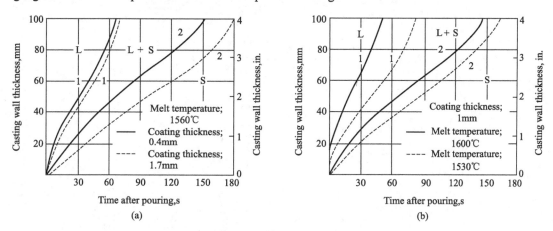

Fig. 1-20 Effect of mold coating thickness (a) and molten metal temperature
(b) on solidification in horizontal centrifugal casting

Wide Range of Available Product Characteristics. The metallurgical characteristics of a tubular product are mainly characterized by its soundness, texture, structure, and mechanical properties. Centrifugal castings can be manufactured with a wide range of microstructures tailored to meet the demands of specific applications.

Dimensional Flexibility. Horizontal centrifugal casting allows the manufacture of pipes with maximum outside diameters close to 1.6m and wall thicknesses to 200mm. Tolerances depend on part size and on the type of mold used.

● **Vocabulary**

cylindrical   adj. 圆柱形的；圆柱体的
horizontal   adj. 水平的；地平线的   n. 水平线，水平面；水平位置
spout   n. 喷口   vt. 喷出；喷射   vi. 喷出；喷射
interchangeable   adj. 可互换的；可交换的；可交替的

calcine   vt. 烧成石灰；煅烧   vi. 煅烧
superheat   vt. 使……过热   n. 过热
longitudinal   adj. 长度的，纵向的；经线的
sliding   adj. 变化的；滑行的   n. 滑；移动   v. 滑动；使滑行
segregation   n. 隔离，分离；偏析

parameter   n. 参数；系数；参量
rotation   n. 旋转；循环，轮流
slag   n. 炉渣；矿渣；熔渣   vt. 使成渣；使变成熔渣   vi. 变熔渣

conductivity   n. 导电性；传导性
anisotropy   n. 各向异性
homogeneous   adj. 均匀的；同质的；同种的

Questions
1. What is horizontal centrifugal casting?
2. Talk about the typical cycle of rotation in horizontal centrifugal casting.

Unit 12
Modeling of Solidification Heat Transfer

    Advantages of Computer Modeling. Computer-aided design (CAD), computer-aided manufacturing (CAM), and computer-aided engineering (CAE) offer a number of advantages for castings. These include:
- Increased casting yield per pound of metal poured.
- Improved casting quality (absence of unsoundness).
- Enhanced productivity of casting system.
- Automated machining of patterns, which in turn reduces costs.
- Easier implementation and evaluation of engineering changes.
- Enhanced ability to deal with batch production of castings of different design.

    The digital computer has had a singularly important impact on the engineering design of complex, multicomponent, high value-added products (for example, aerospace structures).

● **Geometric Description and Discretization**

    To predict freezing history in complex industrial castings, the three-dimensional form must be provided and the correct boundary conditions specified. Even prior to this, there are several valid reasons for defining accurately and unambiguously the geometry and topography of the casting and its rigging:
- Performing the analysis to generate preliminary rigging design.
- Estimating the overall costs for casting production for the purpose of quotation.
- Defining the melting capacity and molding equipment needs within the casting plant.
- Generating the tapes or other information storage forms required to drive machine tools needed for the fabrication of patterns and core boxes and the sinking of wax pattern, permanent mold, and die casting dies.

    The need to provide this geometric representation and to link the chosen form of representation with the process of discretization, that is, the breaking up of the whole into discrete elements, has been recognized as being of prime importance by only a limited number of research groups. Turning first to the problem of overall geometry, much can be gained by examining the capabilities of the many geometric modelers now available. The three most established types of geometric representation are (Fig. 1-21):
- Constructive solid geometry (csg).
- Boundary re presentation (b-rep).
- Wireframe (wf).

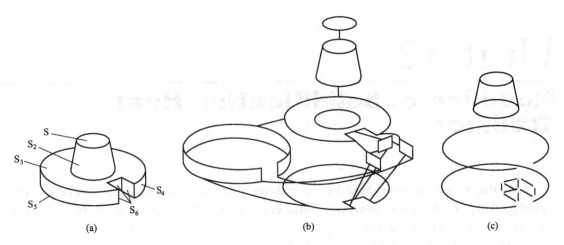

Fig. 1-21 Three types of three-dimensional geometric representation of a simple casting. (a) Constructive solid geometry. (b) Boundary representation. (c) Wireframe

The wireframe is not a true solid modeler, but because it normally forms an important part of many preprocessing packages for commercial finite-element method (FEM) computational codes, it is sometimes listed as a form of geometric modeling. The csg and b-rep approaches are both often incorporated into commercially developed computer-aided design (CAD) packages. Fig. 1-22 shows a csg-based model for a partial section of a casting in the form of a thick-wall cylinder together with its rigging. Many contemporary modeling routines permit not only hidden-line removal but also the use of color and shading.

Before a model of any description can be built and a freezing simulation entered into, the foundry methods engineer must have a reasonably accurate picture of the location and dimensioning of the various components of the rigging system (the gating and risering subsystems) that are to be employed during casting. Two approaches are being followed as alternatives to the age-old art of cut and try. These techniques are both computer based, and one in particular uses (most effectively) the readily available personal computer rather than the mainframe machine demanded by both geometric representational (csg, b-rep, etc.) and numerical computational (FDM, FEM, etc.) programs. The techniques can be referred to as:

- Special-purpose foundry rigging engineering programs.
- Knowledge-based expert systems programs.

Special-Purpose Programs. Many programs fall under the category of special-purpose programs. One of the most versatile, the Novacast program, determines riser sizes by using the well-known Chvorinov rule and locates them by using various other empirically derived feeding range rules. The program will also approximate the geometric features of the gating system using the Bernoulli approximation, together with other empirical axioms. This type of program has met with relatively wide acceptance in foundries around the world. In the United States, the AF Software programs and other routines prepared at the University of Wisconsin are in widespread use.

Knowledge-Based Expert Systems. Microcomputer programs such as those discussed above are often sufficient for designing the rigging of castings of a less critical nature.

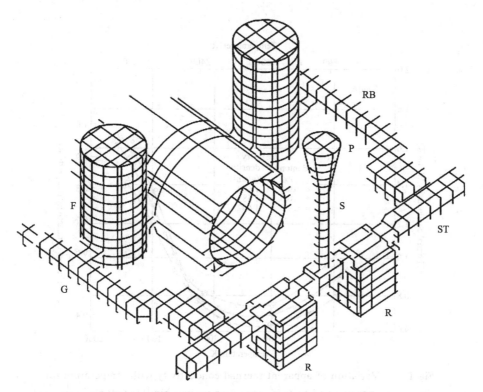

Fig. 1-22 Portion of a geometric model of a casting with rigging, constructed using a csg geometric modeler. F, feeder or riser; G, ingate location; P, pouring basin; R, reaction chamber; RB, runner bar; S, sprue; ST, slag trap

However, for those cast components that form parts of aerospace systems or for the safety features of pressure vessels, and so on, further engineering measures are often necessary.

In such cases, the need arises for a knowledge-based expert system and its associated data base. In any particular organization, a vast amount of the expertise involved in the art of foundry practice often disappears with the retirement of certain employees. Although there is no unique solution to the problem of rigging a particular casting, there are many valuable, although sometimes conflicting, opinions available for consideration.

● **The Data Base**

All mathematical models of the solidification process should possess:
- An accurate representation of geometry.
- An adequate treatment for evolution of latent heat.
- A sensitivity to the thermophysical properties of the materials involved in this process.

The thermophysical property data base for solidification modeling is a vast but sometimes sparsely populated region. By considering the most common molding material in shaped casting (bentonite-bonded silica sand), particularly the relationship that its apparent (or effective) thermal conductivity k has with temperature, one can appreciate part of the problem associated with data base development or expansion. As shown in Fig. 1-23, k is a complex function of temperature. In addition, one must specify the moisture content

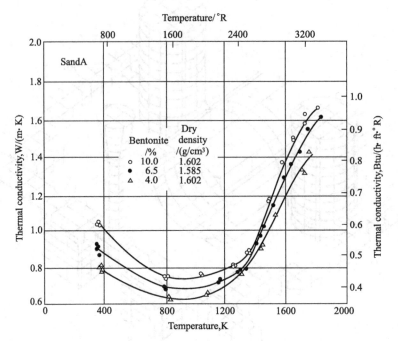

Fig. 1-23 Variation of apparent thermal conductivity with temperature for compacts of silica sand containing various binder contents

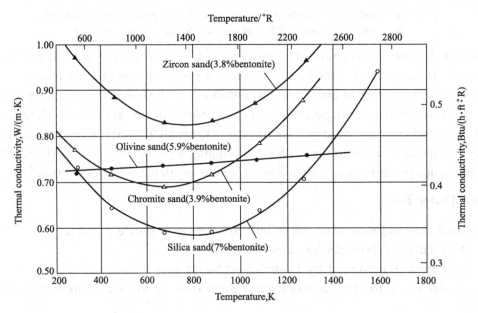

Fig. 1-24 Apparent thermal conductivities of four types of clay-bonded molding sands

(even when considering dried sand), ramming density, average grain fineness, and the sand source. Recognizing the burgeoning number of mold materials, which now include zircon, olivine, and chromite sands (Fig. 1-24), the potential for data base depth seems almost limitless. A collection of such data has been made that includes curve-fitted relationships linking temperature with thermal conductivity, specific heat, and other properties of molding and casting media. If such data were not found to be readily available, estimates were made. This was especially true for the thermophysical properties of metals and alloys above their melting points or ranges.

● Outlook for the Future

As has been indicated, the most successful phase of bringing the computer to the foundry industry has involved the use of first-level personal-computer-supported planning-type software—for example, weight estimation, freezing order, and simple gating and risering calculations rather than full-scale simulation of freezing. Some such software items are now very comprehensive groups of programs and also permit the planning of pattern plate arrangement and part nesting.

Currently, a second, separate growth period is occurring that involves the application of minicomputer-supported, first-generation or subsequent CAD systems. Most of the software used is not tailored to a foundry, die sinking, or patternmaking environment. Therefore, to implement such systems, metal casting plants are undergoing serious changes. These changes involve the recruitment of a new type of computer-literate/technical person into the foundry team. Turning to the software itself, the majority of installations have been concerned with the improvement of tooling design and have only rarely involved solidification simulation. Some installations, however, have incorporated results of the personal-computer-supported software referred to above in connection with rigging design.

● Vocabulary

multicomponent *adj.* 多成分的；多部件的
simulator *n.* 模拟器；模拟装置
rigging *n.* 索具，绳索；装备，传动装置
discretization *n.* 离散化
modeling *n.* 建模，造型；立体感 *adj.* 制造模型的
thermophysical *adj.* 热物理（学）的

simulation *n.* 仿真；模拟；模仿；假装
installation *n.* 安装，装置
finite-element 有限元
topography *n.* 地势；地形学；地志
numerical *adj.* 数值的；数字的；用数字表示的
geometric *adj.* 几何学的；几何学图形的

● Questions

1. Talk about the advantages of computer modeling.
2. What are the three most established types of geometric representation?

Unit 13

Modeling of Fluid Flow

Fluid Flow Modeling is a technique that uses computers to investigate flow phenomena. These flow phenomena, particularly during the initial filling stage, have major effects on the quality of castings. Designers have commonly relied on experience, rule of thumb, and handbook information to achieve their objectives of smooth flow, proper filling time, minimum gas entrapment, elimination of inclusions and dross, and the desired distribution of metal during mold filling. The goal of improving the quality and cost-effectiveness of castings by means of computer-aided design (CAD) and modern process control requires that data be expressed more scientifically, so that they are amenable to computation.

It is difficult to make direct observations of fluid flow inside molds, because the molds and the molten metal are opaque, the temperatures are high, and the conditions are highly transient. Even when observations are made, as by the techniques described later in this article, the location of the metal as a function of time is usually the only information that can be obtained. Not only is fluid flow modeling using computers usually the most economical and practical way to get information about what is going on inside a mold during filling, it is often the only feasible way. Furthermore, it can give information about the velocity and pressure distributions within the molten metal which cannot be obtained by direct observation.

Computational techniques for modeling flow during mold filling can be divided into two categories:

• Energy balance techniques based on the Bernoulli equation and the Saint-Venant equations.

• Momentum balance techniques based on the Navier-Stokes equations as embodied in the Marker-and-Cell group of programs which include the Marker-and-Cell (MAC), Simplified Marker-and-Cell (SMAC), and Solution Algorithm (SOLA) techniques.

The energy balance techniques are most useful for modeling flow through sprues, runners, and gates when the direction of flow is dictated by the configuration of the system. The momentum balance techniques are needed for calculating flow inside mold cavities where the direction of flow and the location of the fluid must be calculated.

● Energy Balance Methods

Because energy is a scalar rather than a vector quantity, these methods are primarily useful in determining flow rates in cases in which the direction of flow is established by the configuration of the system. The Bernoulli equation is used for calculating flow in completely filled channels such as sprues, pressurized runners, and gates, while the Saint-Venant equations are used for partially filled channels such as nonpressurized runners and troughs. Information provided by these calculations is extremely important to the design and manufacture of castings, and industry has used them routinely for many years. Now, CAD programs can apply these techniques to complicated systems with speed and accuracy.

A schematic of a gravity-filled casting system is shown in Fig. 1-25. The Bernoulli equation applicable to this system may be written:

$$\frac{P_j - P_i}{\rho} + \frac{V_j^2}{2b_j} - \frac{V_i^2}{2b_i} + g(z_j - z_i) + E_{f_{i,j}} = 0 \tag{1-12}$$

where P_i and P_j are pressures at positions i and j, V_i and V_j are mean velocities at positions i and j, z_i and z_j are elevations at positions i and j, b_i and b_j are velocity distribution factors (0.5 for laminar flow and 1.0 for highly turbulent flow), g is the acceleration due to gravity, ρ is the fluid density, and $E_{f_{i,j}}$ is the friction energy loss between positions i and j.

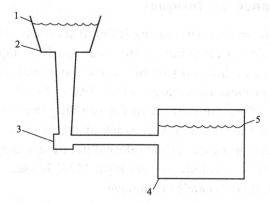

Fig. 1-25 Gravity-filled casting system analyzed by the Bernoulli equation approach. Numbered planes correspond to the subscripts used in Eq (1-12)

The friction energy loss term $E_{f_{i,j}}$ is a function of the velocity, the Reynolds number, and the configuration of the system between positions i and j. The Reynolds (N_{Re}) number is defined by:

$$N_{Re} = \frac{VD_e}{\nu} \tag{1-13}$$

where ν is the kinematic viscosity and D_e is the equivalent diameter.

The configuration of the system may change from point to point resulting in variations of the velocity and the N_{Re}. Thus, $E_{f_{i,j}}$ must be calculated for each segment of the system and then summed for the whole system.

● **Physical Modeling of Mold Filling**

It is important to verify computational models of mold filling with physical experiments. Physical modeling of metal flow is most often done with water in transparent molds. Water is a suitable fluid model because its kinematic viscosity is nearly the same as that of common metals at their normal pouring temperatures, especially if the temperature of the water is properly controlled. For example, the kinematic viscosity of water at 35℃ (95°F) is the same as that of 0.5%C steel at 870℃ (1600°F). To model the flow of liquids influenced by inertial, viscous, and gravitational forces requires N_{Re} and Froude number, N_{Fr}, similarities, in which the Froude number is defined as $N_{Fr} = V^2/gL$, where L is the characteristic dimension of the system. This is obtained when water at the temperature to achieve proper kinematic viscosity is used in models of the same size as the real system.

Recently, computerized data acquisition systems have been used to observe the flow of molten metal into nontransparent three-dimensional molds. Two types of sensors have been used: simple contact wires and thermocouples. The simple contact wires are connected to the digital inputs of the data acquisition unit. Molten metal contacting a bare copper wire completes a circuit, and this is then detected by the data acquisition unit. The digital inputs can be read very rapidly by the computer; it is possible to read hundreds of such contact points many times during the filling of a single mold. An accurate picture of the location of the metal at any time can be developed from these data.

● Momentum Balance Techniques

Fluid flow within the mold cavity during filling is transient; the amount and location of the liquid changes rapidly. Calculation of the location of the liquid and the orientation of its free surface must be an integral part of the computational techniques used to model it. The family of computational techniques called MAC, SMAC, and solution algorithm-volume of fluid (SOLA-VOF) are well suited for handling these problems. Although they differ from each other in the way they keep track of the location of the free surface and the way in which they perform some of the internal iterations, they are based on the same principles. To simplify the discussion, the acronym MAC is used to represent this whole family of computational fluid dynamics techniques.

● MAC Technique Highlights

MAC uses a finite-difference scheme for the mathematical analysis of fluid flow problems (Ref 19). Like most of these techniques, MAC first divides the system (that is, the configuration of the casting cavity under discussion) into a number of subdivisions, called cells, which are usually rectangular. Then a set of imaginary markers (in MAC and SMAC) or fluid function values called F (in SOLA-VOF) is introduced into the system to represent the location of the fluid at any instant. The velocity field of the moving fluid domain can be calculated by the application of fluid dynamics principles. Next, the markers are moved, or the fluid function is updated, according to the calculated velocity field in order to represent the new location of the fluid domain. This procedure can be repeated from the beginning when the cavity is empty until it is completely filled.

● Fluid Domain Identification

In MAC, the cells are designated as full, surface, or empty, based on the location of markers or the distribution of the fluid function. With the marker approach, a full cell is one that contains at least one marker, if all of its neighboring cells contain markers as well. A surface cell contains at least one marker, but has at least one neighbor without any markers. An empty cell is any cell with no markers.

With the fluid function technique, F represents the fraction of the volume of a cell that is filled with fluid. *F* can have values from 0 to 1. *F* is 1 for a full cell, 0 for an empty cell, and some fractional value for surface cells. The fluid function F can also be used to calculate the approximate location and orientation of the free surface of the fluid. Collectively, the full cells constitute the interior region, and the surface cells constitute the surface regions.

● Fluid Flow Phenomena in the Filling of Metal Castings

Fluid flow calculations can help gain an understanding of flow phenomena occurring during mold filling. To illustrate this, the results of MAC calculations applied to some simple mold designs are presented below.

The case is a horizontal square plate 610mm × 610mm, with a 122mm wide ingate at the center of the left wall, through which metal enters at 305 mm/s. The mold fills in 10s. For numerical analysis, the casting was divided into 400 square cells (20 in each direction). Results of the computation (Fig. 1-26) show that as the metal enters the mold, the stream expands slightly before reaching the far wall. Upon reaching the wall, the stream splits in two, building up along the far side of the cavity and then reflecting back toward the ingate. The two vortices that form, one on either side of the gate, are the last regions to fill, and any gases in the mold are squeezed to these areas near the end of the filling process.

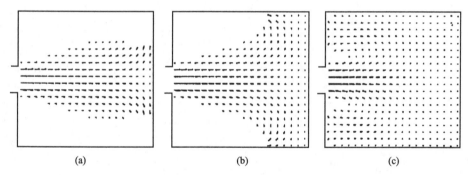

Fig. 1-26 Vector plot showing flow patterns and velocity profiles obtained when filling a horizontal 610 mm × 610mm (2ft × 2ft) square plate casting. Entrance velocity was 305 mm/s (1 ft/s), and vector plots shown are at elapsed times.
(a) 3.95 s; (b) 5.45 s; (c) 9.95 s

● **Vocabulary**

amenable *adj*. 有责任的，应服从的；经得起检验的
momentum *n*. 势头；动量；动力；冲力
configuration *n*. 配置；结构；外形
scalar *adj*. 标量的；数量的 *n*. 标量；数量
laminar *adj*. 层状的；薄片状的；板状的
kinematic *adj*. 运动学上的，运动学的
viscous *adj*. 黏性的；黏的

transient *adj*. 短暂的；路过的 *n*. 瞬变现象
integral *adj*. 积分的；完整的，整体的 *n*. 积分；部分；完整
algorithm *n*. 算法，运算法则
iteration *n*. 迭代；反复；重复
dynamics *n*. 动力学，力学
rectangular *adj*. 矩形的；成直角的
incompressible *adj*. 不能压缩的

Questions
1. Talk about the advantages of modeling of fluid flow.
2. What are the highlights of MAC technique?

Unit 14

Modeling of Combined Fluid Flow and Heat/Mass Transfer

Fluid Flow and Heat/Mass Transfer principles are increasingly gaining acceptance as a means of improving the quality and yield of castings. The benefits to be derived from adopting such an approach range from slag- and dross-free gating system design to a desired microstructure of the finished product. In general, the transport of heat, mass, and momentum during solidification processing controls such varied phenomena as solute macrosegregation, distribution of voids and porosity, shrinkage effects, and overall solidification time. These parameters, in turn, result in a variation of the mechanical, thermophysical, and electrical properties of the solidified product.

The complex nature of the coupling between heat and mass transport with fluid flow during solidification necessitates a fundamental understanding of the processes and the mechanisms of interaction in relation to empirical formulas and charts. Heat transfer by forced convection predominates during the filling stages. Once the mold cavity is filled, buoyancy-generated natural convective heat and mass transfer occur before the phase change.

The principles of heat transfer by forced convection are shown schematically in Fig. 1-27, which is a representation of flowing metal at a superheated pouring temperature T_{01} and a velocity u advancing into a mold channel of width $2d$ and length L, initially at an ambient temperature T_{02}. Stage 1 shows the channel just before the liquid metal enters. Stages 2 and 3 show the liquid region R_1 occupying half and almost full lengths of the channel, respectively. The temperature at the liquid metal/mold wall interface keeps evolving as the flowing metal front advances into the channel. The portion of the mold wall not yet covered by the flowing metal remains at a considerably lower temperature. Stage 4 shows the completely filled channel with conventional steady flow and heat transfer processes.

Subsequent stages during the solidification of a binary alloy involve both phase change heat and mass transfer as well as buoyant thermosolutal convection.

Fig. 1-28 shows a schematic representation of the stages in the solidification of a binary alloy. Solidification begins with cooling across boundary B_{II} between the liquid metal region R_{IV} and the mold region R_I, together with cooling at boundary B_I between the mold and the ambient [Fig. 1-28(a)]. Next, the solid/liquid mushy region R_{III} evolves between boundary B_{II} with the mold and B_{IV} with the liquid metal [Fig. 1-28(b)]. Further cooling leads to a typical steady-state picture showing a solidified crust region R_{II} with boundaries B_{II} and B_{III} with the mold and the mush, respectively, and the mushy region R_{III} with boundaries B_{III} and B_{IV} with the crust and the liquid, respectively [Fig. 1-28(c)]. The final

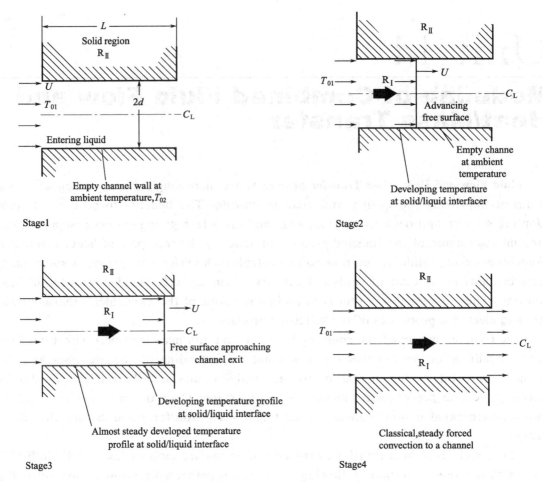

Fig. 1-27 Filling stages in an empty channel

transient stage shows the depletion of the all-liquid region R_{IV} [Fig. 1-28(d)].

● Heat Loss During Filling

Pioneering work on heat loss from the flowing metal to the sand mold runners consisted of obtaining plots of temperature loss versus time, with the ratio of surface area to flow rate used as a parameter. Assuming instantaneous filling and negligible contact resistance between the sand mold and the flowing metal, this method gives good results. A modified version of the method, intended for a constant or linearly decreasing average velocity of the molten metal, indicates that the temperature loss in the runner decreases with time and is proportional to the residence time of the fluid element in the runner. These results can be used to calculate temperature loss for a variety of runner lengths, flow rates, runner diameters, pouring temperatures, and sand mold thermal properties. However, the results are not accurate for metallic molds, nor for very short times after pouring.

● Postfilling Buoyant Convection

The loss of liquid metal superheat in the casting cavity of the mold after the filling transients have died out occurs by buoyancy-generated convection currents. These currents

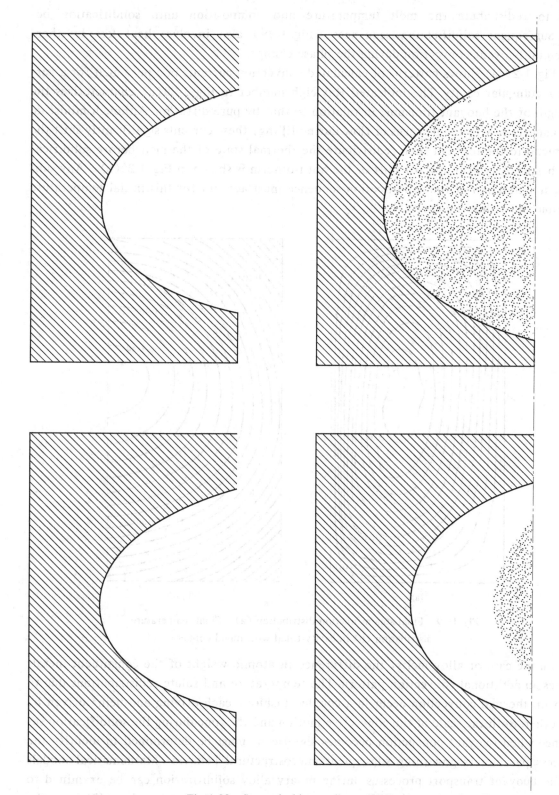

Fig. 1-28 Stages in binary alloy solidification
(a) All liquid. (b) Initial transient. (c) Steady state. (d) Final transient

tend to redistribute the melt temperature and composition until solidification begins. Subsequent solidification sequences (Fig. 1-28) also involves heat loss by thermosolutal buoyant convection during the phase change.

Fig. 1-29(a) shows patterns of calculated convection currents in a pure melt for a vertical rectangular cavity. The indicated Rayleigh number in Fig. 1-29(a) characterizes the strength of the buoyant transport in relation to that by pure diffusion. Although miniscule in comparison with the patterns of flow during filling, these currents significantly shift the hot metal to the top and then redistribute the thermal state of the melt before solidification begins. A typical upward shift of the hot isotherm is shown in Fig. 1-29(b). Any subsequent simulation of the solidification sequence must account for this initial temperature distribution within the cavity.

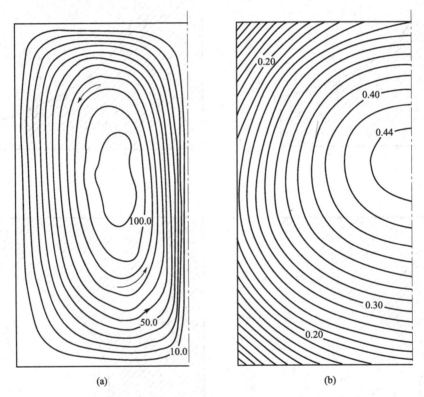

Fig. 1-29 Final steam function distribution (a), Final temperature distribution (b) in cavity filled with liquid copper

In the case of alloy melts, the difference in atomic weight of the constituent metals causes an additional convection pattern. The temperature and solute redistributions due to buoyant thermal convection occur in a coupled fashion, each driving and being driven by the other. Both the scale of the convective motion and the time during the solidification sequence when buoyant convection becomes significant must be determined to identify the process parameters governing subsequent microstructural behavior. Mathematical models of the buoyant transport processes during binary alloy solidification can be examined to obtain the applicable time, length, and motion scales for the liquid, the solid, and the mushy zones depicted in Fig. 1-28. Of these, the most crucial issue from the metallurgical viewpoint is the evolution of the mushy zone and the factors that govern it.

● **Vocabulary**

macrosegregation n. 宏观偏析；巨观沉析；宏观分离	depletion n. 消耗；损耗
void adj. 空的；无效的 n. 空间；空隙 vt. 使无效；排放	miniscule adj. 草写小字的；小字体的
	centerline n. 中心线
	mushy adj. 糊状的；多空隙的
buoyancy n. 浮力；轻快；轻松的心情	isotherm n. 等温线
channel vt. 引导，开导；形成河道 n. 通道	insulating adj. 绝缘的；隔热的 v. 使绝缘；隔离
crust n. 外壳；坚硬外皮 vi. 结硬皮；结成外壳	symmetric adj. 对称的；匀称的

● **Questions**

1. Talk about the principles of heat transfer by forced convection.
2. Please represent the stages in the solidification of a binary alloy.

Unit 15

Modeling of Microstructural Evolution

  The Modeling of Solidification of castings has received increased attention as the computer revolution has matured. The main application of this technique has traditionally been calculation of the path of the isotherms (lines of constant temperature) through shaped castings. In turn, this was used to predict the locations of hot spots in castings and thus to check, using the computer, a proposed gating and risering system, rather than following the classical trial-anderror technique used in foundries.

  This article will discuss techniques used for the simulation of solidification of castings. These techniques combine the modeling of heat transfer (macromodeling) with the modeling of microstructural evolution (micromodeling).

● Modeling of Columnar Structures

  The macroscopic approach can be reasonably applied to columnar solidification because the growth rate of the microstructure (eutectic front or dendrite tips) is more or less equal to the speed at which the corresponding isotherms move (eutectic or liquidus isolines). Therefore, microstructural parameters and undercooling can be directly calculated from the temperature field in this case.

  Columnar growth morphologies are encountered in both dendritic and eutectic alloys. Solidification occurs in a columnar fashion when the growth speed of the dendrite tip or the eutectic front v_s is directly related to the speed v_m of the isotherms calculated from a macroscopic approach. It is therefore necessary to have a positive thermal gradient G at the solid/liquid interface. However, this condition is not sufficient to ensure the formation of columnar structures.

  In a given macroscopic thermal environment, one can calculate:
- The undercooling ΔT_C associated with the formation of a columnar structure;
- The nucleation undercooling ΔT_N at which nuclei are formed within the melt;
- The undercooling ΔT_E required to drive equiaxed solidification.

  Under steady-state growth conditions and considering these three undercoolings, a simple criterion to obtain a fully columnar structure can be defined by:

$$G > A N_0^{1/3} \left[1 - \left(\frac{\Delta T_N}{\Delta T_C} \right)^3 \right] \Delta T_C \tag{1-14}$$

where N_0 is the density of grains nucleated at the undercooling ΔT_N, and A is a constant. Assuming that the thermal gradient G is large enough to ensure that a columnar structure is produced, microstructure formation theories can be easily implemented into macroscopic heat flow calculations if one makes the following hypotheses:
- The kinetics of the eutectic front or the dendrite tip are given by the steady-state growth analysis;

- The velocity of the microstructure v_s is related to the velocity v_m of the corresponding equilibrium isotherm, as shown in Fig. 1-30.

In Fig. 1-30, four different microstructures frequently encountered in solidification are shown: regular and irregular eutectics and cellular and dendritic morphologies. In the first three cases, one has simply:

$$v_s = v_m \tag{1-15}$$

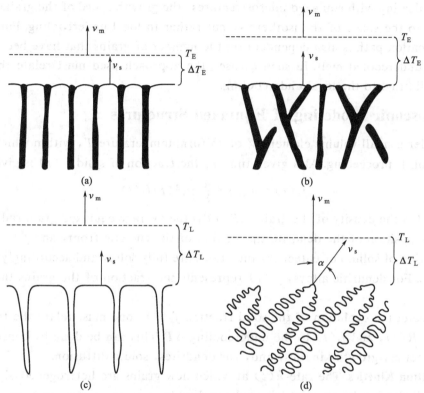

Fig. 1-30　Relationship between growth velocity of the macroscopic isotherms v_m and growth velocity v_s of four different columnar microstructures
(a) and (b) Regular and irregular eutectics, respectively; (c) Cells; (d) Dendrites

For dendritic alloys, the velocity of the dendrite tip is essentially dictated by the trunk orientation, which is imposed more or less by the crystallographic orientation of the solid (for example, ⟨100⟩ for cubic metals). If α is the angle between the trunk orientation and the heat flow direction, then:

$$v_s = \frac{v_m}{\cos\alpha} \tag{1-16}$$

In castings, grain selection will occur such that those grains whose angle α is close to zero will grow preferentially. However, dendritic single-crystal growth or epitaxial dendritic growth from single-crystal substrates can be characterized by an α value that can deviate substantially from zero.

Based on the two hypotheses mentioned previously, the kinetics of microstructure formation can be implemented into macroscopic heat flow calculations according to the following simple scheme. One first calculates the temperature field evolution without taking into account any undercooling. Once the temperature field is known, the velocity of the corresponding isotherms (liquidus or eutectic temperature) can be deduced as well as the thermal gradient at the interface. From these values, the undercooling of the columnar microstructure and the associated parameters of the microstructure (eutectic or dendrite trunk spacings) can be calculated using recent theories of microstructure formation.

● Modeling of Equiaxed Structures

When dealing with equiaxed microstructures, the growth speed of the grains is no longer related to the speed of the isotherms, but rather to local undercooling. Furthermore, the solidification path is also dependent on the number of grains that have been nucleated within the undercooled melt. In such a case, the approach used must relate the fraction that has solidified to the local undercooling.

● Microscopic Modeling of Equiaxed Structures

Consider a small volume element V of uniform temperature T, within which equiaxed solidification is proceeding. At a given time t, the fraction of solid $f_s(t)$ is given:

$$f_s(t) = n(t) \times \frac{4}{3}\pi R^3(t) f_i(t) \tag{1-17}$$

where $n(t)$ is the density of the grains, $R(t)$ is the average equiaxed grain radius characterizing the position of the dendrite tips or that of the eutectic front, and $f_i(t)$ is the internal fraction of solid. For eutectics, the grains are fully solid, and accordingly $f_i(t) = 1$ at any time. For dendritic alloys, $f_i(t)$ represents the fraction of the grains that is really solid.

To predict the evolution of the solid fraction $f_s(t)$, one must relate the three variables $n(t)$, $R(t)$, and $f_i(t)$ to the undercooling ΔT. This can be done by considering nucleation kinetics, growth kinetics, and, for dendrites, solute diffusion.

Nucleation Kinetics. The rate $\dot{n}(t)$ at which new grains are heterogeneously nucleated within the liquid can be given at low undercooling by:

$$\dot{n}(t) = k_1[n_0 - n(t)]\exp\left\{\frac{-k_2}{\Delta T(t)^2}\right\} \tag{1-18}$$

where k_1 is proportional to a collision frequency with nucleation sites, n_0 is the total number of sites present in the melt before solidification, and k_2 is a constant related to the interfacial energy between substrate and nucleated grain. The constants k_1, n_0 and k_2 must be deduced from experiment. Once they are known, the grain density $n(t)$ can be predicted at each time by integrating Eq (1-18) over time or temperature:

$$n(t) = \int_{\tau_0}^{t} \dot{n}(\tau) d\tau = \int_{0}^{\Delta T} \dot{n}(T) \frac{dT}{dT/dt} \tag{1-19}$$

However, this approach fails to predict the correct grain density, in part because the temperature interval within which nucleation proceeds is very narrow. For an undercooling ΔT smaller than a critical value, $\Delta T_N = \sqrt{k_2}$, there is no significant nucleation. When ΔT_N is reached, $n(t)$ increases very rapidly to its saturation limit n_0. Therefore, it is suggested to replace the complex nucleation law of Eq (1-18) by a Dirac function in solidification modeling:

$$\frac{dn}{dT} = n_0 \delta(T - T_N) = n_0 \delta(\Delta T - \sqrt{k_2}) \tag{1-20}$$

Where δ iselongation rate.

Growth. Evolution of the grain radius $R(t)$ can also be related to the undercooling ΔT of the volume element. The speed v of a eutectic front is related to the undercooling through the relationship:

$$v = \frac{dR}{dt} = \mu(\Delta T)^2 \tag{1-21}$$

where μ is a constant depending on the characteristics of the alloy.

For dendritic alloys, a similar relationship has been deduced in the approximation of a hemispherical dendrite tip, which relates the square of the undercooling ΔT to the velocity v of the dendrite tips. Therefore, Eq (1-21), with a different μ value, can be used to predict the evolution of grain size. However, in the case of dendrites, one must still calculate the evolution of the interval volume fraction of solid $f_i(t)$ [Eq (1-17)]. For that purpose, a solute diffusion model has recently been developed. Assuming that there is complete mixing of solute within the interdendritic liquid of the spherical grain envelope outlined by the dendrite tip position, the researchers considered the solute balance at the scale of the equiaxed grain and the solute flow leaving out the grain envelope. They found that:

$$f_i(t) = \Omega(t) g(\delta, R) \tag{1-22}$$

where $\Omega = (C^* - C_0)/[C^*(1-k)]$ is the supersaturation, $g(\delta, R)$ is a correction function that takes into account the solute layer δ around the grain envelope, C^* is the concentration within the interdendritic liquid, C_0 is the initial concentration, and k is the partition coefficient. Because the undercooling ΔT is equal to $m(C^* - C_0)$, where m is the slope of the liquidus, $f_i(t)$ is again directly related to ΔT through Eq (1-22).

● Vocabulary

microstructural   adj. 显微结构的
risering   n. 冒口；浇口杯
evolution   n. 演变；进化；进展
macroscopic   adj. 宏观的；肉眼可见的
conservation   n. 保存，保持；保护；守恒
isoline   n. 等值线；隔离
morphology   n. 形态学，形态论
eutectic   adj. 共熔的；容易溶解的   n. 共熔合金
columnar   adj. 柱状的；圆柱的
equiaxed   adj. 各向等大的；等轴的
supersaturation   n. 过度饱和；过饱和度

hypotheses   n. 假定；臆测（hypothesis 的复数）
gradient   n. 梯度；坡度；倾斜度   adj. 倾斜的；步行的
crystallographic   adj. 结晶的；晶体学的
epitaxial   adj. 外延的；取向附生的
deviate   vi. 脱离；越轨   vt. 使偏离
heterogeneous   adj. 多相的；异种的；不均匀的；由不同成分形成的
saturation   n. 饱和；饱和度；浸透
spherical   adj. 球形的，球面的；天体的
interdendritic   adj. 枝晶间，树枝晶间的

● Questions

1. Please talk about the techniques used for the simulation of solidification of castings.
2. What are the microstructures frequently encountered in solidification?
3. How to calculate the macroscopic heat flow?

Part II
Forming and Forging

Unit 1

Introduction to Forming and Forging Process

  Metal Working consists of deformation processes in which a metal billet or blank is shaped by tools or dies. The design and control of such precesses depend on an understanding of the characteristics of the workpiece material, the conditions at the tool/workpiece interface, the mechanics of plastic deformation (metal flow), the equipment used, and the finished-product requirements. These factors influence the selection of tool geometry and material as well as processing conditions (for example, workpiece and die temperatures and lubrication). Because of the complexity of many metalworking operations, models of various types, such as analytic, physical, or numerical models, are often relied upon to design such processes.

  This article will provide a brief historical perspective, a classification of metalworking processes and equipment, and a summary of some of the more recent developments in the field.

● Historical Perspective

  Metalworking is one of three major technologies used to fabricate metal products; the others are casting and powder metallurgy. However, metalworking is perhaps the oldest and most mature of the three. The earliest records of metalworking describe the simple hammering of gold and copper in various regions of the Middle East around 8000 B. C. . The forming of these metals was crude because the art of refining by smelting was unknown and because the ability to work the material was limited by impurities that remained after the metal had been separated from the ore. With the advent of copper smelting around 4000 B. C. , a useful method became available for purifying metals through chemical reactions in the liquid state. Later, in the Copper Age, it was found that the hammering of metal brought about desirable increases in strength (a phenomenon now known as strain hardening). The quest for strength spurred a search for alloys that were inherently strong and led to the utilization of alloys of copper and tin (the Bronze Age) and iron and carbon (the Iron Age). The Iron Age, which can be dated as beginning around 1200 B. C. , followed the beginning of the Bronze Age by some 1300 years. The reason for the delay was the absence of methods for achieving the high temperatures needed to melt and to refine iron ore.

  Most metalworking was done by hand until the 13th century. At this time, the tilt hammer was developed and used primarily for forging bars and plates. The machine used water power to raise a lever arm that had a hammering tool at one end; it was called a tilt hammer because the arm tilted as the hammering tool was rised. After raising the hammer, the blacksmith let it fall under the force of gravity, thus generating the forging blow. This relatively simple device remained in service for some centuries.

The development of rolling mills followed that of forging equipment. Leonardo da Vinci's notebook includes a sketch of a machine designed in 1480 for the rolling of lead for stained glass windows. In 1945, da Vinci is reported to have rolled flat sheets of precious metal on a hand-operated two-roll mill for coin-making purposes. In the following years, several designs for rolling mills were utilized in Germany, Italy, France, and England. However, the development of large mills capable of hot rolling ferrous materials took almost 200 years. This relatively slow progress was primarily due to the limited supply of iron. Early mills employed flat rolls for making sheet and plate, and until the middle of the 18th century, these mills were driven by water wheels.

During the Industrial Revolution at the end of the 18th century, processes were devised for making iron and steel in large quantities to satisfy the demand for metal products. A need arose for forging equipment with larger capacity. This need was answered with the invention of the high-speed steam hammer, in which the hammer is raised by steam power, and the hydraulic press, in which the force is supplied by hydraulic pressure. From such equipment came products ranging from firearms to locomotive parts. Similarly, the steam engine spurred developments in rolling, and in the 19th century, a variety of steel products were rolled in significant quantities.

The past 100 years have seen the development of new types of metalworking equipment and new materials with special properties and applications. The new types of equipment have included mechanical and screw presses and high-speed tandem rolling mills. The materials that have benefited from such developments in equipment range from the ubiquitous low-carbon steel used in automobiles and appliances to specialty aluminum-, titanium-, and nickel-base alloys. In the last 20 years, the formulation of sophisticated mathematical analyses of forming processes has led to higher-quality products and increased efficiency in the metalworking industry.

● Classification of Metalworking Processes

In metalworking, an initially simple part—a billet or a blanked sheet, for example—is plastically deformed between tools(or dies) to obtain the desired final configuration. Metal-forming processes are usually classified according to two broad categories:
- Bulk, or massive, forming operations;
- Sheet forming operations.

In both types of process, the surfaces of the deforming metal and the tools are in contact, and friction between them may have a major influence on material flow. In bulk forming, the input material is in billet, rod, or slab form, and the surface-to-volume ratio in the formed part increases considerably under the action of largely compressive loading. In sheet forming, on the other hand, a piece of sheet metal is plastically deformed by tensile loads into a three-dimensional shape, often without significant changes in sheet thickness or surface characteristic.

Processes that fall under the category of bulk forming have the following distinguishing features:
- The deforming material, or workpiece, undergoes large plastic (permanent) deformation, resulting in an appreciable change in shape or cross section.

- The portion of the workpiece undergoing plastic deformation is generally much larger than the portion undergoing elastic deformation; therefore, elastic recovery after deformation is negligible.

Examples of generic bulk forming processes are extrusion, forging, rolling, and drawing.

The characteristics of sheet metal forming processes are as follows:
- The workpiece is a sheet or a part fabricated from a sheet.
- The deformation usually causes significant changes in the shape, but not the cross-sectional area, of the sheet.
- In some cases, the magnitudes of the plastic and the elastic (recoverable) deformations are comparable; therefore, elastic recovery or springback may be significant.

Examples of processes that fall under the category of sheet metal forming are deep drawing, stretching, bending, and rubber-pad forming.

● Types of Metalworking Equipment

The various forming processes discussed above are associated with a large variety of forming machines or equipment, including the following:
- Rolling mills for plate, strip, and shapes.
- Machines for profile rolling from strip.
- Ring-rolling machines.
- Thread-rolling and surface-rolling machines.
- Magnetic and explosive forming machines.
- Draw benches for tube and rod; wire- and rod-drawing machines.
- Machines for pressing-type operations (presses).

Among those listed above, pressing-type machines are the most widely used and are applied to both bulk and sheet forming processes. These machines can be classified into three types: load-restricted machines (hydraulic presses), stroke-restricted machines (crank and eccentric, or mechanical, presses), and energy-restricted machines (hammers and screw presses). The significant characteristics of pressing-type machines comprise all machine design and performance data that are pertinent to the economical use of the machine. These characteristics include:
- Characteristics for load and energy: Available load, available energy, and efficiency factor (which equals the energy available for workpiece deformation/energy supplied to the machine).
- Time-related characteristics: Number of strokes per minute, contact time under pressure, and velocity under pressure.
- Characteristics for accuracy: For example, deflection of the ram and frame, particularly under off-center loading, and press stiffness.

● New Processes

A number of processes have recently been introduced or accepted. These include a variety of forging processes, such as radial, precision, rotary, metal powder, and isothermal forging, as well as sheet forming processes, such as superplastic forming.

Radial Forging is a technique that is most often used to manufacture axisymmetrical parts, such as gun barrels. Radial forging machines use the radial hot- or cold-forging principle with three, four, or six hammers to produce solid or hollow round, square, rectangular, or profiled sections. The machines used for forging large gun barrels are of a horizontal type and can size the bore of the gun barrel to the exact rifling that is machined on the mandrel. Products produced by radial forging often have improved mechanical and metallurgical properties as compared to those produced by other, more conventional techniques.

Precision Forging, also known as draftless forging, is a relatively recent development that is distinguished from other types of forging principally by finished products with thinner and more detailed geometric features, virtual elimination of drafted surfaces and machining allowances, varying die parting line locations, and closer dimensional tolerances. These types of parts are most commonly manufactured from light metals, such as aluminum, and more recently from titanium for aerospace applications in which weight, strength, and intricate shaping are important considerations, along with price and delivery.

Superplastic Forming is the sheet forming counterpart to isothermal forging. The isothermal, low strain rate conditions in superplastic forming result in low workpiece flow stress. Therefore, gas pressure, rather than a hard punch, is most often used to carry out a stretching-type operation; the only tooling requirement is a female die. The very high tensile ductilities characteristic of superplastically formed sheet alloys such as Ti-6Al-4V, Zn-22Al enable the forming of parts of very complex shape. Although cycle times for superplastic forming are relatively long (of the order of 10min per part), economies of manufacture are realized primarily through reduced machining and assembly costs.

● Vocabulary

deformation   n. 变形
billet   n. 方钢，坯锭，坯料
blank   n. 毛坯，坯料
workpiece   n. 工件；轧件；工件壁厚
lubrication   n. 润滑；润滑作用；润滑剂
metalworking   n. 金属加工；金属制造
   adj. 金属制造的
hammering   n. 锤击；锤打   v. 锤打；锤锻
rolling   n. 旋转；轧制；滚轧
bulk   n. 体积，容量；大部分；大块
massive   adj. 大量的；巨大的，厚重的；块状的

tensile   adj. 拉力的；张力的；可伸长的
extrusion   n. 挤出；挤压；挤制加工
forging   n. 锻造；锻件   v. 锻造；打制
drawing   n. 拉，拔，牵引，拉延
springback   n. 回弹，反弹，回跳
stretching   n. 拉伸；伸展   v. 拉伸
bending   n. 弯曲度；弯曲；折弯   v. 弯曲
crank   n. 曲柄；曲柄轴   vt. 装曲柄
stroke   n. 冲程；行程
deflection   n. 偏向；挠曲；偏差
superplastic   adj. 超塑性的   n. 超塑性；超塑性材料
mandrel   n. 心轴；轴柄

● Questions

1. What are the distinguishing features of bulk forming?
2. Please tell the characteristics of sheet metal forming processes.
3. Please give some types of forming machines or equipment for plastic forming.

Unit 2
Open-Die Forging

Open-Die Forging, also referred to as hand, smith, hammer, and flat-die forging, can be distinguished from most other types of deformation processes in that it provides discontinuous material flow as opposed to continuous flow. Forgings are made by this process when:
- The forging is too large to be produced in closed dies.
- The required mechanical properties of the worked metal that can be developed by open-die forging cannot be obtained by other deformation processes.
- The quantity required is too small to justify the cost of closed dies.
- The delivery date is too close to permit the fabrication of dies for closed-die forging.

All forgeable metals can be forged in open dies.

● **Shapes**

Highly skilled hammer and press operators, with the use of various auxiliary tools, can produce relatively complex shapes in open dies. However, the forging of complex shapes is time consuming and expensive, and such forgings are produced only under unusual circumstances. Generally, most open-die forgings can be grouped into four categories: cylindrical (shaft-type forgings symmetrical about the longitudinal axis), upset or pancake forgings, hollow (including mandrel and shell-type forgings), and contour-type forgings.

● **Hammers and Presses**

Because the length of the hammer ram stroke and the magnitude of the force must be controllable over a wide range throughout the forging cycle, gravity-drop hammers and most mechanical presses are not suitable for open-die forging. Power forging hammers (air or steam driven) and hydraulic presses are most commonly used for the production of open-die forgings that weigh up to 4.5 Mg (5 tons). Larger forgings are usually made in hydraulic presses.

● **Dies**

Most open-die forgings are produced in a pair of flat dies—one attached to the hammer or to the press ram, and the other to the anvil. Swage dies (curved), V-dies, V-die and flat-die combinations, FM (free from Mannesmann Effect) dies and FML (free from Mannesmann Effect with low load) dies are also used. The Mannesmann Effect refers to a tensile stress state as a result of compressive stresses in a perpendicular orientation. These die sets are shown in Fig. 2-1. In some applications, forging is done with a combination of a flat die and a swage die. The dies are attached to platens and rams by either of the methods shown in Fig. 2-1 (a) and (b).

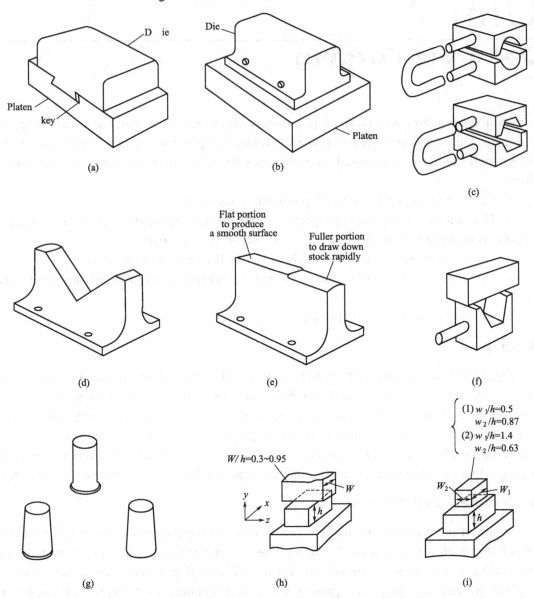

Fig. 2-1 Typical dies and punches used in open-die forging

(a) Die mounted with dovetail and key. (b) Flange-mounted die. (c) Swages for producing smooth round and hexagonal bars. (d) V-die. (e) Combination die (bar die). (f) Single loose die with flat top for producing hexagonal bars. (g) Three styles of hole-punching tools. (h) FM process. (i) FML process

● **Auxiliary Tools**

Mandrels, saddle supports, sizing blocks (spacers), ring tools, bolsters, fullers, punches, drifts (expansion tools), and a wide variety of special tools (for producing shapes) are used as auxiliary tools in forging production. Because most auxiliary tools are exposed to heat, they are usually made from the same steels as the dies.

Saddle Supports. An open-die forging can be made with an upper die that is flat, while the lower die utilizes another type of tool. Two or more hammers or presses and die setups are often needed to complete a shape (or operations are done at different times in the same hammer or press by changing the tooling). For example, large rings are made by upsetting the stock between two flat dies, punching out the center, and then saddle forging.

Sizing Blocks. A sizing block can be used between the mandrel and the ram to prevent the cross section of the workpiece from being forged too thin. Most state-of-the-art presses have automatic sizing or thickness controls.

Ring Tools. A tonghold can be retained on a forging so that the forging can be more easily handled after upsetting. A ring tool with a center opening is placed on the workpiece. During the upsetting, the hot work metal at the ring tool opening is protected from being upset, and it is back extruded to a tonghold with a length equal to the thickness of the ring tool. Alternatively, the tonghold can be forged on one end of the workpiece prior to upsetting; a hole in the lower die protects the tonghold during the upsetting operation.

Punches. To make holes, punches are placed on the hot workpiece and are driven through, or partly through, by a ram. A hole can also be made by punching from both sides. Relatively deep holes can be produced by punching from both sides until only a thin center section remains.

● Ingot Structure and Its Elimination

Ingots are extensively used as forging stock in the open-die forging of large components. Whenever ingots are used, it is desirable (and often mandatory) to adopt a forging procedure that will remove the cast structure (ingotism) in the finished forging. Fig. 2-2 shows a schematic cross section of a large ferrous forging ingot. Because of the large diameter of heavy forging ingots (up to 4.1m, or 160in.), the solidification process is extremely slow, often taking as long as 2 to 3 days. Unfortunately, the slow cooling rate causes considerable macrosegregation, especially in the ingot center toward the top of the

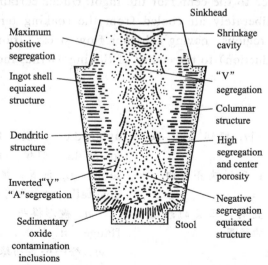

Fig. 2-2 Schematic illustrating macrosegregation in a large steel ingot

ingot. Consequently, the center of the ingot must be mechanically worked during the forging operation to redistribute the segregated elements and to heal internal porosity.

The segregated regions are usually associated with a coarse dendritic structure; therefore, breaking up these regions by using hot deformation leads to refined microstructures. Compression of the dendritic arms reduces the local diffusion distance, which can enhance homogenization during subsequent heat treatment. Repeated hot deformation also causes grain refinement through static and/or dynamic recrystallization of the austenite. Finer austenitic grain sizes promote finer microstructures during subsequent transformation to ferrite, pearlite, and bainite or martensite or both. Finer microstructures lead to more uniform mechanical properties and, in general, improved tensile properties coupled with greater toughness. However, nonuniform hot deformation can lead to undesirable duplex microstructures, that is, mixed fine and coarse grain size/transformation products. Segregated regions containing higher alloy concentrations can also lead to nonuniform recrystallization and grain growth.

Various approaches are available for minimizing the undesirable effects of segregation. In some forgings, the centerline is actually removed from the finished product in the form of a core bar by machine trepanning. This is permissible for some symmetrical rotating machinery; however, many forgings are not symmetrical, and the center region cannot be removed. In these cases, the thermal and thermomechanical treatments must be optimized in order to redistribute the solute elements. Long homogenization treatments at temperatures approaching 1290 ℃ are frequently conducted to allow some diffusion of alloying elements. However, redistribution (homogenization) of the substitutional solid-solution elements, such as manganese, silicon, nickel, chromium, molybdenum, and vanadium, would require several weeks at temperature, which is far too long to be economically feasible. The other alternative is to put as much hot work as possible into the segregated regions.

Hot deformation in the center of the ingot is enhanced when there is a temperature gradient from the surface to the center of the ingot. Under certain circumstances in production, ingots are deliberately air cooled from the soaking temperature before forging. The cooler surface regions, having a higher flow stress, translate the forces of the draft (percentage of reduction) to the center of the ingot, thus increasing centerline consolidation.

● Vocabulary

smith　n. 铁匠；锻工　vt. 锻制　vi. 锻打金属；当锻工
swage　vt. 型铁；铁模；用型铁弄弯曲　n. 型砧；冲模
perpendicular　adj. 垂直的，正交的；直立的　n. 垂线；垂直的位置
platens　n. 滚筒；压板
bolster　n. 垫板；长枕；上下模板
punch　n. 冲压机；冲头；冲子

upper die　上模；上模板
lower die　凹模；下模
setup　n. 设置；机构；安装
dovetail　vt. 用鸠尾榫接合；与……吻合　n. 楔形榫头
flange　n. 法兰；凸缘；边缘　vt. 给……装凸缘
tonghold　n. 夹头
ingotism　n. 巨晶

recrystallization   n. 再结晶；重结晶
austenitic   adj. 奥氏体的
pearlite   n. 珠光体
bainite   n. 贝氏体

martensite   n. 马氏体
thermomechanical   adj. 热机的，热机械的

● **Questions**

1. Please tell some special tools that used as auxiliary tools in forging production.
2. Talk about the macrosegregation in a large steel ingot.

Unit 3

Closed-Die Forging in Hammers and Presses

Closed-Die Forging, or impression-die forging, is the shaping of hot metal completely within the walls or cavities of two dies that come together to enclose the workpiece on all sides. The impression for the forging can be entirely in either die or can be divided between the top and bottom dies.

The forging stock, generally round or square bar, is cut to length to provide the volume of metal needed to fill the die cavities, in addition to an allowance for flash and sometimes for a projection for holding the forging. The flash allowance is, in effect, a relief valve for the extreme pressure produced in closed dies. Flash also acts as a brake to slow the outward flow of metal in order to permit complete filling of the desired configuration.

● Capabilities of the Process

With the use of closed dies, complex shapes and heavy reductions can be made in hot metal within closer dimensional tolerances than are usually feasible with open dies. Open dies are primarily used for the forging of simple shapes or for making forgings that are too large to be contained in closed dies. Closed-die forgings are usually designed to require minimal subsequent machining.

Closed-die forging is adaptable to low-volume or high-volume production. In addition to producing final, or nearly final, metal shapes, closed-die forging allows control of grain flow direction, and it often improves mechanical properties in the longitudinal direction of the workpiece.

● Forging Materials

In closed-die forging, a material must satisfy two basic requirements. First, the material strength (or flow stress) must be low so that die pressures are kept within the capabilities of practical die materials and constructions, and, second, the forgeability of the material must allow the required amount of deformation without failure. By convention, closed-die forging refers to hot working. The forging material influences the design of the forging itself as well as the details of the entire forging process. For a given metal, both the flow stress and the forgeability are influenced by the metallurgical characteristics of the billet material and by the temperatures, strains, strain rates, and stresses that occur in the deforming material.

In most practical hot-forging operations, the temperature of the workpiece material is higher than that of the dies. Metal flow and die filling are largely determined by the resistance and the ability of the forging material to flow, that is, flow stress and forgeability; by the friction and cooling effects at the die/material interface; and by the complexity of the forging shape. Of the two basic material characteristics, flow stress represents the resistance of a metal to plastic deformation, and forgeability represents the ability of a metal to deform without failure, regardless of the magnitude of load and stresses required for deformation.

● Friction and Lubrication in Forging

In forging, friction greatly influences metal flow, pressure distribution, and load and energy requirements. In addition to lubrication effects, the effects of die chilling or heat transfer from the hot material to colder dies must be considered. For example, for a given lubricant, friction data obtained from hydraulic press forging cannot be used for mechanical press or hammer forging even if die and billet temperatures are comparable.

In forging, the ideal lubricant is expected to:

• Reduce sliding friction between the dies and the forging in order to reduce pressure requirements, to fill the die cavity, and to control metal flow.

• Act as a parting agent and prevent local welding and subsequent damage to the die and workpiece surfaces.

• Possess insulating properties so as to reduce heat losses from the workpiece and to minimize.

temperature fluctuations on the die surface.

• Be nonabrasive and noncorrosive so as to prevent erosion of the die surface.

• Be free of residues that would accumulate in deep impressions.

No single lubricant can fulfill all of the requirements listed above; therefore, a compromise must be made for each specific application.

Various types of lubricants are used, and they can be applied by swabbing or spraying. The simplest is a high flash point oil swabbed onto the dies. Colloidal graphite suspensions in either oil or water are frequently used. Synthetic lubricants can be employed for light forging operations. The water-base and synthetic lubricants are extensively used primarily because of cleanliness.

● Classification of Closed-Die Forgings

Closed-die forgings are generally classified as blocker-type, conventional, and close-tolerance.

Blocker-Type Forgings are produced in relatively inexpensive dies, but their weight and dimensions are somewhat greater than those of corresponding conventional closed-die forgings. A blocker-type forging approximates the general shape of the final part, with relatively generous finish allowance and radii. Such forgings are sometimes specified when only a small number of forgings are required and the cost of machining parts to final shape is not excessive.

Conventional Closed-Die Forgings are the most common type and are produced to comply with commercial tolerances. These forgings are characterized by design complexity and tolerances that fall within the broad range of general forging practice. They are made closer to the shape and dimensions of the final part than are blocker-type forgings; therefore, they are lighter and have more detail.

Close-Tolerance Forgings are usually held to smaller dimensional tolerances than conventional forgings. Little or no machining is required after forging, because close-tolerance forgings are made with less draft, less material, and thinner walls, webs, and ribs. These forgings cost more and require higher forging pressures per unit of plan area than conventional forgings. However, the higher forging cost is sometimes justified by a reduction in machining cost.

● Shape Complexity in Forging

Metal flow in forging is greatly influenced by part or die geometry. Several operations (preforming or blocking) are often needed to achieve gradual flow of the metal from an initially simple shape (cylinder or round-cornered square billet) into the more complex shape of the final forging. In general, spherical and blocklike shapes are the easiest to forge in impression or closed dies. Parts with long, thin sections or projections (webs and ribs) are more difficult to forge because they have more surface area per unit volume. Such variations in shape maximize the effects of friction and temperature changes and therefore influence the final pressure required to fill the die cavities. There is a direct relationship between the surface-to-volume ratio of a forging and the difficulty in producing that forging.

The ease of forging more complex shapes depends on the relative proportions of vertical and horizontal projections on the part. Fig. 2-3 shows a schematic of the effects of shape on forging difficulties. The parts illustrated in Fig. 2-3(c) and (d) would require not only higher forging loads but also at least one more forging operation than the parts illustrated in Fig. 2-3(a) and (b) in order to ensure die filling.

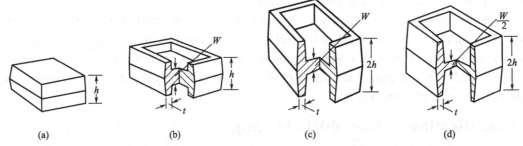

Fig. 2-3 Forging difficulty as a function of part geometry. Difficulty in forging increases from (a) to (d). (a) Rectangular shape. (b) Rib-web part. (c) Part with higher rib. (d) Part with higher rib and thinner web

● Design of Blocker (Preform) Dies

One of the most important aspects of closed-die forging is proper design of preforming operations and of blocker dies to achieve adequate metal distribution. Therefore, in the finish-forging operation, defect-free metal flow and complete die filling can be achieved, and metal losses into the flash can be minimized. In preforming, round or round-cornered square stock with constant cross section is deformed such that a desirable volume distribution is achieved prior to the final closed-die forging operation. In blocking, the preform is die forged in a blocker cavity before finish forging.

The primary objective of preforming is to distribute the metal in the preform in order to:
- Ensure defect-free metal flow and adequate die filling.
- Minimize the amount of material lost into flash.
- Minimize die wear in the finish-forging cavity by reducing metal movement in this direction.
- Achieve desired grain flow and control mechanical properties.

Common practice in preform design is to consider planes of metal flow—that is, selected cross sections of the forging. Several preforming operations may be required before a part can be successfully finish forged. In determining the various forging steps, it is first necessary to obtain the volume of the forging, based on the areas of successive cross sections throughout the forging. A volume distribution can be obtained by using the following procedure:
- Lay out a dimensioned drawing of the finish configuration, complete with flash.
- Construct a baseline for area determination parallel to the centerline of the part.
- Determine maximum and minimum cross-sectional areas perpendicular to the centerline of the part.
- Plot these areas at proportional distances from the baseline.
- Connect these points with a smooth curve. In cases in which it is not clear how the curve would best show the changing cross-sectional areas, plot additional points to assist in determining a smooth representative curve.
- Above this curve, add the approximate area of the flash at each cross section, giving consideration to those sections where the flash should be widest. The flash will generally be of a constant thickness, but will be widest at the narrower sections and smallest at the wider sections.
- Convert the maximum and minimum area values to round or rectangular shapes having the same crosssectional areas.

● Vocabulary

valve　n. 阀；阀门　vt. 装阀于；以活门调节
forging stock　锻坯；锻造用坯
bar　n. 条，棒材
tolerance　n. 公差；宽容；工差
low-volume　小容量的
forgeability　n. 可锻性；锻造性

chilling　adj. n. 冷却；寒冷　v. 冷却
welding　n. 焊接　v. 焊接；锻接
fluctuation　n. 起伏，波动
swabbing　n. 擦（抹）；（起模前）刷水；润滑处理
spraying　n. 喷涂；喷镀　v. 喷射；飞溅
perform　vt. 预先形成　n. 粗加工的成品

● Questions

1. Please tell the capabilities of the closed-die forging process.
2. Why should the lubricant be used in forging?
3. What types of closed-die forgings are generally classified?

Unit 4

Extrusion

● Cold Extrusion

Cold Extrusion is so called because the slug or preform enters the extrusion die at room temperature. Any subsequent increase in temperature, which may amount to several hundred degrees, is caused by the conversion of deformation work into heat. Cold extrusion involves backward (indirect), forward (direct), or combined backward and forward (indirect-direct) displacement of metal by plastic flow under steady, though not uniform, pressure. Backward displacement from a closed die is in the direction opposite to punch travel. Workpieces are often cup-shaped and have wall thicknesses equal to the clearance between the punch and die. In forward extrusion, the work metal is forced in the direction of the punch travel. These two basic methods of extrusion are sometimes combined so that some of the work metal flows backward and some forward.

In cold extrusion, a punch applies pressure to the slug or preform, causing the work metal to flow in the required direction. The relative motion between punch and die is obtained by attaching either one (almost always the die) to the stationary bed and the other to the reciprocating ram. The axis of the machine can be vertical or horizontal. The pressure can be applied rapidly as a sharp blow, as in a crank press or header (impact extrusion), or more slowly by a squeezing action, as in a hydraulic press. The pressure exerted by the punch can be as low as 34.5MPa (5ksi) for soft metals or as high as 3100MPa (450ksi) for extrusion of alloy steel.

Work Hardening of Metals. Metals are work hardened when they are deformed at temperatures below their recrystallization temperatures. This can be an advantage if the service requirements of a part allow its use in the as-formed condition. (Under some conditions, heat treatment is not needed.) Work hardening, however, raises the ratio of yield strength to tensile strength and lowers ductility. Therefore, when several severe cold extrusion operations follow one another, ductility must be restored between operations by annealing. Any scale formed during annealing must be removed by blasting or pickling before subsequent extrusion.

In spite of the high pressure applied to it, the metal being extruded is not compressed to any measurable amount. Except for scale losses in annealing or the inadvertent formation of flash, constancy of volume throughout a sequence of operations is ensured. For all practical purposes, volumetric calculations can be based on the assumption that there is no loss of metal.

Cold-Extruded Metals. Aluminum and aluminum alloys, copper and copper alloys, low-carbon and medium-carbon steels, modified carbon steels, low-alloy steels, and stainless steels are the metals that are most commonly cold extruded. The above listing is in the order of decreasing extrudability. The equipment and tooling are basically the same regardless of the metal being extruded.

Cold Extrusion Versus Alternative Processes. Cold extrusion competes with such alternative metal-forming processes as cold heading, hot forging, hot extrusion, machining, and sometimes casting. Cold extrusion is used when the process is economically attractive because of:

• Savings in material.

• Reduction or elimination of machining and grinding operations, because of the good surface finish and dimensional accuracy of cold-extruded parts.

• Elimination of heat-treating operations, because of the increase in the mechanical properties of cold-extruded parts.

Cold extrusion is sometimes used to produce only a few parts of a certain type, but it is more commonly used for mass production because of the high cost of tools and equipment.

● **Hot Extrusion**

Hot Extrusion is the process of forcing a heated billet to flow through a shaped die opening. The temperature at which extrusion is performed depends on the material being extruded. Hot extrusion is used to produce long, straight metal products of constant cross section, such as bars, solid and hollow sections, tubes, wires, and strips, from materials that cannot be formed by cold extrusion. The three basic types of hot extrusion are nonlubricated, lubricated, and hydrostatic (Fig. 2-4).

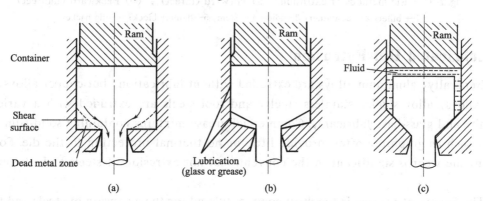

Fig. 2-4 Schematics of the nonlubricated(a), lubricated(b), and hydrostatic(c) extrusion processes

In nonlubricated hot extrusion, the material flows by internal shear, and a dead-metal zone is formed in front of the extrusion die [Fig. 2-4(a)]. Lubricated extrusion, as the name implies, uses a suitable lubricant (usually glass or grease) between the extruded billet and the die [Fig. 2-4(b)]. In hydrostatic extrusion, a fluid film present between the billet and the die exerts pressure on the deforming billet [Fig. 2-4(c)]. The hydrostatic extrusion process is primarily used when conventional lubrication is inadequate—for example, in the extrusion of special alloys, composites, or clad materials. For all practical purposes, hydrostatic extrusion can be considered an extension of the lubricated hot extrusion process.

● Nonlubricated Hot Extrusion

Nonlubricated hot extrusion is a relatively straightforward process once the conditions have been defined. However, a large number of metallurgical and processing factors interact and affect the mechanical properties, surface finish, and corrosion resistance of the final extruded shape. This extrusion method uses no lubrication on the billet, container, and die, and it can produce very complex sections, with mirror surface finishes and close dimensional tolerances, that are considered to be net extrusions. A flat-face (shear-face) die is often used in nonlubricated hot extrusion.

There are basically two methods of hot extruding materials without lubrication:
- Forward, or direct, extrusion.
- Backward, or indirect, extrusion.

In forward extrusion [Fig. 2-5(a)], the ram travels in the same direction as the extruded section, and there is relative movement between the billet and the container. In backward extrusion [Fig. 2-5(b)], the billet does not move relative to the container, and a die or punch is pushed against the billet to produce solid parts.

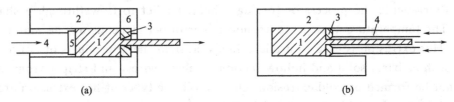

Fig. 2-5 Basic methods of extrusion. (a) Forward (direct) . (b) Backward (indirect)
1— billet; 2— container; 3— die; 4— stem; 5—dummy block; 6—die backer

● Lubricated Hot Extrusion

Generally, aluminum alloys are extruded without lubrication, but copper alloys, titanium alloys, alloy steels, stainless steels, and tool steels are extruded with a variety of graphite and glass-base lubricants. Commercial grease mixtures containing solid-film lubricants, such as graphite, often provide little or no thermal protection to the die. For this reason, die wear is significant in the conventional hot extrusion of steels and titanium alloys.

The Sejournet process is the most commonly used for the extrusion of steels and titanium alloys. In this process, the heated billet is rolled over a bed of ground glass or is sprinkled with glass powder to provide a layer of low-melting glass on the billet surface. Before the billet is inserted into the hot extrusion container, a suitable lubricating system is positioned immediately ahead of the die. This lubricating system can be a compacted glass pad, glass wool, or both. The prelubricated billet is quickly inserted into the container, along with the appropriate followers or a dummy block. The extrusion cycle is then started.

● Metal Flow in Hot Extrusion

Metal flow varies considerably during extrusion, depending on the material, the material/tool interface friction, and the shape of the section. Figure 3 shows the four types of flow patterns that have been observed.

Flow Pattern S [Fig. 2-6(a)] is characterized by the maximum possible uniformity of flow in the container. Plastic flow takes place primarily in a deformation zone directly in front of the die. The major part of the nonextruded billet, pushed as a rigid body through the die, remains undeformed; therefore, the front of the billet moves evenly into the deformation zone.

Flow Pattern A [Fig. 2-6(b)] occurs in homogeneous materials when there is virtually no friction between the container and the billet but significant friction at the surface of the die and its holder. This retards the radial flow of the peripheral zones and increases the amount of shearing in this region. The result is a slightly larger dead-metal zone than that in flow type S, along with a correspondingly wider deformation zone. However, deformation in the center remains relatively uniform. Flow patterns of this type are seldom observed in nonlubricated extrusion; instead, they occur during the lubricated extrusion of soft metals and alloys, such as lead, tin, α-brasses, and tin bronzes, and during the extrusion of copper billets covered with oxide (which acts as a lubricant).

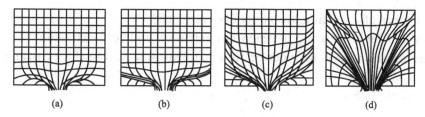

Fig. 2-6 Four types of flow patterns observed in the extrusion of metals
(a) Flow pattern S. (b) Flow pattern A. (c) Flow pattern B. (d) Flow pattern C

Flow Pattern B [Fig. 2-6(c)] occurs in homogeneous materials if friction exists at both the container wall and at the surfaces of the die and die holder. The peripheral zones are retarded at the billet/container interface, while the lower resistance causes the material in the center to be accelerated toward the die. The shear zone between the retarded regions at the surface and the accelerated material in the center extends back into the billet to an extent that depends on the extrusion parameters and the alloy. Therefore, the dead-metal zone is large. At the start of extrusion, the shear deformation is concentrated in the peripheral regions, but as deformation continues, it extends toward the center. This increases the danger of material flowing from the billet surface-with impurities or lubricant-along the shear zone and finishing up under the surface of the extrusion. In addition, the dead-metal zone is not completely rigid and can influence, even if to a limited degree, the flow of the metal. Flow type B is found in single-phase (homogeneous) copper alloys that do not form a lubricating oxide skin and in most aluminum alloys.

Flow Pattern C [Fig. 2-6(d)] occurs in the hot extrusion of materials having inhomogeneous properties when the friction is high (as in flow pattern B) and when the flow stress of the material in the cooler peripheral regions of the billet is considerably higher than that in the center. The billet surface forms a relatively stiff shell. Therefore, the conical dead-metal zone is much larger and extends from the front of the billet to the back. At the start of extrusion, only the material inside the funnel is plastic, and it is severely deformed, especially in the shear zone, as it flows toward the die. The stiff shell and the dead-metal zone are in axial compression as the billet length decreases; consequently, the displaced material of the outer regions follows the path of least resistance to the back of the billet, where it turns toward the center and flows into the funnel.

● Vocabulary

cup-shaped　*adj*. 杯状的；壳斗状的
squeezing　*n*. 推挤　*v*. 挤压　*adj*. 挤压的
grinding　*n*. 磨削；研磨
annealing　*n*. 热处理；低温退火　*v*. 退火
pickling　*n*. 酸洗；浸酸
volumetric　*adj*. 体积的；容积的；测定体积的

hydrostatic　*adj*. 流体静力学的；静水力学的
shear　*vt*. 剪；修剪　*vi*. 剪；剪切
dummy　*adj*. 虚拟的；假的
stainless　*adj*. 不锈的；纯洁的，无瑕疵的
peripheral　*adj*. 外围的；次要的
funnel　*n*. 漏斗；烟囱　*vt*. 使成漏斗形

● Questions

1. What types of extrusion are generally classified?
2. Please tell the difference between hot extrusion and cold extrusion.
3. Please describe the four types of flow patterns observed in the extrusion of metals.

Unit 5
Precision Forging

The Term Precision Forging does not specify a distinct forging process but rather describes a philosophical approach to forging. The goal of this approach is to produce a net shape, or at least a near-net shape, in the as-forged condition.

The term net indicates that no subsequent machining or finishing of a forged surface is required. Thus, a net shape forging requires no further work on any of the forged surfaces, although secondary operations may be required to produce minor holes, threads, and other such details. A near-net shape forging can be either one in which some but not all of the surfaces are net or one in which the surfaces require only minimal machining or finishing. Precision forging is sometimes described as close-tolerance forging to emphasize the goal of achieving, solely through the forging operation, the dimensional and surface finish tolerances required in the finished part.

● Advantages of Precision Forging

Due to difficulties in achieving close tolerance and acceptable surface finish, hot forgings have traditionally been designed with a generous machining allowance, sometimes 3mm (1/8in) or more. The motivation for precision forging is the elimination, or at least the reduction, of the costs associated with this machining allowance. These costs include not only the labor and indirect costs of the machining and finishing operations but also the cost of the excess raw material that is lost during machining.

The savings achieved through material conservation may not be as obvious as the savings obtained by eliminating production machining operations, but it can be quite substantial. Material costs are a significant fraction (often more than half) of the total cost of a forging. The cost of excess material includes not only the purchase price of that material but also the cost associated with handling it in the plant and the energy cost associated with heating it to the forging temperature.

The weight of a traditional forging is often more than twice the weight of the finished part after machining. The machining allowance is responsible for some of this excess material. Significant amounts are also associated with the forging flash. Generous allowances are made in traditional forging for excess material to escape from the die cavity as flash. A study performed by the Forging Industry Association estimated that 20% to 40% of the weight of conventional closed-die forgings is expended as flash. Although flash is sometimes considered necessary for trapping the metal in the die and for ensuring that tight corners or other details are filled, the design of a precision forging usually minimizes and sometimes completely eliminates the flash.

Applications of Precision Forging

After it has been decided that a given part will be manufactured by forging, either a traditional or a precision forging process must be selected. Not all part designs are candidates for precision forging.

As presented above, the precision of a forging is defined in terms of its conformity to finished-part requirements concerning overall geometry, dimensional tolerance, and surface finish. These requirements should be derived from the performance of the part that is desired in service. The impact of the requirements on manufacturing options should also be included in the design analysis. Specifically, the application of precision forging can be enhanced by considering the capabilities of the technology during the design process.

Given the nature of forging technology and the wide range of geometries that are forged, the determination of appropriate applications for precision forging processes is best begun through a process of elimination, that is, through consideration of those characteristics that tend not to favor precision forging.

Physical Considerations. A primary consideration is that the forging must be able to be removed from the tooling after the forging process is completed. Thus, geometries that would interlock with the forging dies cannot be forged net. Furthermore, surfaces parallel to the forging axis will often generate high frictional forces with the tooling during ejection of the part. Therefore, forgings are often designed with a slight draft added to such surfaces to facilitate ejection. Although forgings with no draft have been demonstrated, elimination of draft is limited by:

- The capacity of the ejection mechanism of the forging equipment to provide the increased load that will be required.
- The strength of the workpiece material at the ejection temperature; the workpiece must also.

accommodate the increased ejection loads.

- Wear of the tooling and/or damage to the surface of the workpiece that might occur because of friction.

Economic Considerations also affect the application of precision forging. If only the costs of the forging process itself are considered, precision forging will generally be more costly than traditional forging. This is due to the large number of factors that must be considered in a precision forging process. Many of these factors are ignored in traditional forging.

The increased cost associated with precision forging will be offset by savings in subsequent manufacturing steps, as discussed above. However, if the number of parts required is relatively small, the savings in material, machining, and so on, may not be sufficient to offset the increased costs of precision forging. This may occur because a significant portion of the cost differential associated with precision forging is a fixed cost, that is, independent of the actual number of pieces forged.

Precision forging is especially attractive in the case of parts with complex surfaces that are difficult or costly to machine. Turning is a relatively inexpensive operation in comparison with milling, grinding, or gear cutting. Not surprisingly, many precision forging applications involve gears and similar types of parts.

● Tooling Design Considerations

The design of the forging tools must include analysis of all effects that could impact on the precision of the process. Allowance should be made for the thermal expansion of the tooling because it is generally at some elevated temperature during the forging process. Similar allowance should be made for contraction of the workpiece as it cools after forging. Thermal contraction is estimated from the workpiece temperature at die closure. These allowances are typically of the order of hundredths of a millimeter (thousandths of an inch) —comparable to the tolerances desired in the precision forging process.

The Dimensions of the Forged Part will be decreased relative to the dimensions of the die cavity by the thickness of the forging lubricant at die closure. The thickness at die closure will generally be less than the thickness applied to the dies and/or forging preform. In many cases, the lubricant layer is very thin and can be neglected. In other cases, it may be significant. Thicker coatings are sometimes applied to billets prior to forging as protection against oxidation during subsequent heating. Buildup of the lubricant in the tooling can also be a problem in some cases.

The Workability of the Workpiece Material is a quantitative measure of how much deformation can be accommodated without cracking or other forms of failure. Workability is more critical in precision forging than in conventional forging because higher deformation levels may be required to achieve the tolerances required in precision forging. Deformation levels can be especially high in localized areas. Furthermore, the workability index of the material can be decreased in a precision forging process if the forging temperature is decreased in an effort to improve precision.

In practice, consideration of the above-mentioned factors is extremely difficult for all but the simplest forging geometries. Accurate calculation of the temperature gradients in the workpiece and tooling requires a heat transfer analysis. Calculation of elastic deflections requires knowledge of the forging loads and a stress analysis of the tooling and associated fixturing. Calculation of metal flow for preform design is even more complex.

● Process Control Considerations

After a candidate part for precision forging is identified and the tooling is designed, implementation requires increased attention to detail and process control at every step of the manufacturing process. At a minimum, all of the factors discussed below usually must be considered. The significance of a given factor depends on the geometry and tolerance requirements of a given forging. In addition, there may be other factors not listed here that are unique to a particular application.

Precision of the Tooling. A precision forging requires precision tooling. The tolerance achieved in the forging will clearly be no better than the tolerance of the tooling. Because many factors influence the forging tolerance, it will typically be significantly worse than the tooling tolerance. Therefore, the tolerance bands for precision forge tooling must be set at a small fraction (for example, to 1/3) of the desired forging tolerances. This is similar to the rule of statistical process control that the capability (variation) of a gage must be an order of magnitude better than the allowable variation of the machine or workpiece being measured.

Precision of the Setup. Control of the alignment and setup of the tooling in the forging press is just as important as the tolerance of the tooling itself. The fixtures used to hold the die blocks for precision forging in presses are frequently designed with posts or similar devices for maintaining alignment.

The setup of the tooling affects the thickness of the forged part. Thickness may be important in its own right, if there is a close tolerance on any of the thickness dimensions of the part. However, thickness is also important because the overall volume of the forged part is dependent on thickness. Because precision forgings are usually designed with little or no flash, the volume of the finish forging in relation to the volume of the preform is critical. If the tooling is set up so that the volume of the finish forging would be too great, a lack of fill in the corners would generally result. If the setup is such that the volume of the finish forging cannot accommodate the entire preform, the tooling or the forging equipment could be damaged.

Precision of the Preform. In a one-hit precision forging process, the preform is simply the slug of raw material sheared or cut from bar or coil stock. In a progressive forging operation, the preform is the product of a series of intermediate forging operations. In both cases, the quality of the preform is of concern because it limits the precision of the finished forging.

As discussed above in connection with the setup of the tooling, the relationship between the volume of the preform and the volume of the finish forging is critical. If the geometry of the preform is complex, the distribution of volume in the preform may also be important to ensure the proper metal flow in the finish forging. Thus, precision forging requires a precision preform. In progressive forging, each forging step must be considered to be a precision operation.

Control of Lubrication. Of all forging variables, the performance of the lubricant may be the most difficult to quantify. However, lubrication is also recognized as one of the factors that is most critical to the success of any forging process, precision or otherwise. Lubrication influences the total forging load, the degree to which the metal will fill the cavities of the dies, the uniformity of the resultant metallurgical microstructure, and the surface quality of the forged product.

Control of lubrication in precision forging can be approached indirectly by stressing consistency in the lubricant composition and application. Samples of the lubricant should be taken upon delivery from the supplier and after any dilution. Samples should also be taken to ensure consistency during production.

● **Vocabulary**

as-forged　n. 锻造状态；黑皮锻件
finishing　n. 精加工；最后的修整；表面加工　v. 完成
machining allowance　机械加工余量
handling　n. 处理；操作　adj. 操作的
flash　n. (模锻) 飞边　v. 去毛刺
milling　n. 铣削；研磨　v. 碾磨；滚 (碾轧) 金属

gear cutting   切齿；齿轮切制；齿轮加工
die closure   模具闭合量
contraction   n. 收缩，紧缩
workability   n. 可使用性；施工性能；可加工性
fixturing   n. 紧固，定位；夹具
deflection   n. 偏向；挠曲；偏差
statistical   adj. 统计的；统计学的
uniformity   n. 均匀性；一致；同样
dilution   n. 稀释，冲淡；稀释法

● Questions

1. Please talk about the advantages of precision forging.
2. What is precision forging?
3. Please tell the difference between precision forging and conventional forging.

Unit 6

Hammers and Presses for Forging

Forging Machines can be classified according to their principle of operation. Hammers and high-energy-rate forging machines deform the workpiece by the kinetic energy of the hammer ram; they are therefore classed as energy-restricted machines. The ability of mechanical presses to deform the work material is determined by the length of the press stroke and the available force at various stroke positions. Mechanical presses are therefore classified as stroke-restricted machines. Hydraulic presses are termed force-restricted machines because their ability to deform the material depends on the maximum force rating of the press.

● Hammers

Historically, hammers have been the most widely used type of equipment for forging. They are the least expensive and most flexible type of forging equipment in the variety of forging operations they can perform. Hammers are capable of developing large forces and have short die contact times. The main components of a hammer are a ram, frame assembly, anvil, and anvil cap. The anvil is directly connected to the frame assembly, the upper die is attached to the ram, and lower die is attached to the anvil cap.

In operation, the workpiece is placed on the lower die. The ram moves downward, exerting a force on the anvil and causing the workpiece to deform. Forging hammers can be classified according to the method used to drive the ram downward. Various types of hammers are described in the following sections.

● Die Forger Hammers

The ram is held at the top of the stroke by a constant source of pressurized air, which is admitted to and exhausted from the cylinder to energize the blow. The die forger hammers from one manufacturer are capable of delivering 5.5 to 89.5kJ of energy per blow.

● Counterblow Hammers

These hammers develop striking force by the movement of two rams, simultaneously approaching from opposite directions and meeting at a midway point. Some hammers are pneumatically or hydraulically actuated; others incorporate a mechanical-hydraulic or a mechanical-pneumatic system.

A vertical counterblow hammer with a steam-hydraulic actuating system is illustrated in Fig. 2-7 (air-hydraulic systems are also available). In this hammer, steam is admitted to the upper cylinder and drives the upper ram downward. At the same time, pistons connected to the upper ram act through a hydraulic linkage in forcing the lower ram upward. Retraction speed is increased by steam (or air) pressure acting upward on the piston. Through proper design relative to weights (including tooling and workpiece) and hydraulics (slower lower-assembly velocities), the kinetic energy of the upper and lower assemblies can be balanced at impact.

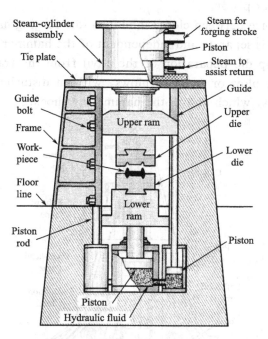

Fig. 2-7 Principal components of a vertical counter-blow hammer
with a steam-hydraulic actuating system

The rams of a counterblow hammer are capable of striking repeated blows; they develop combined velocities of 5 to 6m/s. Compared to single-action hammers, the vibration of impact is reduced, and approximately the full energy of each blow is delivered to the workpiece, without loss to an anvil. As a result, the wear of moving hammer parts is minimized, contributing to longer operating life. At the time of impact, forces are canceled out, and no energy is lost to foundations. In fact, counterblow hammers do not require the large inertia blocks and foundations needed for conventional power-drop hammers.

● Open-Die Forging Hammers

Open-die forging hammers are made with either a single frame (often termed C-frame or single-arch hammers) or a double frame (often called double-arch hammers) (Fig. 2-8). Open-die forging hammers are used to make a large percentage of open-die forgings. The rated sizes of double-frame open-die forging hammers range from about 2720 to 10,900kg, although larger hammers have been built.

A typical open-die forging hammer is operated by steam or compressed air—usually at pressures of 690 to 825kPa for steam and 620 to 690kPa for air. These pressures are similar to those used for power-drop hammers.

There are two basic differences between power-drop hammers used for closed-die forging and those used for open-die forging. First, a modern power-drop hammer has blow-energy control to assist the operator in setting the intensity of each blow. In hammers for closed-die forging, the hammer stroke is limited by the upper die surface contacting the surface of the lower die face. In open-die forging, the upper and lower dies do not make contact; stroke-position control is provided through control of the air or steam valve that actuates the hammer piston.

The second difference between closed- and open-die forging hammers is that the anvil of an open-die hammer is separate and independent of the hammer frame that contains the striking ram and the top die. Separation of the anvil from the frame allows the anvil to give way under a heavy blow or series of blows, without disturbing the frame. The anvil may rest on oak timbers, which absorb the hammering shock.

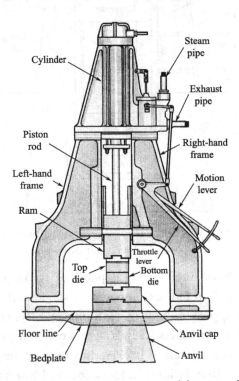

Fig. 2-8 Double-frame power hammer used for open-die forging

● Mechanical Presses

All mechanical presses employ flywheel energy, which is transferred to the workpiece by a network of gears, cracks, eccentrics, or levers. Driven by an electric motor and controlled by means of an air clutch, mechanical presses have a full-eccentric type of drive shaft that imparts a constant-length stroke to a vertically operating ram. Various mechanisms are used to translate the rotary motion of the eccentric shaft into linear motion to move the ram. The ram carries the top, or moving, die, while the bottom, or stationary, die is clamped to the die seat of the main frame. The ram stroke is shorter than that of a forging hammer or a hydraulic press. Ram speed is greatest at the center of the stroke, but force is greatest at the bottom of the stroke.

Mechanical forging presses have principal components that are similar to those of eccentric-shaft, straight-side, single-action presses used for forming sheet metal. In detail, however, mechanical forging presses are considerably different from mechanical presses that are used for forming sheet. The principal differences are:

• Forging presses, particularly their side frames, are built stronger than presses for forming sheet metal.

• Forging presses deliver their maximum force within 3.2mm of the end of the stroke, because.

maximum pressures is required to form the flash.

• The slide velocity in a forging press is faster than in a sheet metal deep-drawing press, because in forging it is desirable to strike the metal and retrieve the ram quickly to minimize the time the dies are in contact with the hot metal.

Unlike the blow of a forging hammer, a press blow is more of a squeeze than an impact and is delivered by uniform stroke length. The character of the blow in a forging press resembles that of an upsetting machine, thus combining some features of hammers and upsetters. Mechanical forging presses use drive mechanisms similar to those of upsetters, although an upsetter is generally a horizontal machine.

● Advantages and Limitations

Compared to hammer forging, mechanical press forging results in accurate close-tolerance parts. Mechanical presses permit automatic feed and transfer mechanisms to feed, pick up, and move the part from one die to the next, and they have higher production rates than forging hammers (stroke rates vary from 30 to 100 strokes per minute). Because the dies used with mechanical presses are subject to squeezing forces instead of impact forces, harder die materials can be used in order to extend die life. Dies can also be less massive in mechanical press forging.

One limitation of mechanical presses is their high initial cost-approximately three times as much as forging hammers that can do the same amount of work. Because the force of the stroke cannot be varied, mechanical presses are also not capable of performing as many preliminary operations as hammers. Generally, mechanical presses forge the preform and final shape in one, two, or three blows; hammers are capable of delivering up to ten or more blows at varying intensities.

● Hydraulic Presses

Hydraulic presses are used for both open- and closed-die forging. The ram of a hydraulic press is driven by hydraulic cylinders and pistons, which are part of a high-pressure hydraulic or hydropneumatic system. After a rapid approach speed, the ram (with upper die attached) moves at a slow speed while exerting a squeezing force on the work metal. Pressing speeds can be accurately controlled to permit control of metal-flow velocities; this is particularly advantageous in producing close-tolerance forgings. The principal components of a hydraulic press are shown in Fig. 2-9.

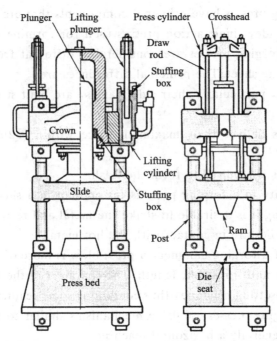

Fig. 2-9 Principal components of a four-post hydraulic press for closed-die forging

● Vocabulary

hammer   n. 铁锤；锤子   vt. 锤击；锤打
flexible   adj. 有弹性的的；柔韧的；易弯曲的
exhaust   vt. 排出   vi. 排气   n. 排气；排气装置
pneumatically   adv. 充气地；气动地，由空气作用
air-hydraulic   气动液压的
linkage   n. 连接；连杆结构；联动装置
assembly   n. 装配；组装，组配
inertia   n. 惯性；惯量；不活动

eccentric   adj. 偏心的   n. 偏心轮；偏心盘
clutch   n. 控制；离合器   vt. 抓住；紧握
lever   n. 杠杆；控制杆；手柄   vt. 用杠杆撬动；把……作为杠杆
shaft   n. 轴；传动轴   vt. 在……上装杆
single-action press   单动压力机
sheet metal forming   板料成形；冲压成形；金属板材成形
upsetter   n. 镦锻机，顶锻机；杆端锻粗机

● Questions

1. Please tell the differences between power-drop hammers used for closed-die forging and those used for open-die forging.

2. Talk about the principal differences between mechanical forging presses and mechanical presses that are used for forming sheet.

3. Please describe the principal components of a hydraulic press.

Unit 7
Selection of Forging Equipment

Forging Equipment influences the forging process because it affects deformation rate, forging temperature, and rate of production. The forging engineer must have sound knowledge of the different forging machines in order to:
- Use existing machinery more efficiently.
- Define the existing plant capacity accurately.
- Communicate better with, and at times request improved performance from, the machine builder.
- Develop, if necessary, in-house proprietary machines and processes not available in the machine tool market.
- Utilize them in the most cost-effective mannery.

This article will detail the significant factors in the selection of forging equipment for a particular process.

● Classification and Characterization of Forging Machines

Forging machines can be classified into three types:
- Force-restricted machines (hydraulic presses).
- Stroke-restricted machines (mechanical presses).
- Energy-restricted machines (hammers and screw presses).

The significant characteristics of these machines constitute all machine design and performance data that are pertinent to the economical use of the machine, including characteristics of load and energy, time-related characteristics, and characteristics of accuracy.

● Hydraulic Presses

The operation of hydraulic presses is relatively simple and is based on the motion of a hydraulic piston guided in a cylinder. Hydraulic presses are essentially force-restricted machines; that is, their capability for carrying out a forming operation is limited mainly by the maximum available force.

The operational characteristics of a hydraulic press are essentially determined by the type and design of its hydraulic drive system. The two types of hydraulic drive systems—direct drive and accumulator drive—provide different time-dependent characteristic data.

In both direct and accumulator drives, a slowdown in penetration rate occurs as the pressure builds and the working medium is compressed. This slowdown is larger in direct oil-driven presses, mainly because oil is more compressible than a water emulsion.

From a practical point of view, in a new installation, the choice between direct and accumulator drive is based on the capital cost and the economics of operation. The accumulator drive is usually more economical if one accumulator system can be used by several presses or if very large press capacities are considered. In direct-drive hydraulic presses, the maximum press load is established by the pressure capability of the pumping system and is available throughout the entire press stroke. Therefore, hydraulic presses are ideally suited to extrusion-type operations requiring very large amounts of energy. With adequate dimensioning of the pressure system, an accumulator-drive press exhibits only a slight reduction in available press load as the forming operation proceeds.

● **Mechanical Presses**

The drive system used in most mechanical presses is based on a slider-crank mechanism that translates rotary motion into reciprocating linear motion. The eccentric shaft is connected, through a clutch and brake system, directly to the flywheel. In designs for larger capacities, the flywheel is located on the pinion shaft, which drives the eccentric shaft.

Kinematics of the Slider-Crank Mechanism. The slider-crank mechanism is illustrated in Fig. 2-10(a). The following valid relationships can be derived from the geometry illustrated.

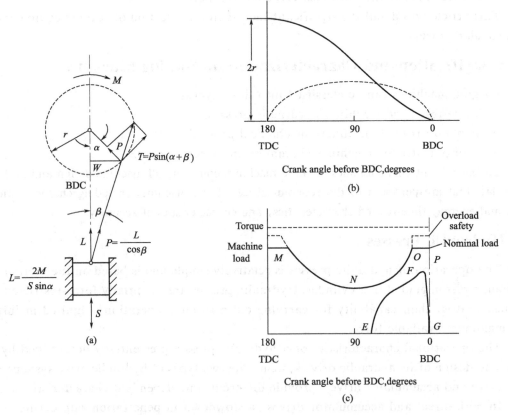

Fig. 2-10 Load, displacement, velocity, and torque in a simple slider-crank mechanism.
(a) Schematic of slider-crank mechanism. (b) Displacement (solid curve) and velocity (dashed curve). (c) Clutch torque M and machine load L_M

Load and Energy Characteristics. An exact relationship exists between the torque M of the crankshaft and the available load L at the slide [Fig. 2-10(a) and (c)]. The torque M is constant, and for all practical purposes, angle is small enough to be ignored [Fig. 2-10 (a)]. A very close approximation then is given by:

$$L = \frac{2M}{S\sin\alpha} \qquad (2\text{-}1)$$

Eq (2-1) gives the variation of the available slide load L with respect to the crank angle above bottom dead center [Fig. 2-10(c)]. From Eq (2-1), it is apparent that as the slide approaches bottom dead center—that is, as angle approaches zero—the available load L may become infinitely large without exceeding the constant clutch torque M or without causing the friction clutch to slip.

The following conclusions can be drawn from the observations that have been made thus far. Crank and the eccentric presses are displacement-restricted machines. The slide velocity V and the available slide load L vary accordingly with the position of the slide before bottom dead center. before bottom dead center. For different applications, the nominal load can be specified at different positions before bottom dead center, according to the standards established by the American Joint Industry Conference. If the load required by the forming process is smaller than the load available at the press—that is, if curve EFG in Fig. 2-10(c) remains below curve NOP—then the process can be carried out, provided the flywheel can supply the necessary energy per stroke.

● Screw Presses

The screw press uses a friction, gear, electric, or hydraulic drive to accelerate the flywheel and the screw assembly, and it converts the angular kinetic energy into the linear energy of the slide or ram.

Load and Energy. In screw presses, the forging load is transmitted through the slide, screw, and bed to the press frame. The available load at a given stroke position is supplied by the stored energy in the flywheel. At the end of the downstroke after the forging blow, the flywheel comes to a standstill and begins its reversed rotation. During the standstill, the flywheel no longer contains any energy. Therefore, the total flywheel energy EFT has been transformed into:

- Energy available for deformation E_p to carry out the forging process.
- Friction energy E_f to overcome frictional resistance in the screw and in the gibs.
- Deflection energy E_d to elastically deflect various parts of the press.

At the end of a downstroke, the deflection energy E_d is stored in the machine and can be released only during the upward stroke.

The flywheel in Fig. 2-11(a) is accelerated to such a velocity that at the end of downstroke the deformation is carried out, and no unnecessary energy is left in the flywheel. This is done by using an energy-metering device that controls flywheel velocity. The flywheel shown in Fig. 2-11(b) has excess energy at the end of the downstroke. The excess energy from the flywheel stored in the press frame at the end of the stroke is used to begin the acceleration of the slide back to the starting position immediately at the end of the stroke. The screw is not self-locking and is easily moved.

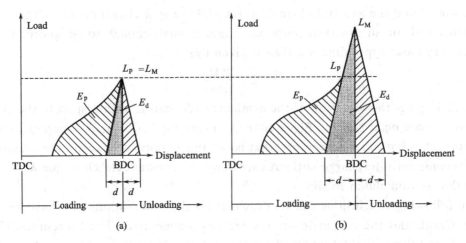

Fig. 2-11 Load versus displacement curves for die forging using a screw press.
(a) Press with energy or load metering. (b) Press without energy or load metering.
E_p, energy required for deformation; L_p, load required for deformation; L_M, maximum machine load; E_d, elastic deflection energy; d, elastic deflection of the press

● Hammers

The hammer is the least expensive and most versatile type of equipment for generating load and energy to carry out a forming process. Hammers are primarily used for the hot forging, coining, and, to a limited extent, sheet metal forming of parts manufactured in small quantities—for example, in the aircraft industry. The hammer is an energy-restricted machine. During a working stroke, the deformation proceeds until the total kinetic energy is dissipated by plastic deformation of the material and by elastic deformation of the ram and anvil when the die faces contact each other. Therefore, the capacities of these machines should be rated in terms of energy. The practice of specifying a hammer by its ram weight, although fairly common, is not useful for the user. Ram weight can be regarded only as model or specification number.

There are basically two types of anvil hammers: gravity-drop and power-drop. In a simple gravity-drop hammer, the upper ram is positively connected to a board (board-drop hammer), a belt (belt-drop hammer), a chain (chain-drop hammer), or a piston (oil-, air-, or steam-lift drop hammer). The ram is lifted to a certain height and then dropped on the stock placed on the anvil. During the downstroke, the ram is accelerated by gravity and builds up the blow energy. The upstroke takes place immediately after the blow; the force necessary to ensure quick lift-up of the ram can be three to five times the ram weight.

The operation principle of a power-drop hammer is similar to that of an air-drop hammer. In the downstroke, in addition to gravity, the ram is accelerated by steam, cold air, or hot air pressure.

● Vocabulary

machinery   *n*. 机械；机器；机构；机械装置

motion   *n*. 动作；移动   *vi*. 运动   *vt*. 运动

slowdown　　n. 减速；急工；降低速度
penetration　　n. 渗透；穿透；侵入
installation　　n. 安装，装置；安装方式
pumping　　n. 抽吸；泵送　v. 抽水
slider-crank　　滑件曲柄；曲柄型；曲柄滑块
reciprocating　　adj. 往复的；摆动的
　　n. 往复　v. 往复运动
standstill　　n. 停顿；停止

brake　　vi. 刹车　n. 闸，刹车；制动；制动器　vt. 刹车
flywheel　　n. 飞轮，惯性轮；调速轮
torque　　n. 转矩，扭矩；力矩；扭力
downstroke　　n. 下行程；下行冲程
electrohydraulic　　adj. 电动液压的
upstroke　　n. 上升冲程；上行程；上行运动

● Questions

1. Why do the forging engineer must have sound knowledge of the different forging machines?

2. How many types of forging machines are classified? Talk about the characteristics of each type of forging machines.

Unit 8

Dies and Die Materials for Hot Forging

● Open Dies

Most open-die forgings are produced in a pair of flat dies—one attached to the hammer or to the press ram, and the other to the anvil. Swage (semicircular) dies and V-dies are also commonly used. These different types of die sets are shown in Fig. 2-12. In some applications, forging is done with a combination of a flat die and a swage die.

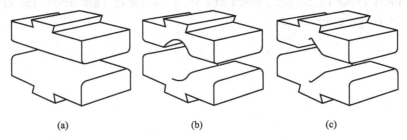

Fig. 2-12 Three types of die sets used for open-die forging

Flat Dies. The surfaces of flat dies [Fig. 2-12(a)] should be parallel to avoid tapering of the workpiece. Flat dies may range from 305 to 510 mm in width, although most are from 405 to 455 mm in width. The edges of flat dies are rounded to prevent pinching or tearing of the workpiece and the formation of laps during forging.

Flat dies are used to form bars, flat forgings, and round shapes. Wide dies are used when transverse flow (sideways movement) is desired or when the workpiece is drawn out using repeated blows. Narrower dies are used for cutting off or for necking down larger cross sections.

Swage dies are basically flat dies with a semicircular shape cut into their centers [Fig. 2-12(b)]. The radius of the semicircle corresponds to the smallest-diameter shaft that can be produced. Swage dies offer the following advantages over flat dies in the forging of round bars:

- Minimal side bulging.
- Longitudinal movement of all metal.
- Greater deformation in the center of the bar.
- Faster operation.

Disadvantages of swage dies include the inability to:

- Forge bars of more than one size, in most cases.
- Mark or cut off parts (in contrast to flat-die use).

V-dies [Fig. 2-12(c)] can be used to produce round parts, but they are usually used to forge hollow cylinders from a hollow billet. A mandrel is used with the V-dies to form the inside of the cylinder. The optimum angle for the V is usually between 90° and 120°.

● Impression Dies

Dies for closed-die (impression-die) forging on presses are often designed to forge the part in one blow, and some sort of ejection mechanism (for example, knockout pins) is often incorporated into the die. Dies may contain impressions for several parts.

Hammer forgings are usually made using several blows in successive die impressions. A typical die used for hammer forging is shown in Fig. 2-13. Such dies usually contain several different types of impressions, each serving a specific function. These are discussed below.

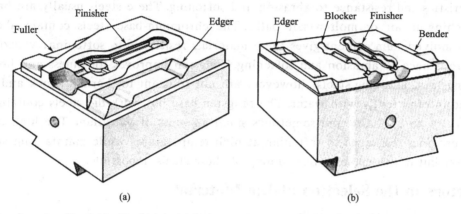

Fig. 2-13 Typical multiple-impression dies for closed-die forging

Fullers. A fuller is a die impression used to reduce the cross section and to lengthen a portion of the forging stock. In longitudinal cross section, the fuller is usually elliptical or oval to obtain optimum metal flow without producing laps, folds, or cold shuts. Fullers are used in combination with edgers or rollers, or as the only impression before use of the blocker or finisher.

Because fullering usually is the first step in the forging sequence, and generally uses the least amount of forging energy, the fuller is almost always placed on the extreme edge of the die, as shown in Fig. 2-13(a).

Edgers are used to redistribute and proportion stock for heavy sections that will be further shaped in blocker or finisher impressions. Thus, the action of the edger is opposite to that of the fuller. A connecting rod is an example of a forging in which stock is first reduced in a fuller to prepare the slender central part of the rod and then worked in an edger to proportion the ends of the boss and crank shapes [Fig. 2-13(a)].

Flatteners are used to widen the work metal, so that it more nearly covers the next impression or, with a 90° rotation, to reduce the width to within the dimensions of the next impression. The flattener station can be either a flat area on the face of the die or an impression in the die to give the exact size required.

Benders. A portion of the die can be used to bend the stock, generally along its longitudinal axis, in two or more planes. There are two basic designs of bender impressions: free-flow and trapped-stock. In bending with a free-flow bender [Fig. 2-13(b)], either one end or both ends of the forging are free to move into the bender. A single bend is usually made. This type of bending may cause folds or small wrinkles on the inside of the bend.

Splitters. In making fork-type forgings, frequently part of the work metal is split so that it conforms more closely to the subsequent blocker impression. In a splitting operation, the stock is forced outward from its longitudinal axis by the action of the splitter. Generous radii should be used to prevent the formation of cold shuts, laps, and folds.

● Die Materials

Hot-work die steels are commonly used for hot-forging dies subjected to temperatures ranging from 315 to 650℃. These materials contain chromium, tungsten, and in some cases, vanadium or molybdenum or both. These alloying elements induce deep hardening characteristics and resistance to abrasion and softening. These steels usually are hardened by quenching in air or molten salt baths. The chromium-base steels contain about 5% Cr. High molybdenum content gives these materials resistance to softening; vanadium increases resistance to abrasion and softening. Tungsten improves toughness and hot hardness; tungsten-containing steels, however, are not resistant to thermal shock and cannot be cooled intermittently with water. The tungsten-base hot-work die steels contain 9% to 18% W, 2% to 12% Cr, and sometimes small amounts of vanadium. The high tungsten content provides resistance to softening at high temperatures while maintaining adequate toughness, but it also makes water cooling of these steels impossible.

● Factors in the Selection of Die Materials

Properties of materials that determine their selection as die materials for hot forging are:
- Ability to harden uniformly.
- Wear resistance (ability to resist the abrasive action of hot metal during forging).
- Resistance to plastic deformation (ability to withstand pressure and resist deformation under load).
- Toughness.
- Resistance to thermal fatigue and heat checking.
- Resistance to mechanical fatigue.

Ability to Harden Uniformly. The higher the hardenability of a material, the greater the depth to which it can be hardened. Hardenability depends on the composition of the tool steel. In general, the higher the alloy content of a steel, the higher its hardenability, as measured by the hardenability factor D_1 (in inches). The D_1 of a steel is the diameter of an infinitely long cylinder which would just transform to a specific microstructure (50% martensite) at the center if heat transfer during cooling were ideal, that is, if the surface attained the temperature of the quenching medium instantly. A larger hardenability factor D_1 means that the steel will harden to a greater depth on quenching, not that it will have a higher hardness.

Wear Resistance. Wear is a gradual change in the dimensions or shape of a component caused by corrosion, dissolution, or abrasion and removal or transportation of the wear products. Abrasion resulting from friction is the most important of these mechanisms in terms of die wear. The higher the strength and hardness of the steel near the surface of the die, the greater its resistance to abrasion. Thus, in hot forming, the die steel should have a high hot hardness and should retain this hardness over extended periods of exposure to elevated temperatures.

Resistance to Plastic Deformation. As shown in Fig. 2-14, the yield strengths of steels decrease at higher temperatures. However, yield strength also depends on prior heat treatment, composition, and hardness. The higher the initial hardness, the greater the yield strength at various temperatures. In normal practice, the level to which a die steel is hardened is determined by toughness requirements: the higher the hardness, the lower the toughness of a steel. Thus, in metal-forming applications, the die block is hardened to a level at which it should have enough toughness to avoid cracking.

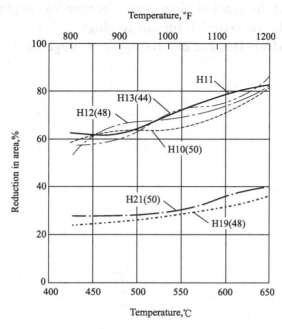

Fig. 2-14 Elevated-temperature ductilities of various hot-work die steels

Toughness can be defined as the ability to absorb energy without breaking. The energy absorbed before fracture is a combination of strength and ductility. The higher the strength and ductility, the higher the toughness. Ductility, as measured by reduction in area or percent elongation in a tensile test, can therefore be used as a partial index of toughness at low strain rates.

● **Vocabulary**

swage vt. 用型铁弄弯曲   n. 型砧；冲模；旋锻工具

tapering adj. 尖端细的；锥状的；锥形的   v. 逐渐变尖细

transverse adj. 横向的；横断的   n. 横断面；贯轴

semicircular adj. 半圆的；半环形的

bulging n. 膨胀，凸出；胀形；折皱

knockout adj. 击倒的   n. 脱模；脱模装置；敲除

lengthen vt. 使延长；加长   vi. 延长；变长

flatten vt. 击败，摧毁；使……平坦   vi. 变平

finisher n. 整理工；修整器

bending n. 弯曲度   v. 弯曲；折弯

bender n. 弯曲机；弯机
abrasion n. 磨损；磨耗；研磨
blocker n. 雏形锻模，预锻模
quenching n. 淬火；抑制；猝熄 v. 扑灭；压倒
molybdenum n. 钼

hardenability n. 可硬化性；淬硬性；淬透性；可淬性
toughness n. 韧性；韧度；有黏性
ductility n. 延展性；柔软性
elongation n. 伸长；伸长率；延伸率；延长

● Questions

1. Please talk about the types of die sets used in open-die forgings.
2. How to select the die materials for hot forging?
3. Please tell the advantages and disadvantages of swage dies.

Unit 9
Forging Process Design

The Traditional Build-and-Test Methods of developing a complete manufacturing process were heavily experience based, because the analytical approach to process design was inadequately developed. The part geometries are generally quite complex, and the simpler analytical methods (as opposed to the computer-aided numerical methods) could not handle the task of providing accurate solutions to engineering problems. The advent of numerical methods such as general-purpose finite-element method (FEM) codes to handle large deformation plasticity has made accurate analysis possible, but these techniques still have several limitations. FEM codes such as ALPID (developed under programs funded by the U. S. Air Force) are analysis tools, not design tools, and are quite expensive to use in terms of required computer time and facilities. Because the potentially viable processing routes are numerous, many FEM process simulations would be necessary to identify optimal processing methods unless some means of restricting the solution space are implemented.

In the design and manufacture of forging dies, two methodologies can be used. In the first method, the design of the die is obtained by making use of a computer-aided engineering (CAE) systems approach. This approach integrates dynamic materials behavior modeling, geometric modeling, and analytical process modeling. Advanced process modeling is the heart of this approach, and the understanding of dynamic materials behavior in a quantitative way for all materials—composites, metals, alloys, polymers, and ceramics—makes the integration possible and generic.

In the second method, well-established empirical rules are used to arrive at an acceptable design alternative. Currently, both of these procedures follow a trial-and-error approach to achieve the required goal. Either one used by itself is a time-consuming and costly process. The CAE procedure lacks empirical aids during the selection of an initial design, and the experience-based method lacks analytical aids for verification of the final design. The optimum die design procedure would be to use both of these methods.

An initial design can be selected on the basis of empirical rules; such a design can be further refined by computation involving analysis and simulation as followed in the CAE approach. This procedure is complex because it involves two fundamental types of activities, information handling and problem solving. This can be made easier if an intelligent system that makes use of the techniques is available from software engineering (SE), data base management systems (DBMS), operating systems (OS), analytical modeling (AM), or artificial intelligence (AI) .

To summarize, automation of engineering methodology in forging design and manufacture should address the following basic issues:

- Engineering disciplines of significant diversity are involved and need to be integrated in a uniform fashion.
- The potential design solution space is large and needs to be intelligently reduced so that the design-analysis iterations remain practical.

The global approach to automation is conceptually straightforward, and is suitable for incremental implementation as newer software tools become available. The automation of the initial-guess design is done through the use of knowledge-based expert systems (KBES); when possible, a rough analysis (for example, using slab analysis for plasticity) is provided as a pre-screen to detail analysis (usually FEM), and the detail analysis is used primarily as a verification tool. It is useful at this point to note that the solution space is reducible through two means:

- The use of KBES rough analysis-detail analysis iterations can provide a local reduction of admissible solutions, that is, in a specific domain such as plasticity, heat transfer, or material engineering.
- The use of a knowledge-based integration shell provides a more global reduction of the solution space by implementing a methodology that controls design procedures across interdisciplinary domains; this approach embeds procedural knowledge in the integration shell, and also provides a uniform user interface.

● Tasks Performed in Forging Manufacture

If the overall procedure in the production of forgings in a typical company were examined, the following major tasks would be found to be necessary components of the manufacturing operation:

- Receive and interpret request for quotation (RFQ).
- Input part geometry into computer-aided design (CAD) system.
- Identify constraints imposed by specifications in RFQ.
- Identify billet stock sources.
- Check incoming billet stock for quality.
- Prepare billet for heating/forging.
- Determine forging sequence (blocking, preforming, and so forth).
- Design dies.
- Select forging temperatures and strain-rates.
- Choose forging technique (hot-die, isothermal, and so forth).
- Select forging equipment.
- Manufacture dies.
- Ascertain furnace cycles and environments (atmosphere control, and so forth).
- Determine lubricants required.
- Select intermediate operations such as trimming of preforms.
- Inspect finish forging.
- Use identification method (serial numbers, and so forth) to track workpieces, drawings, dies, and so on.
- Determine heat treating and finishing operations.
- Test finish forging to see it meets customer specifications.

• Verify packing and shipping requirements.

Software Tools Available to Support Task Automation

Five classes of tools are necessary for the implementation of an integrated system for forging process design:

  • Geometry Representation Tools. A significant portion of the design and analysis task is manipulation and definition of geometry.

  • Knowledge-based expert systems (KBES) provide experience-based initial guesses to design problems. These initial guesses can then be iterated upon by rough and detailed analysis tools.

  • Rough analysis tools are fast and cost effective: They prescreen initial guesses provided by the KBES so that inappropriate designs are not passed to more expensive detail analysis tools.

  • High-accuracy detail analysis tools serve mainly to validate selected designs.

  • An intelligent DBMS stores all data used by the aforementioned tools. Access to this data, whether it be by the user or by one of the aforementioned tools, should be guided and controlled; the forging knowledge-based DBMS must control the sequence of creation and use of the data by users and tools according to the dictates of the methodology.

Geometry Representation Tools

CAD Systems. It is necessary to provide geometry information to the simulation and expert systems programs in an appropriate fashion. Much of the U. S. manufacturing industry has already started to use computer-aided drafting systems, and it would be ideal to use this computerized geometry representation for forging process design.

Computer-aided design commercialization is fairly mature, and options range from low-cost PC-based systems to full-function mainframe software. The choice is mostly a matter of performance versus cost.

  • Input requirement: Interactive geometry creation, or geometry data files.

  • Output: Engineering drawings, cross sections for analysis, section geometric properties, solid model geometric properties, numerical control (NC) machining "tapes".

Callable Graphics Libraries. The above-mentioned CAD software is generally highly proprietary and, as such, is not readily useable in applications software. Furthermore, CAD systems offer a capability exceeding the requirements of graphics application codes. It is therefore necessary to use callable graphics libraries that can be integrated into graphics application routines. Several such graphics libraries are commercially available.

  • Input: These are not used directly by the end-user, rather, they are programming tools for the software applications developer.

  • Output: Graphics output to and input from the user.

Knowledge-Based Expert Systems

Automated Forging Design (AFD) is a knowledge-based system implementing rules for establishing stock allowances to a finished part for the various manufacturability criteria, such as forgeability, machining, die mismatch, and so forth. In addition, it establishes a suitable parting line.

The program can currently handle two-dimensional geometries; thus, for general three-dimensional components, the designer has to determine which set of two-dimensional sections should be provided to the AFD expert system.

• Input requirements: Material specification, two-dimensional geometry of the required part.

• Output: Two-dimensional geometry of the required part with a forging envelope applied as well as a parting line for final forging operation.

Blocker Initial Design (BID). This program adds allowances to the finish forging according to experience guidelines that generate a preform geometry for the finish forging.

BID could be used iteratively to work back all the way to a starting billet requirement. The program can currently handle two-dimensional geometries; thus, for general three-dimensional components, the designer has to determine which set of two-dimensional sections should be provided to the AFD expert system.

It is worth noting that the use of a two-dimensional section is quite appropriate, because this is in fact the way experts currently handle design. It would be advantageous to attempt to identify the two-dimensional sections that should be given to the KBES.

• Input requirements: Geometry at the end of a forging step, and material specification.

• Output: Preform geometry for the forging step.

● Rough Analysis Tools

Finishr. This Fortran program is intended to give approximate load distributions on the forging dies using the slab method. Again, this program operates on two-dimensional sections; however, this is consistent with the functionality of the KBES.

• Input requirements: Geometry at the end of forging step, and material specification.

• Output: Estimated load distribution on the dies.

● Vocabulary

finite-element 有限元
simulation *n.* 仿真；模拟；模仿；假装
implement *vt.* 实施，执行；实现 *n.* 工具，器具
plasticity *n.* 塑性，可塑性；适应性
methodology *n.* 方法学，方法论；研究方法
integrate *vt.* 使……完整；使……成整体 *adj.* 整合的；完全的
verification *n.* 确认，查证；核实
artificial *adj.* 人造的；仿造的；仿真的
knowledge-based *adj.* 知识型的；基于知识的

reducible *adj.* 可降低的，可还原的；可缩小的
interdisciplinary *adj.* 各学科间的；跨学科的；跨领域的
procedural *adj.* 程序上的；程序性的
trimming *n.* 整理；修边；去毛边
manipulation *n.* 操纵；操作；处理；操控
aforementioned *adj.* 上述的；前面提及的
mainframe *n.* 主机；大型主机；主机架
graphics *n.* 制图学；图像；图表算法
forgeability *n.* 可锻性；锻造性
mismatch *vt.* 使配错 *n.* 错配；偏模

Questions

1. What classes of tools are necessary for the implementation of an integrated system for forging process design?

2. Please talk about the overall procedure in the production of forgings.

Unit 10

Modeling Techniques Used in Forging Process Design

An Understanding of the flow behavior of the workpiece material under processing conditions is necessary in order to exploit the full potential of process modeling techniques. Mechanistic and dynamic material modeling approaches are being used to understand the fundamentals of flow, fracture, and workability. The former approach is based on activation energy analysis and is limited to processes that can be described by steady-state equations applied to pure, crystalline, and simple alloys. The latter approach is based on continuum and thermodynamic fundamentals and is used to understand the intrinsic workability of simple as well as complex alloys. Dynamic material modeling is required for obtaining realistic predictions of the total performance of any nonlinear deformation process and for reducing the cost of the design process.

● Constitutive Equations for Material Modeling

Constitutive equations describe the nonlinear relationship that exists among such process variables as effective stress, effective strain rate, and temperature at different deformation levels. They are required for the development of dynamic material models and for the realistic modeling of various unit processes. They are unique for each material under each processing condition. Therefore, these equations are developed by using data, obtained under simplified experimental conditions, that can be extended to complex situations by means of well-known hypotheses or, for the case of plastic deformation, such criteria as the von Mises yield criterion. These equations affect the convergence and accuracy of finite-element modeling and must satisfy certain requirements, including the following:

- The constitutive equations must be continuous.
- The surface generated by the constitutive equations must have the same characteristics as the surface generated by the function that describes the dissipation of power applied to a specimen under testing conditions.
- The equations are to be generated to cover the range of processing conditions experienced during the production process.
- The equations should be represented in a form compatible with a finite-element analysis program.

● Dynamic Material Modeling

Control of microstructure during any material-processing operation requires answers to two fundamental questions:

- What conditions does the process require the workpiece material to withstand?

- How does the workpiece material respond to the demands imposed by the process?

The first question can be answered by modeling the process with finite-element methods. The second question, which deals with how the workpiece material responds to the demands of the process, can be answered only if the flow behavior of the workpiece material has been adequately characterized under processing conditions. This necessitates an understanding of how the workpiece will dissipate the instantaneous power applied to it by the process.

The workpiece will dissipate the instantaneous power applied by a metallurgical process commensurate with the level of power supplied. For example, when energy is supplied at a very high strain rate, the material dissipates it by fracture processes. On the other hand, when energy is supplied at a lower and more controlled rate, the material dissipates it by superplastic flow if the material has the correct microstructure and is deformed under superplastic conditions. The efficiency of energy dissipation of these metallurgical processes in both cases may be the same, but the variation of efficiency with respect to strain rate may not be favorable for achieving a steady-state condition.

The applied power also sets up an entropy production rate by a material system. This rate is controlled by the second law of thermodynamics and is directly related to grain size. The rate of entropy production by the material system reaches a maximum level when the material system has the potential to develop very fine grain structure. The rate of entropy production begins decreasing when grain growth takes place. To study this phenomenon, a parameter known as entropy rate ratio has been defined by the dynamic material modeling approach. Therefore, to control microstructures and to avoid defect formation, a new type of material behavior model termed a dynamic material model is required in order to understand how the workpiece dissipates power while producing entropy to satisfy the demands of the process. This model is capable of producing information consistent with the unifying aspects of the finite-element model in such a way that it can become a nonholonomic constraint in the finite-element model for obtaining optimal solutions during the design of various unit processes.

● Analytical Process Modeling of Forging Operations

Several methods are available for the analytical modeling of the forging process. Generally, they fall into the following categories:

- The slab method, which restricts the change of stress to only one direction.
- The uniform deformation energy method, which neglects redundant work involved in internal shearing due to nonuniform deformation.
- The slip-line field solution, which is limited to rigid-plastic materials under plane-strain conditions.
- The bounding methods, which can provide fairly good estimates of upper and lower limits of the deformation force but cannot provide details of local stress and strain distributions.
- The finite-element method, which provides the information required for die design and process control.

All of the above approaches, except the finite-element method, are capable of providing approximate solutions to processing problems, but are subject to some limitations. Therefore, the following discussion will consider the most commonly used approximate methods separately from the finite-element method.

● Approximate and Closed Form Solutions

In general, the boundary conditions in metal-forming operations are too complicated to be accounted for by analytical solutions to the plasticity problem. The need to obtain at least approximate solutions has been satisfied by simplifying assumptions, but each of the analytical approaches has its limitations. The most commonly used approximate methods will be briefly discussed without attempting a rigorous description of the equations that are solved, because this information is available in several other sources. These methods are described in detail with examples in the above references and are presented in increasing order of complexity.

The Sachs (Slab) Method. In this approach, the deformation is assumed to be homogeneous, and the force equilibrium equations are set up and solved using an appropriate yield criterion. The major deficiencies of this approach are:

- Redundant work is not accounted for.
- Stress and strain gradients are accounted for in only one direction and are assumed to be uniform in the perpendicular direction.

The slab method is a quick way of obtaining approximate load and strain estimates in axisymmetric and plane-strain problems and is therefore widely used.

The Slip-Line Field Approach was developed for plane-strain problems. It assumes that the material is rigid and ideally plastic (that is, the material does not strain harden). The theory is based on the fact that any state of stress in plane strain can be represented as the sum of a hydrostatic stress and a pure shear stress. Given the force and velocity boundary conditions, this slip-line field is constructed. The main advantage of this method over the slab method is that it can provide local stress calculations even when the deformation is not homogeneous. The major limitations of the slip-line field approach are:

- It is usable only for plane-strain problems.
- It assumes rigid and ideally plastic materials.
- The method is tedious, and solutions are difficult to verify.

The Upper Bound Method is based on the limit theorem stating that the power dissipated by the boundary forces at their prescribed velocities is always less than or equal to the power dissipated by the same forces under any other kinematically acceptable velocity field. A kinematically acceptable velocity field must satisfy the velocity boundary conditions and material incompressibility. This method allows kinematically admissible velocity fields to be set up as a function of an unknown parameter. Power dissipation is then minimized with respect to the unknown parameter to yield a reasonable estimate of load.

The main disadvantage of this method is that the choice of velocity field is rather arbitrary, and the poorer the selection, the more the estimated load will exceed the true load. Another limitation is that no local stress field is compared.

The Lower Bound Method is not of great practical significance, because forming loads are underestimated. However, it does provide an indication of how conservative the upper bound solution is if the lower bound solution is known.

The lower bound approach is based on the limit theorem stating that the power dissipation of the actual surface forces at their prescribed velocities is always greater than the power dissipation of the surface tractions corresponding to any other statically admissible stress field. A statically admissible stress field must satisfy force equilibrium and not violate the yield criterion.

● Finite-Element Methods

Because of the rapid advancement of high-speed digital computer technology, numerical methods of analysis have been developed. These include the finite-element method (FEM) and the finite-difference method (FDM). Due to the complexity of material flow during metal forming, the finite-element method is the most suitable for analyzing such problems. Finite-element methods, as applied to metal-forming analysis, can be classified into either elastic-plastic or rigid-viscoplastic methods, depending on the assumptions made with regard to the material flow behavior.

The Elastic-Plastic Method assumes that the material deformation includes a small, recoverable elastic part and a much larger, nonrecoverable plastic part. It can give details regarding deformation loads, stresses and strains, and residual stresses. This method has been applied to a large variety of problems, including upsetting, indentation, extrusion, and expansion of a hole in a plate. However, because of the large change in the material flow behavior between elastic and plastic deformation and the need to check the status of each element, the deformation steps must be small, and this makes the method uneconomical.

The Rigid-Viscoplastic Method assumes that the deformation stresses are primarily dependent on deformation (strain) rates. Several programs based on the variational approach have been written by various researchers and have been applied to the same range of problems as the elastic-plastic finite-element method. Although predictions regarding residual stresses cannot be made with the rigid-viscoplastic finite-element method, the larger steps that can be used in modeling metal-forming procedures make the method very economical, especially for modeling hot deformation.

● Vocabulary

workability   n. 可使用性；施工性能；可加工性
constitutive   adj. 基本的；制定的；构成的
entropy   n. 熵
analytical   adj. 分析的；解析的；善于分析的
rigorous   adj. 严格的，严厉的；严密的
slab   n. 厚板，平板；板坯
yield   vt. 屈服；出产   vi. 屈服   n. 产量
axisymmetric   adj. 轴对称的

slip-line   滑移线
tedious   adj. 沉闷的；冗长乏味的
kinematically   adv. 运动学上地
viscoplastic   adj. 黏塑性的
residual   n. 剩余   adj. 剩余的；残留的
upsetting   n. 缩锻，镦锻；镦粗；顶锻
indentation   n. 压痕，刻痕；缩排；呈锯齿状
convergence   n. 收敛；会聚，集合

Questions

1. What conditions does the process require the workpiece material to withstand?
2. How does the workpiece material respond to the demands imposed by the process?
3. What methods are available for the analytical modeling of the forging process?

Unit 11

Blanking

A Blank is a shape cut from flat or preformed stock. Ordinarily, a blank serves as a starting workpiece for a formed part; less often, it is a desired end product. This article will discuss the production of blanks from low-carbon steel sheet and strip in dies in a mechanical or hydraulic press.

● Methods of Blanking in Presses

Cutting operations that are done by dies in presses to produce blanks include cutoff, parting, blanking, notching, and lancing. The first three of these operations can produce a complete blank in a single press stroke. In progressive dies, two or more of these five operations are done in sequence to develop the complete outline of the blank and to separate it from the sheet, strip, or coil stock.

Trimming is defined as the cutting off of excess material from the periphery of a workpiece. It is usually done in dies and is similar to blanking. It is often the final operation on a formed or drawn part.

Cutoff. This operation consists of cutting along a line to produce blanks without generating any scrap in the cutting operation, most of the part outline having been developed by notching or lancing in preceding stations. The cutoff line can take almost any shape—straight, broken, or curved. After being cut off, the blanks fall onto a conveyor or into a chute or container.

A cutoff die can be used to cut the entire outline of blanks whose shape permits nesting in a layout that uses all of the material (except possibly at the ends of the strip), as shown in Fig. 2-15. Alternating positions can sometimes be used in nesting (middle, Fig. 2-15) to avoid producing scrap except at strip ends. Cutoff is also used to cut blanks from strip that has already been notched to separate the blanks along part of their periphery, as described in the following example.

Advantages of cutoff in making blanks include:
- The die has few components and is relatively inexpensive.
- Waste of material in blanking is minimized or eliminated.
- The die can be resharpened easily, and maintenance costs are low.

Disadvantages of cutoff include:
- It can be used only to make blanks that nest in the layout without waste.
- Cutting of one edge causes one-way deflection and stress.
- Accuracy may be affected adversely by the method of feeding.

Parting (Fig. 2-16) is the separation of blanks by cutting away a strip of material between them. Like cutoff, it can be done after most of the part outline has been developed

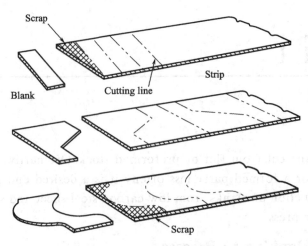

Fig. 2-15 Nested layouts for making blanks by cutoff

by notching or lancing. It is used to make blanks that do not have mating adjacent surfaces for cutoff (Fig. 2-16) or to make blanks that must be spaced for ease of handling in order to avoid distortion or to allow room for sturdy tools. Some scrap is produced in making blanks by parting; therefore, this method is less efficient than cutoff in terms of material use.

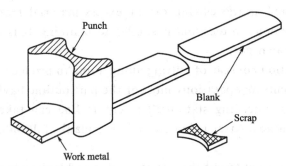

Fig. 2-16 Use of a parting punch to make blanks not having mating adjacent surfaces

Blanking (also called punching) is the cutting of the complete outline of a workpiece in a single press stroke. Because a scrap skeleton is usually produced, blanking involves some material waste. However, blanking is usually the fastest and most economical way to make flat parts, particularly in large quantities.

The skeleton left by blanking sometimes has only scrap-metal value, but many shops have organized programs to maximize the use of cutouts and sizable scrap skeletons in making other production parts. Material waste is completely avoided by using the scrap skeleton that remains from certain blanking operations to provide perforated stock for such items as air filters for forced-air furnaces.

Piercing (with a flat-end punch), also called punching or perforating, is similar to blanking except that the punched-out (blanked) slug is the waste and the surrounding metal is the workpiece.

Notching is an operation in which the individual punch removes a piece of metal from the edge of the blank or strip (Fig. 2-17). Notching is done for such reasons as the follow-

ing:
- To free some metal for drawing [Fig. 2-17(a)] and for forming [Fig. 2-17(b)] while the workpiece remains attached to the strip.
- To remove excess metal before forming [Fig. 2-17(c)].
- To cut part of the outline of a blank that would be difficult to cut otherwise.

The piercing of holes of any shape in a strip to free metal for subsequent forming or to produce surfaces that later coincide with the outline of a blanked part is sometimes called seminotching. The pierced area may outline a portion of one part or of two or more adjacent parts in a strip.

Lancing is a press operation in which a single-line cut or slit is made part way across the strip stock without removing any metal. Lancing is usually done to free metal for forming. The cut does not have a closed contour and does not release a blank or a piece of scrap. In addition to its use in freeing metal for subsequent forming, lancing is also used to cut partial contours for blanked parts, particularly in progressive dies.

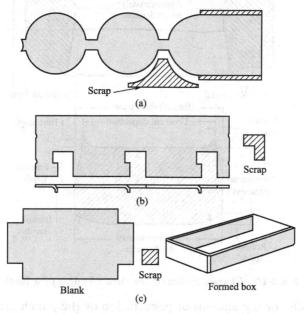

Fig. 2-17 Notched work illustrating the use of notching for freeing metal before drawing (a), and before forming (b), and for removing excess metal before forming (c)

Trimming is an operation for removing excess metal (such as deformed and uneven metal on drawn or formed parts) and metal that was used in a previous operation (such as a blankholding flange for a draw operation). Trimming is done in several ways, depending on the shape of the workpiece, the accuracy required, and the production quantity.

● **Characteristics of Blanked Edges**

The sheared edges of a blank produced in a conventional die are not smooth and vertical for the entire thickness of the part, but exhibit the characteristics represented on an exaggerated scale in Fig. 2-18. The blank is shown in the position in which it would be cut from the work metal by the downward motion of the punch. A portion of the stock remaining after removal of the blank is shown at the top of the illustration.

Rollover on the lower edges of the blank develops by plastic deformation of the work metal as it is forced into the die by the punch. Compression of the metal above the rollover zone against the walls of the die opening burnishes a portion of the edge of the blank, as shown in Fig. 2-18. As the punch completes its stroke, the remaining portion of the blank edge is broken away or fractured (resulting in die break), and a tensile burr is formed along the top of the blank edge.

The angle of the fractured portion of the edge is identified in Fig. 2-18 as the breakout angle. The breakout dimension of the blank and the burnish dimension of the hole in the scrap skeleton are approximately equal to the corresponding punch dimension, and the burnish dimension of the blank is very close to the corresponding die dimension. Therefore, the punch determines the hole size, and the die governs the blank size.

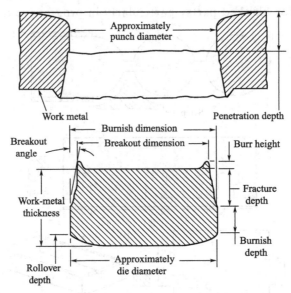

Fig. 2-18 Characteristics of the sheared edges of a blank

Penetration depth, or the amount of penetration of the punch into the work metal before fracture occurs, is shown on the edge of the remaining stock or scrap skeleton in Fig. 2-18. This depth is approximately equal to the sum of the rollover depth and the burnish depth on the blank, except when low die clearance produces secondary burnish. It is usually expressed as a percentage of the work metal thickness.

● **Die Clearance**

The terms clearance, die clearance, and punch-to-die clearance are used synonymously to refer to the space between punch and die. Clearance is important for the reliable operation of the blanking equipment, the quality and type of cut edges, and the life of the punch and die. The data in that illustration can serve as a guide for selecting clearances for blanking. All clearance values given in this article are per side, except where indicated.

Optimal blanking clearance may sometimes be less than optimal piercing clearance. This is partly because the blanked edge is generally close to the stock edge, and material expansion is therefore less restricted. A piercing tool must move a great deal of material away from its cutting edge, and for longest life, the clearance should be selected to eliminate as much compressive loading on the work metal as possible.

A part blanked using clearance much greater than normal may exhibit double shear, which is ordinarily evident only with extremely small clearance. In addition, a part blanked using large clearances will be smaller than the die opening (except for a deeply dished blank), and it is difficult to correct the tooling to compensate for this. In some applications, retaining the blank becomes almost as great a problem as expelling the slugs into a die cavity after piercing, because of the increased clearance.

● **Vocabulary**

blank n. 毛坯；坯料	cutoff n. 切掉；切断；截断 adj. 截止的；中断的
sheet n. 薄片，纸张；薄板	
strip n. 带；条状	scrap n. 碎片；废料；废品
blanking n. 消除；切断；下料	conveyor n. 输送机，传送机；传送带
cutting n. 切断；切削；切削加工	chute n. 斜槽；溜槽；斜道
parting n. 分断加工；分离 v. 分开；断裂	punching n. 穿孔；冲孔；冲切
	piercing adj. 刺穿的 n. 冲孔加工；冲孔
notching n. 切口；冲口加工；开槽	burr n. 毛刺；利口
lancing n. 切口；气切割 v. 切开	penetration n. 渗透；突破；穿透；穿入
clearance n. 清除；空隙；间隙	

● **Questions**

1. Please give some methods of blanking in presses.
2. What are the advantages and disadvantages of cutoff in making blanks?
3. Please talk about the characteristics of blanked edges.

Unit 12
Piercing

Piercing is the cutting of holes in sheet metal, generally by removing a slug of metal, with a punch and die. Piercing is similar to blanking, except that in piercing the work metal that surrounds the piercing punch is the workpiece and the punched-out slug is scrap, while in blanking the workpiece is punched out.

The term piercing is used in this article, to denote the production of a hole by removing a slug of metal with a punch and die. However, some prefer the terms punching or perforating, limiting the term piercing to the use of a pointed punch that tears and extrudes a hole without cutting a slug of metal. The term perforating is also sometimes used in the special sense of cutting many holes in a sheet metal workpiece by removing slugs with several punches.

Piercing is ordinarily the fastest method of making holes in steel sheet or strip and is generally the most economical method for medium-to-high production. Pierced holes can be almost any size and shape; elongated holes are usually called slots. The accuracy of conventional tool steel or carbide dies provides pierced holes with a degree of quality and accuracy that is satisfactory for a wide variety of applications.

● **Characteristics of Pierced Holes**

Pierced holes are different from through holes that are produced by drilling or other machining methods. A properly drilled or otherwise machined through hole has a side-wall that is straight for the full thickness of the work metal, with a high degree of accuracy in size, roundness, and straightness. The sidewall of a pierced hole is generally straight and smooth for only a portion of the thickness, beginning near the punch end of the hole; the rest of the wall is broken out in an irregular cone beyond the straight portion of the hole, producing fracture, breakout, or die break (Fig. 2-19).

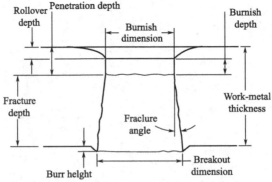

Fig. 2-19 Characteristics of a pierced hole. Curvature and angles are exaggerated for emphasis

The piercing operation typically begins as a cut that produces a burnished surface on the hole wall and some rollover (curved surface caused by deformation of the workpiece before cutting begins), as illustrated in Fig. 2-19. The punch completes its stroke by breaking and tearing away the metal that was not cut during the beginning of the piercing operation.

The combined depth of rollover and burnish is a measure of the penetration depth of the stroke, also shown in Fig. 2-19. This is the part of the stroke during which the cutting force is exerted, before the metal fractures or breaks away.

The amount of penetration before fracture is commonly expressed as a percentage of the stock thickness. In general, the percentage of penetration depends more on the material than on other factors, such as punch-to-die clearance.

● Quality of Hole Wall

If the sidewall of a pierced hole is not smooth or straight enough for the intended application, it can be improved by shaving in a die or by reaming. When done in quantity, shaving is the least expensive method of improving the sidewall of a pierced hole. Shaving in one or two operations generally makes the sidewall of a hole uniform and smooth through 75% to 90% of the stock thickness.

Superior accuracy and smoothness of hole walls can be obtained by fine edge piercing. With this method, one stroke of a triple-action press pierces holes with smooth and precise edges for the entire thickness of the material.

Burr height is an important element in hole quality, and a maximum burr height is usually specified. For most applications, the limit on burr height is between 5% and 10% of stock thickness. Burr height in piercing a given workpiece is primarily governed by punch-to-die clearance and tool sharpness.

Burr condition and limits usually determine the length of run before the punch and die are resharpened. With good practice, burr height generally ranges from 0.013 to 0.076mm, but may be much greater, depending on workpiece material and thickness, clearance, and tool condition.

● Selection of Die Clearance

Clearance, or the space between the punch and the sidewall of the die, affects the reliability of operation of piercing (and blanking) equipment, the characteristics of the cut edges, and the life of the punch and die. Published recommendations for clearances have varied widely, with most suggesting a clearance per side of 3% to 12.5% of the stock thickness for steel.

Establishment of the clearance to be used for a given piercing or blanking operation is influenced by the required characteristics of the cut edge of the hole or blank and by the thickness and the properties of the work metal. Larger clearances prolong tool life. An optimal clearance can be defined as the largest clearance that will produce a hole or blank having the required characteristics of the cut edge in a given material and thickness. Because of differences in cut-edge requirements and in the effect of tool life on overall cost, clearance practices vary among plants and for different applications.

No single table or formula can specify an optimal clearance for all situations encountered in practice. Starting with general guidelines, trial runs using several different clearances may be needed to establish the most desirable clearance for a specific application. The following general principles are useful in making adjustments:

- Rollover (plastic deformation) and burnish depths are greater in thick material than in thin material and are greater in soft material than in hard material.
- Clearance (in decimal parts of an inch) needed to produce a given type of edge should vary directly with material thickness and hardness, and inversely with ductility.

● Effect of Tool Dulling

The sharpness of punch and die edges has an important effect on cut-edge characteristics in piercing and blanking. At the beginning of a run, with punch and die equally sharp, the hole profile is the same as that of the slug or blank. As the run progresses, dulling of the punch increases the rollover and the burnish depth on the hole wall and increases the burr height on the slug or blank. Dulling of the die increases burnish depth and burr height on the hole edge. The punch dulls faster than the die; therefore, the changes in hole characteristics related to punch dulling proceed more rapidly than those related to die dulling.

On average, the following differences between hole edge and blank edge are observed in production work on sheet metal:

- Rollover is greater on hole edge than on slug or blank edge.
- Burnish depth is greater on hole edge than on slug or blank edge.
- Fracture depth is smaller (and fracture angle greater) on hole edge than on slug or blank edge.
- Burr height on hole edge is less than that on slug or blank edge, and varies with tool sharpness.

● Clearance and Tool Size

In blanking, the die opening is usually made to the desired size of the blank, and the punch size is then equal to the die opening minus twice the specified clearance per side. Conversely, in piercing, the punch is usually made to the desired size of the hole, and the die opening is then equal to the punch size plus twice the specified clearance per side.

Clearance per side for blanking dies is ordinarily calculated from the desired percentage of clearance and the nominal thickness of the stock. However, to keep the inventory of piercing tools from becoming too large, some manufacturers use a modified practice for stocking piercing punches and die buttons in commonly used diameters. Punches are ordered to size. Work metal thickness is classified into several ranges, and die buttons are ordered to the specified clearance per side for the median stock thickness of the range to which the work metal for the given application belongs.

● Presses

Presses used in piercing are the same as those used in other pressworking operations. Open-back gap-frame presses of the fixed upright, fixed inclined, or inclinable type are common. The stock can be fed from the side with minimal interference from the press frame, and the parts can be removed from the front by the operator or ejected out the back by gravity or air jets.

Adjustable-bed or horn presses are used for piercing holes in tubing and in the sides of drawn or formed shells and boxes. Adjustable-bed and gap-frame presses are generally rated at capacities of less than 1.8MN.

Straight-side presses are commonly used for compound-die and progressive-die operations. Increased accuracy, speed, and stability are required for these operations.

The turret punch press is a special machine in which the punches and dies are mounted in synchronized indexing tables. Several sets of punches and dies are mounted in the table, which can be manually or automatically indexed into operating position. A flat blank is pierced and notched in a turret punch press by positioning it under the operating punch and tripping the punching mechanism. The blank is secured to a free-floating table on which a template containing the hole pattern is also attached. Each hole size and shape is coded so that all such holes can be pierced before indexing a new punch-and-die set under the press ram. The table is moved so that a pin will drop into a hole in the template; this places the blank in the proper position for piercing a hole. After the holes of one size and shape have been pierced, a new punch and die are indexed into operating position, and piercing continues in this manner until the part is finished. Almost any size or shape of hole can be pierced, within the capacity of the machine.

Turret punch presses can be programmed for tape control for increased production. Turret movement can also be controlled semiautomatically or automatically, on numerical control (NC) or computer numerical control (CNC) punch presses. A closed-loop direct or alternating current drive connected to both the upper and lower turret assemblies provides the automatic turret with either unidirectional or bidirectional movement. Selected CNC presses even offer an optimization feature that automatically determines the most efficient and most cost-effective punching sequence for a specific workpiece.

● Vocabulary

perforating　*adj*. 穿孔的；贯穿的　*v*. 穿孔；刺穿；打孔
drilling　*n*. 钻孔　*v*. 钻孔；钻削
roundness　*n*. 圆；球形；真圆度
sidewall　*n*. 边墙，侧壁
cone　*n*. 圆锥体，圆锥形　*vt*. 使成锥形
rollover　*n*. 翻转；反转
reaming　*n*. 铰刀；纹孔；扩孔　*v*. 钻孔；铰除
shaving　*n*. 削；缺口修整加工

smoothness　*n*. 平滑；柔滑；平坦
establishment　*n*. 确立，制定；机构
dulling　*n*. 钝化　*v*. 使变钝
inventory　*n*. 存货，存货清单；库存
pressworking　*n*. 压制成品，冲压成品；压力加工
synchronized　*adj*. 同步的　*v*. 使协调；同时发生；校准
template　*n*. 模板，样板
bidirectional　*adj*. 双向的；双向作用的

Questions

1. What is piercing?
2. What is clearance? How to select die clearance?
3. How to improve the quality of hole wall in piercing?

Unit 13
Press-Brake Forming

Press-Brake Forming is a process in which the workpiece is placed over an open die and pressed down into the die by a punch that is actuated by the ram portion of a machine called a press brake. The process is most widely used for the forming of relatively long, narrow parts that are not adaptable to press forming and for applications in which production quantities are too small to warrant the tooling cost for contour roll forming.

Simple V-bends or more intricate shapes can be formed in a press brake. Operations such as blanking, piercing, lancing, shearing, straightening, embossing, beading, wiring, flattening, corrugating, and flanging can also be carried out in a press brake.

● Principles

In press-brake forming, as in other forming processes, when a bend is made, the metal on the inside of the bend is compressed or shrunk, and that on the outside of the bend is stretched. The applied forces create a strain gradient across the thickness of the work metal in the area of die contact. Tensile strain occurs in the outer fiber, and compressive strain in the inner fiber; both decrease in magnitude toward the neutral axis.

The setup and tooling for press-brake forming are relatively simple (Fig. 2-20). The distance the punch enters the die determines the bend angle and is controlled by the shut height of the machine. The span width of the die, or the width of the die opening, affects the force needed to bend the workpiece. The minimum width is determined by the thickness of the work and sometimes by the punch-nose radius. After the tools have been set up and the shut height has been adjusted, the press brake is cycled, and the work metal is bent to the desired angle around the nose radius of the punch.

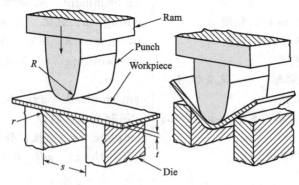

Fig. 2-20 Typical setup for press-brake forming in a die with a vertical opening

● Dies and Punches

V-bending dies and their corresponding punches [Fig. 2-21(a) and (d)] are the tools most commonly used in press-brake forming. The width of the die opening [s, Fig. 2-21 (a)] is usually a minimum of 8t (eight times the thickness of the work metal).

The nose radius of the punch should not be less than $1t$ for bending low-carbon steel, and it must be increased as the formability of the work metal decreases. The radius of the V-bending die must be greater than the nose radius of the punch by an amount equal to or somewhat greater than the stock thickness in order to allow the punch to bottom. Optimal dimensional control is obtained by bottoming the punch to set the bend.

When producing 90° bends in a bottoming die, the V-die is ordinarily provided with an included angle of 85° to 87°. Several trials are often necessary, and various adjustments must be made on the punch setting before the required 90° bend can be obtained.

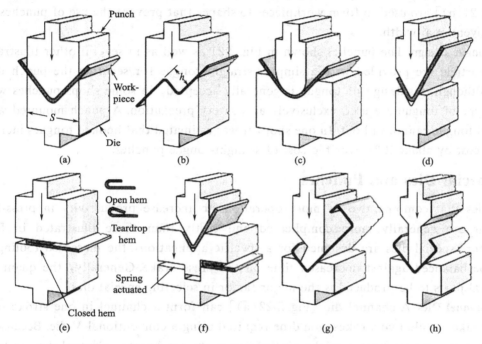

Fig. 2-21 Dies and punches most commonly used in press-brake forming
(a) 90° V-bending; (b) Offset bending; (c) Radiused 90° bending; (d) Acute-angle bending;
(e) Flattening for three types of hems; (f) Combination bending and flattening;
(g) Gooseneck punch for multiple bends; (h) Special clearance punch for multiple bends

Offset Dies. Punch and die combinations such as the one shown in Fig. 2-21(b) are often used to produce offset bends. Because an offset bend requires about four times as much force as a 90° V-bend, offset bending is usually restricted to relatively light-gage metal. The depth of offset [h, Fig. 2-21(b)] should be a minimum of six times the work metal thickness to provide stability at the bends.

Radius Forming is done with a 90° die and a punch, each having a large radius [Fig. 2-21(c)]. When the punch is at the bottom position, the inside radius of bend in the workpiece conforms to the radius of the punch over a part of the curve. The harder the punch bottoms, the more closely the work metal wraps around the punch nose, resulting in a smaller radius of bend and less springback. Uniformity of bend angle depends greatly on the uniformity of the work metal thickness.

Acute Angles are formed by the die and punch shown in Fig. 2-21(d). The air-bending technique is often used to produce acute angles. Acute angles are formed as the first step in making a hem. For this purpose, the die is often bottomed to make the bend angle as acute as possible. A disadvantage of bottoming is that the metal becomes work hardened, so that the hem is likely to crack when formed.

Flattening Dies, shown in Fig. 2-21(e), are used to produce three types of hems after the metal has been formed into an acute angle. The combination die shown in Fig. 2-21(f) produces an acute angle on one workpiece and a hem on another, so that a piece is started and a piece completed with each stroke of the press brake.

Gooseneck Punches [Fig. 2-21(g)] and narrow-body, or special clearance, punches [Fig. 2-21(h)] are used to form workpieces to shapes that prevent the use of punches having conventional width.

Tongue Design. The punches shown in Fig. 2-21 as well as in several other illustrations in this article are provided with a simple, straight tongue for securing the punch to the ram. Although this design of tongue is generally accepted, in some shops punches with a hook type of tongue are used exclusively as a safety precaution. A punch mounted with a hooked tongue cannot fall out. In one shop, it was estimated that hooked tongues increased punch cost by about 10% over the cost of straight-tongue punches.

● Special Dies and Punches

Dies that combine two or more operations to increase productivity in press-brake forming are generally more complicated and costly than those illustrated in Fig. 2-22. Before special dies are designed for a specific application, the increased tooling cost must be balanced against decreased time on the press brake. Generally, the quantity of identical parts to be produced is the major factor in selecting special dies.

Channel Dies. A channel die [Fig. 2-22(a)] can form a channel in one stroke of the press brake, while two strokes would be required using a conventional V-die. Because it is necessary to have an ejector in the die to extract the workpiece, channel dies cost more than conventional dies. This higher cost can be justified only on the basis of large-quantity

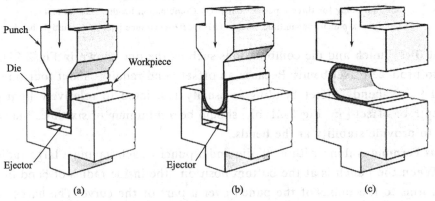

Fig. 2-22 Three types of special punches and dies for press-brake forming
(a) Forming a channel in one stroke; (b) Forming a U-bend in one stroke;
(c) Flattening to remove springback after U-bending

production. It is ordinarily not necessary to have a stripper on the punch, because springback usually causes the part to release. The ejector in the die may be of the spring, hydraulic, or air-return type. The stripper for the punch (if needed) is a release-wedge device or a knockout piece. The use of a channel die, regardless of production quantities, is limited by work metal thickness, corner radii, and required flatness of the web.

A modification of the channel die is the U-bend die [Fig. 2-22(b)]. Springback is a common problem with this type of die; one means of overcoming it is to perform a secondary operation on flat dies, as shown in Fig. 2-22(c).

Air Bending. In air bending, the die is deep enough that setting does not take place at the bottom of the stroke. The die can have a V shape (Fig. 2-23), or the sides can be vertical (Fig. 2-20). The shape and nose radius of the punch are varied to suit the workpiece. The required angle is produced on the workpiece by adjusting the depth to which the punch enters the die opening. This permits the operator to overbend the metal sufficiently to produce the required angle after springback.

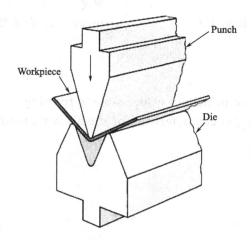

Fig. 2-23 Setup for air bending with an acute-angle punch and die in a press brake

When metal is bent beyond its yield strength, the radius formed bears a definite relationship to the opening in the die. A small die opening produces a small radius; the use of a large die opening increases the radius, but also increases the amount of springback. Springback must be compensated for by overbending. Changing the size of the die opening also changes the amount of force needed to make the bend. As the die opening is increased, less force is required; as the die opening decreases, the bending leverage is less, and more force is therefore required.

The principal advantage of the air-bend method is the variety of forming that can be done with a minimum number of punches and dies. Air bending also requires less force for a given bend, thus preventing excessive strain on the press brake.

The primary disadvantage of air bending is the possible inconsistency in the bends. Because of variations in dimensions and temper of the work metal as it is received from the mill, springback can vary throughout a production run. However, the operator can adjust the ram to compensate for these irregularities. When air bending in a hydraulic press brake, the operator can use a preset pressure, check each part with a gage, and restrike if necessary. With a mechanical press brake, the shut height can be easily adjusted for a restrike and then reset for the next part.

● **Vocabulary**

press-brake forming　折弯成形
contour　*n*. 轮廓；等高线；等位线
straightening　*v*. 矫直；校正　*n*. 校正
embossing　*n*. 压纹，压花，模压加工；凸起
flattening　*n*. 整平；压扁作用　*v*. 压扁
corrugating　*n*. 波纹成形；波纹板加工　*v*. 起皱
flanging　*n*. 折边；翻口；翻边　*v*. 作凸缘
leverage　*n*. 杠杆作用；杠杆效率

stretch　*vt*. 伸展，张开　*vi*. 伸展　*n*. 伸展，延伸
tooling　*n*. 工具；模具；机床安装　*v*. 使用工具；用工具加工
formability　*n*. 成形性，成型性能；可成形性；成型
springback　*n*. 回弹，反弹
hem　*n*. 边，边缘　*vt*. 包围；给……缝边
hooked　*adj*. 钩状的；钩形的　*v*. 用钩固定
stripper　*n*. 剥离器；脱模机；推板

● **Questions**

1. Please talk about the principles of press-brake forming.
2. What are the principal characteristics of the air-bend method?

Unit 14
Deep Drawing

Deep Drawing of metal sheet is used to form containers by a process in which a flat blank is constrained while the central portion of the sheet is pressed into a die opening to draw the metal into the desired shape without folding of the corners. This generally requires the use of presses having a double action for hold-down force and punch force. The process is capable of forming circular shapes, such as cooking pans, box shapes, or shell-like containers. The term deep drawing implies that some drawing-in of the flange metal occurs and that the formed parts are deeper than could be obtained by simply stretching the metal over a die. Clearance between the mate punch and the female die is closely controlled to minimize the free span so that there is no wrinkling of the sidewall. This clearance is sufficient to prevent ironing of the metal being drawn into the sidewall in the deep-drawing process. If ironing of the walls is to be part of the process, it is done in operations subsequent to deep drawing.

Suitable radii in the punch bottom to side edge, as well as the approach to the die opening, are necessary to allow the metal sheet to be formed without tearing. In most deep-drawing operations, the part has a solid bottom to form a container and a retained flange that is trimmed later in the processing. In some cases, the cup shape is fully drawn into the female die cavity, and a straight-wall cup shape is ejected through the die opening. To control the flange area and to prevent wrinkling, a hold-down force is applied to the blank to keep it in contact with the upper surface of the die. A suitable subpress or a double-action press is required. Presses can be either hydraulic or mechanical devices, but hydraulic presses are preferred because of better control of the rate of punch travel.

Any metal that can be processed into sheet form by a cold-rolling process should be sufficiently ductile to be capable of deep drawing. Both hot- and cold-rolled sheet products are used in deep-drawing processes. The cold-work effects introduced during processing of the sheet products for deep-drawing applications must be removed (by annealing, for example), and the as-delivered coils should be free of any aging. This would imply that an aluminum-killed drawing-quality steel, for example, would be preferred over a rimmed steel. After the deep-drawing operation, ductility can be returned to that of the original sheet by in-process annealing, if necessary. In many cases, however, metal that has been deep drawn in a first operation can be further reduced in cup diameter by additional drawing operations, without the need for intermediate annealing.

The properties considered to be important in sheet products designed for deep drawing include:

• Composition, with a minimum amount of inclusions and residual elements contributing to better drawability.

- Mechanical properties, of which the elongation as measured in a tension test, the plastic-strain ratio r, and the strain-hardening exponent n are of primary importance. The strength of the final part as measured by yield strength must also be considered, but this is more a function of the application than forming by deep drawing.
- Physical properties, including dimensions, modulus of elasticity, and any special requirements for maintaining shape after forming.

● Fundamentals of Drawing

A flat blank is formed into a cup by forcing a punch against the center portion of a blank that rests on the die ring. The progressive stages of metal flow in drawing a cup from a flat blank are shown schematically in Fig. 2-24. During the first stage, the punch contacts the blank [Fig. 2-24(a)], and metal section 1 is bent and wrapped around the punch nose [Fig. 2-24(b)]. Simultaneously and in sequence, the outer sections of the blank (2 and 3, Fig. 2-24) move radially toward the center of the blank until the remainder of the blank has bent around the punch nose and a straight-wall cup is formed [Fig. 2-24(c) and(d)]. During drawing, the center of the blank [punch area, Fig. 2-24 (a)] is essentially unchanged as it forms the bottom of the drawn cup. The areas that become the sidewall of the cup (1, 2, and 3, Fig. 2-24) change from the shape of annular segments to longer parallel-side cylindrical elements as they are drawn over the die radius. Metal flow can occur until all the metal has been drawn over the die radius, or a flange can be retained.

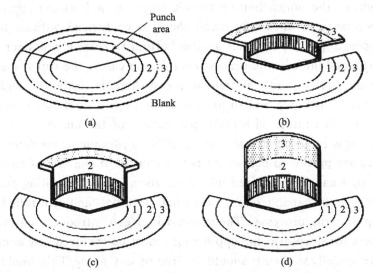

Fig. 2-24 Progression of metal flow in drawing a cup from a flat blank

A blankholder is used in a draw die to prevent the formation of wrinkles as compressive action rearranges the metal from flange to sidewall. Wrinkling starts because of some lack of uniformity in the movement or because of the resistance to movement in the cross section of the metal. A blankholder force sufficient to resist or compensate for this nonuniform movement prevents wrinkling. Once a wrinkle starts, the blankholder is raised from the surface of the metal so that other wrinkles can form easily. The force needed to hold the blank flat during drawing of cylindrical shells varies from practically zero for relatively thick blanks to about one-third of the drawing load for a blank 0.76mm thick. Thinner blanks often require proportionally greater blankholder force.

Conditions for drawing without a blankholder depend on the ratio of the supported length of the blank to its thickness, the amount of reduction from blank diameter to cup diameter, and the ratio of blank diameter to stock thickness. For thick sheets, the maximum reduction of blank diameter to cup diameter in drawing without a blankholder is about 25%. This ratio approaches zero for thin foil-like sheet. If a blankholder is employed, the maximum reduction is increased to about 50% for metals of maximum drawability and 25% to 30% for metals of marginal drawability in the same equipment.

● Dies

Dies used for drawing sheet metal are usually one of the following basic types or some modification of these types:
- Single-action dies.
- Double-action dies.
- Compound dies.
- Progressive dies.
- Multiple dies with transfer mechanism.

Selection of the die depends largely on part size, severity of draw, and quantity of parts to be produced.

Single-action Dies [Fig. 2-25(a)] are the simplest of all drawing dies and have only a punch and a die. A nest or locator is provided to position the blank. The drawn part is pushed through the die and is stripped from the punch by the counterbore in the bottom of the die. The rim of the cup expands slightly to make this possible. Single-action dies can be used only when the forming limit permits cupping without the use of a blankholder.

Double-action Dies have a blankholder. This permits greater reductions and the drawing of flanged parts. Fig. 2-25(b) shows a double-action die of the type used in a double-action press. In this design, the die is mounted on the lower shoe; the punch is attached to the inner, or punch slide; and the blankholder is attached to the outer slide. The pressure pad is used to hold the blank firmly against the punch nose during the drawing operation and to lift the drawn cup from the die. If a die cushion is not available, springs or air or hydraulic cylinders can be used; however, they are less effective than a die cushion, especially for deep draws.

Fig. 2-25(c) shows an inverted type of double-action die, which is used in single-action presses. In this design, the punch is mounted on the lower shoe; the die on the upper shoe. A die cushion can supply the blankholding force, or springs or air or hydraulic cylinders are incorporated into the die to supply the necessary blankholding force. The drawn cup is removed from the die on the upstroke of the ram, when the pin like extension of the knockout strikes a stationary knockout bar attached to the press frame.

Compound Dies. When the initial cost is warranted by production demands, it is practical to combine several operations in a single die. Blanking and drawing are two operations commonly placed in compound dies. With compound dies, workpieces can be produced several times as fast as by the simple dies shown in Fig. 2-25.

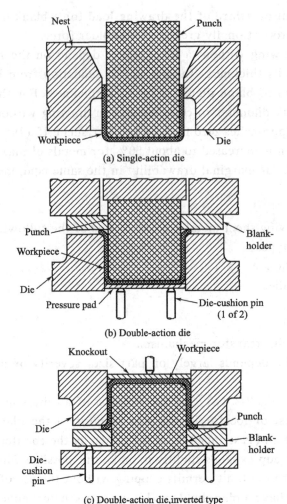

Fig. 2-25 Components of three types of simple dies shown in a setup used for drawing a round cup

Progressive Dies. The initial cost and length of bed needed for progressive dies usually limit their application to relatively small workpieces. Fig. 2-26 shows a typical six-station progression for making small shell-like workpieces on a mass-production basis. However, larger parts, such as liners for automobile headlights, have been drawn in progressive dies.

The total number of parts to be produced and the production rate often determine whether or not a progressive die will be used when two or more operations are required. There are, however, some practical considerations that may rule against a progressive die, regardless of quantity:

- The workpiece must remain attached to the scrap skeleton until the final station, without hindering the drawing operations.
- Drawing operations must be completed before the final station is reached.
- In deep drawing, it is sometimes difficult to move the workpiece to the next station.
- If the draw is relatively deep, stripping is often a problem.

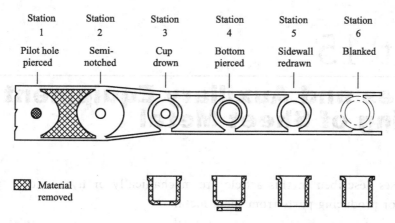

Fig. 2-26 Production of a small ferrule in a six-station progressive die

- The length of press stroke must be more than twice the depth of draw.

● Vocabulary

deep drawing 深冲压，深拉
flange n. 法兰；凸缘；边缘 vt. 给……装凸缘
wrinkling n. 起皱现象；起皱纹 v. 起皱纹
tearing adj. 撕裂的 v. 撕开；裂开
subpress n. 小压力机；半成品压力机
in-process adj. 进程内的；同进程的
drawability n. 可拉性，回火性，压延性
annular adj. 环形的，环状的

blankholder 防皱压板；压边圈
proportionally adv. 成比例地；相称地，适当地
compound die 复合模
progressive die 级进模；顺序冲模
counterbore n. 埋头孔，扩孔
rim n. 边，边缘 vt. 作……的边，装边于……
cushion n. 垫子 vt. 给……安上垫子；缓和……的冲击

● Questions

1. What is the concept of drawing?
2. What properties should be considered in sheet products designed for deep drawing?
3. Please talk about the fundamentals of drawing?

Unit 15

Presses and Auxiliary Equipment for Forming of Sheet Metal

The Presses described in this article are mechanically or hydraulically powered machines used for producing parts from sheet metal.

● Mechanical Presses

In most mechanical presses, a flywheel is the major source of energy that is applied to the slides by cranks, gears, eccentrics, or linkages during the working part of the stroke. The flywheel runs continuously and is engaged by the clutch only when a press stroke is needed. In some very large mechanical presses the drive motor is directly connected to the press shaft, thus eliminating the need for a flywheel and a clutch.

Two basic types of drive, gear and nongeared, are used to transfer the rotational force of the flywheel to the main shaft of the press.

Nongeared Drive. In a nongeared drive (also known as a flywheel drive), the flywheel is on the main shaft [Fig. 2-27(a)], and its speed, in revolutions per minute, controls the slide speed. Usually press speeds with this type of drive are high, ranging from 60 to 1000 strokes per minute. The main shaft can have a crankshaft, as shown in Fig. 2-27(a), or an eccentric.

Energy stored in the flywheel should be sufficient to ensure that the reduction in the speed of the flywheel will be no greater than 10% per press stroke. If the energy in the flywheel is not sufficient to maintain this minimum in speed reduction, a gear-driven press should be used.

Gear drives [Fig. 2-27(b),(c), and (d)] have the flywheel on an auxiliary shaft that drives the main shaft through one or more gear reductions. Either single-reduction or multiple-reduction gear drives are used, depending on size and tonnage requirements. In gear-driven presses, there is more flywheel energy available for doing work than there is in the nongeared presses, because the speed of the flywheel is higher than that of the main shaft. The flywheel shaft of a gear-driven press often is connected to the main shaft at both ends [Fig. 2-27(c)], which results in a more efficient drive.

A single-reduction gear drive develops speeds of 30 to 100 strokes per minute. Speed for a multiple-reduction twin gear drive [Fig. 2-27(d)] is usually 10 to 30 strokes per minute, which provides exceptionally steady pressure.

● Hydraulic Presses

Hydrostatic pressure against one or more pistons provides the power for a hydraulic press. Most hydraulic presses have a variable-volume, variable-pressure, concentric-piston

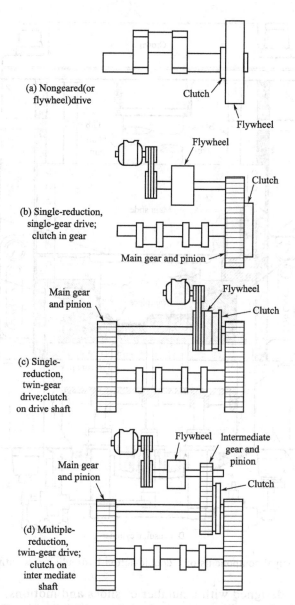

Fig. 2-27 Four types of drive and clutch arrangements for mechanical presses

pump to provide them with a fast slide opening and closing speed. It also provides a slow working speed at high forming pressure.

The principal components of a typical hydraulic press are shown in Fig. 2-28. A bolster plate is attached to the bed to support the dies and to guide the pressure pins between the die cushion and the pressure pad.

The capacity of a hydraulic press depends on the diameter of the hydraulic pistons and on the rated maximum hydraulic pressure, the latter being a function of the pump pressure and related mechanisms. Hydraulic presses with capacities up to 445MN have been built, but most have a capacity of less than 133MN. The typical hydraulic press is rated at 900kN to 9MN. Gap-frame presses are rated at 45 to 450kN.

Because of their construction, hydraulic presses can be custom designed at a relatively

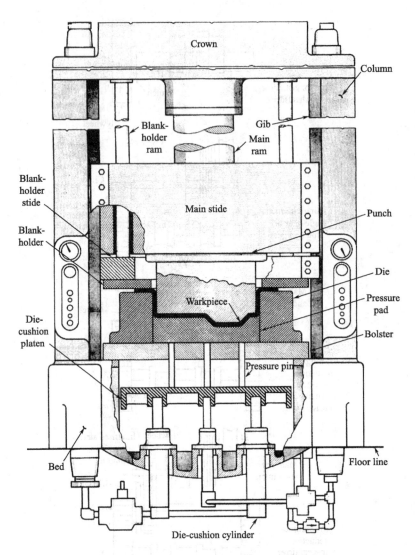

Fig. 2-28 Principal components of a double-action hydraulic press with a die cushion

low cost. They can be designed with a number of slides and motions, or separate hydraulic circuits can be used for various independent actions. In addition, side action can be provided within the frame of the press by means of separate cylinders. Such side action in a mechanical press is usually provided by cams and is complex and expensive. Most hydraulic presses are straight-side models, but small, fast, gap-type presses designed to compete with mechanical open-back inclinable presses have been developed.

Hydraulic press slides, or platens, are actuated by numerous combinations of hydraulic drives. Hydraulic presses usually have a longer stroke than mechanical presses, and force can be constant throughout the stroke. Hydraulic presses have an adjustable stroke for one or more slides. Accumulators or large-volume pumps can provide fast motion for a slide to open and close. High-pressure pumps provide the working force at a slower speed.

Usually all slides are operated by one pumping system. The relation of each action to the others, interaction, and timing all depend on the controls.

● Press Selection

Proper selection of a press is essential for successful and economical operation. Important factors influencing the selection of a press include size, force, energy, and speed requirements. The press must be capable of exerting force in the amount, location, and direction, as well as for the length of time, needed to perform the specified operation or operations. Other necessary considerations include the size and geometry of the workpieces, the workpiece material, operation or operations to be performed, number of workpieces to be produced, production rate needed, accuracy and finish requirements, equipment costs, and other factors.

Size, Force, and Energy Requirements. Bed and slide areas of the press must be large enough to accommodate the dies to be used and provide adequate space for die changing and maintenance. Space is required around the dies for accessories such as keepers, pads, cam return springs, and gages; space is also needed for attaching the dies to the press. Shut height of the press, with adjustment, must also be suitable for the dies.

Presses with as short a stroke as possible should be selected because they permit higher-speed operation, thus increasing productivity. Stroke requirements, however, depend upon the height of the parts to be produced. Blanking can be done with short strokes, but some forming and drawing operations require long strokes, especially for ejection of parts.

Size and type of press to be selected also depend upon the method and direction of feeding; the size of sheet, coil stock, blank, or workpiece to be formed; the type of operation; and the material being formed and its strength. Material or workpiece handling and die accessibility generally determine whether the press should be of gap-frame or straight-side construction, and whether it should be inclined or inclinable.

The force required to perform the desired operations determines press capacity, expressed in tons or kilonewtons (kN). The position on the stroke at which the force is required and the length of stroke must be considered.

Energy or work (force times distance), expressed in inch-tons or joules (J), varies with the operation. Blanking and punching require the force to be exerted over only a short distance; drawing, forming, and other operations require force application over a longer distance. The major source of energy in mechanical presses is the flywheel, the energy varying with the size and speed of the flywheel. The energy available increases with the square of the flywheel speed. Possible problems are minimized by selecting a press that has the proper frame capacity, drive motor rating, flywheel energy, and clutch torque capacity.

Speed Requirements. Press speed is a relative term that varies with the point of reference. Fast speeds are generally desirable, but they are limited by the operations performed, the distances above stroke bottoms where the forces must be applied, and the stroke lengths. High speed, however, is not necessarily the most efficient or productive. Size and configuration of the workpiece, the material from which it is made, die life, maintenance costs, and other factors must be considered to determine the highest production rate at the lowest cost per workpiece. A lower speed may be more economical because of possible longer production runs with less downtime.

Mechanical Versus Hydraulic Presses. Mechanical presses are the most frequently used for the blanking, forming, and drawing of sheet metal, but hydraulic presses are being increasingly applied. There are applications for which hydraulic presses offer certain advantages and, in some cases, are the only machines that can be used. For example, very high force requirements can only be met with hydraulic presses.

● **Vocabulary**

actuation n. 冲动，驱使；行动
tonnage n. 吨位，吨数，载重量
crankshaft n. 机轴；曲柄轴
rotational adj. 转动的；回转的；轮流的
auxiliary n. 辅助物；附属机构 adj. 辅助的；附加的
downtime n. 停工期；故障停机时间

shaft n. 柏杆；轴；传动轴 vt. 在……上装杆
concentric adj. 同轴的；同中心的
bolster n. 垫板；上下模板
inclinable adj. 倾向于……的；可倾斜的
accessory n. 配件；附件 adj. 附属的

● **Questions**

1. Please give the comparison of characteristics and preferred uses for both mechanical and hydraulic presses.
2. How to select presses for sheet metal forming?

Unit 16
CAD/CAM Applications in sheet Forming

Computer-Aided Design and Manufacture (CAD/CAM) typically involves the use of graphic displays, which allow the interactive creation and modification of geometric shapes, but CAD/CAM is not limited to this technique. In its broadest definition, CAD/CAM can be the application of any software program--batch or interactive--that facilitates product design and manufacture.

There are two principal advantages of applying CAD to the design of dies for sheet metal stamping. First is the generation of computer surface data for downstream CAM applications to generate numerically controlled (NC) cutter paths and to eliminate the need for die models. Second is the reduction of downstream die tryout time and the reduction of die construction aids by producing more geometrically accurate data. These advantages can result in both time and cost savings. This article will discuss the application of CAD/CAM to the diemaking process, first in general terms and then in a specific case study.

● **Computer-Aided Design**

Computer-aided design has been defined as the technique by which geometrical descriptions of three-dimensional objects can be created and stored in the form of mathematical models in a computer system; once created, the models can then be displayed, manipulated, and analyzed in a number of ways on a CRT. This Section will describe typical CAD equipment and processes used for sheet forming die design.

● **Advantages Associated With CAD**

Within the design phase itself, most advantages derive from enhanced productivity in terms of speed and accuracy. Depending on the specific task, productivity can typically increase from three to ten times for particular functions. As mentioned above, standardized components help tremendously in raising this figure; other factors include the complexity of the part, the degree of part symmetry, and its similarity to previously designed components. Another element of productivity gain is found in the reaction time to any changes in input, which may range from days to literally moments.

As important as productivity increases may be, perhaps the greatest contribution of CAD is in design accuracy. On one hand, there is dimensional control that is often well above that attainable by manual drafting. A designer can precisely scale and view the work from any perspective, rotating the design on the screen at will. Further, with this three-dimensional capability, when an alteration is made to a design in one dimension, the computer automatically makes the equivalent change in the remaining views, thus preserving continuity and minimizing the possibility of errors. These features lead to vastly improved comprehension by the designers, because they are not required to assemble a series of two-dimensional drawings into a mental three-dimensional image. On the other hand, CAD systems provide the opportunity to avoid errors in drafting and documentation because the computer maintains records and continuity. In addition, computer tolerances are much closer than those of a drafter; inconsistencies that may be difficult to detect on paper are immediately obvious to the system.

● When to Use CAD

Not all die design work is currently suitable for CAD; even if CAD is capable of handling the design work, it is not always economically feasible to do so. As noted previously, it is often more expensive to design a die with CAD than manually. However, economies can be achieved for large families of similar parts, for which a library can be maintained and accessed often. Poor candidates for CAD are unique items, or those requiring a sizable amount of individual attention, for which library entries do not exist and will not be useful in the future. Ideal candidates are repeat commodities. In the automotive industry, these include hood inner and outer panels, roofs, fenders, doors, and quarter panels.

Even where CAD is used, only 80% to 90% of the designing is done on-screen. Functions still frequently done manually include such tasks as double checking and detailing the designs. Computer detailing requires exorbitant amounts of computer memory, but it is a relatively simple task to perform manually. Thus, there are not enough advantages to justify performing this operation on the computer. This may change, however, as newer and more powerful software and hardware become available.

To use CAD, it is necessary to obtain three-dimensional wireframe diagrams of the finished part from the customer. Not all parts are available as wireframes; perhaps 95% of all new outer-skin prints in the automotive industry have such diagrams available. However, virtually 100% of all new automotive parts can be found in the computer. Surface data are not required for CAD, although they are necessary for CAM.

● Die Design Using CAD

Obtaining and Storing Data. The designing of sheet forming dies for automotive stampings usually begins with a telephone link to the data center of the automaker. Using the direct link, the die designer can obtain the data necessary to generate a wireframe of the panel. Once obtained from the computer of the automaker, the data can be used immediately or stored on magnetic disk or tape for later reference.

Laying Up the Design. In the design process, models are summoned from the library and compared to the current workpiece. The designer enlarges or reduces the size of the details of the standard model to fit the new part. Guide pins, wear plates, air cylinders, air headers, and other die details are included in the standard model. With the full three dimensions available, the panel and die representation can be rotated in any direction for a better view of the part. Because the model is still in a wireframe format, sections initially appear as a series of unconnected dots. The points are connected by the designer. Currently, there is no automatic routine for connecting the points. Because the computer does not know which points to connect, a skilled designer is needed. In laying up the design, hidden lines also must be indicated by the designer. This is done by altering line fonts on each view or section that contains hidden design features.

Creating Views and Detailing. To create a view, the three-dimensional wireframe is dissected in a manner that allows viewing of specific areas within the die. A three-dimensional image seen on the workstation screen is projected onto a flat plane. At this time, the designer can remove hidden lines and otherwise enhance the projection (for example, add dimensions, finish marks, and so on) to suit his needs. When this process is completed, the depiction is transferred to the plotter. The resulting drawing (s) are then used for manual detailing and checking and filing for future reference. The final drawing is used as a medium to convey the information from the computer to the shop floor.

● Computer-Aided Manufacture

Computer-aided manufacture is defined as the use of computers (or, in this case, stand-alone workstations) for partial or complete control of the manufacturing processes; in practice, the term is usually applied only to computer-based developments or NC technology.

● Advantages Associated With CAM

Again, like CAD, the benefits derived from the use of CAM are difficult, and sometimes impossible, to quantify. Some stem from the reduction in man-hours required for machining; even more come from the greater accuracy and product quality achieved from the use of the system. Among the specific advantages are:

- Time savings from the reduction of multiple setups.
- Greater productivity in the cutting process itself (due primarily to the elimination of drag imposed by the tracer on the model surface; improvements of up to 50% may be achieved).
- Elimination of inaccuracies in models due to warpage.
- Accurate cutter paths for profiling from computer data instead of from templates.
- Less subsequent handwork required.
- Reduction in tryout time due to reduced part errors.
- More productive use of employees.

Computer-aided manufacturing allows the machine to perform the routine functions, thus enabling the diemaker to concentrate on more complex tasks. The main theme of the above list of advantages is the avoidance of errors, and this is what makes the quantification of benefits associated with the use of CAM so difficult. It is difficult to place a value on errors and slowdowns that never occur.

In addition, the use of true CAM is impossible without CAD. Computer-aided design inputs the data that allow the cutter paths to be generated by computer. Without CAD, CAM must create all of its own data, slowing the overall process.

● When to Use CAM

Two-And-One-Half Dimensional Work. Some aspects of die manufacture are relatively straightforward, requiring only two-dimensional representations for cutter path generation. In the case of casting millwork (flat surfaces that require simple mill cutting), it remains easier to input much of the data manually, particularly for straight areas. Operators can use their experience and judgment to determine cutter paths quickly; therefore, it is not economical to use CAM for this process. However, for angled millwork, the operator would have to perform excessive calculations and programming. With CAD/CAM, the process is effortless and accurate. The overall is a net reduction in design and manufacturing time.

Three-Dimensional Work. To program three-dimensional surfaces, data must be available in wireframe; surface data are more desirable, but are not always available. If a surface model does not exist, it must be created. The more complex the part geometry, the greater the number of patches required, and the longer it takes to create the surface. If surfaces are available, a small amount of trimming of the surface patches is required in order to eliminate patch extension and/or overlap. Outer surface parts have relatively simple geometries with critical surface and dimensional requirements, and CAM is a must with or without supplied surfaces. Existing CAD/CAM systems can handle the data and create excellent cutter paths in a timely, efficient manner. On inner parts, where surfaces are complex with multiple patches, the effectiveness of cutting the shape by CAM is questionable because of the current limitations of surface mathematics. The surface is seldom supplied. The task of creating a surface on a panel such as a hood inner is an 8-week program before cutter paths can start to be generated. If the programming for CAM takes too long or creates gouges, the net effect is lost time and money. A directive cannot be set that all machining be programmed and cut using CAM. Because CAD/CAM is an emerging technology that does certain items well, it should be used only for those applicable items, such as outer panels, hoods, and fenders. Applications can be expanded as new software allows.

● Vocabulary

batch   n. 批次；批量   vt. 分批处理
cutter   n. 刀具，切割机
tryout   n. 试验；试用
diemaking   n. 开模，制模
idling   n. 空载；空运转
fender   n. 挡泥板；叶子板；翼子板
panel   n. 仪表板；嵌板；平板

exorbitant   adj. 过高的；过分的
summon   vt. 召唤；召集；鼓起；振作
plotter   n. 绘图机；绘图仪
profiling   n. 性能分析；压型；仿形切削
millwork   n. 水车机械；磨光工作
stamping   v. 冲压   n. 冲击制品；压模

● Questions

1. What are the principal advantages of applying CAD to the design of dies for sheet metal stamping?

2. What are the advantages of applying CAM to the design of dies for sheet metal stamping?

Unit 17
Statistical Analysis of Forming Processes

Statistics are becoming important tools in the operation of press shops, providing numerical process analysis capabilities that far exceed the more traditional recording of simple breakage rates. The most common use of statistics in the press shop is the area of statistical process control (SPC). Though utilized in many formats, SPC is simply the use of statistical techniques such as control charts to analyze a process or its output and thus enable appropriate actions to be taken to achieve and maintain a state of statistical control. The use of statistical process control instead of traditional quality control methods such as inspection/sorting is beneficial in a number of ways. Statistical process control:

- Decreases scrap, rework, and inspection costs by controlling the process.
- Decreases operating costs by optimizing the frequency of tool adjustments and tool changes.
- Maximizes productivity by identifying and eliminating the causes of out-of-control conditions.
- Allows the establishment of a predictable and consistent level of quality.
- Eliminates or reduces the need for receiving inspection by the purchaser because it produces a more reliable, trouble-free product, resulting in increased customer satisfaction.

● **The Forming Process**

A wide range of forming processes are currently in use. Although the details of these processes differ significantly, most forming processes share certain characteristics. Each forming process, however simple, can be viewed as a system. For sheet metal forming, one common breakdown of the system consists of the following components:
- Material.
- Lubricant.
- Tooling.
- Press.

Each of these major components can be further broken down into subcomponents.

The components of forming systems are highly interactive. A change in one component can produce significant changes in the effects of other components. Not only are the changes within a single component difficult to trace and understand, but the interaction of the components makes the task even more difficult. Small changes made in one or more components of the system can cause very large changes in the output of the system (the finished part). These synergistic changes may not be predictable or even possible to anticipate.

Ideally, the forming system should be a continuous process. For many processes, the system appears to be continuous. The tools are inserted into the designated press and remain there for the production life cycle of the part, which often spans several years. Changes made during the production life cycle may in fact create major disruptions in the continuous nature of the process. These changes can include engineering modifications, tooling replacement, routine maintenance, process improvements, and other seemingly minor modifications to the process.

Many forming processes are conducted on a batch basis, typically with large volumes. Tooling is inserted into a press, a specific number of pieces are made, and the tooling is removed from the press. This type of process is often considered to be an interrupted or segmented form of a continuous process. In reality, however, a new forming system is created each time the tooling is inserted into the press. This is evidenced by the extended period of trial-and-error adjustments necessary to the tooling before the production of satisfactory parts can begin.

● The Statistical Approach

Statistical process control programs are becoming commonplace in industry. An entire science has been developed to deal with the problem of defining, analyzing, correcting, and controlling production processes. By providing data on the capabilities and output of a process, statistical methods provide a rational, rather than an emotional, basis for problem solving and decision making. Other benefits of statistical process control have been listed in the introduction to this article.

As a system, the forming process is amenable to system analysis and the techniques of system control. Various statistical techniques, many of which have their origins in quality control practices, can be applied to the forming process. In this article, these statistical techniques are divided into two broad categories: historical tracking and statistical deformation control (process design).

● Historical Tracking

Historical tracking is a long-term process of measuring, recording, and analyzing one or more specific characteristics of a process. This record then becomes the basis upon which the current state of the process can be assessed and the future state of the process predicted. Numerous statistical techniques are applicable to historical tracking; one is the control chart and another is statistical deformation control.

● Control Charting

The heart of many SPC systems is the control chart. The control chart is a method of monitoring process output through the measurement of a selected characteristic and the analysis of its performance over time. Because the output from one process is often the input to the next process, the physical location of the measurement can be at either end of the transfer link. For example, the output from a blanking press—the blanks—becomes the input to the next stage, which is the press itself.

A control chart can be a very powerful statistical tool. Information from the control chart can be used to inform the operator when to adjust the process and, perhaps more important, when not to adjust the process. This places the operator in control of the process, based on statistically valid numbers instead of trial and error.

For example, the operator is given a machine capable of producing the required parts and is then given the means to measure the characteristics of output (the finished parts) in real time. Thus, the operator knows the quality of the part coming off the machine on a real time basis. In addition, the operator has control limits for the process. These control limits tell the operator when to adjust the process and when not to adjust the process, which permits the operator to prevent rather than detect defects.

● Statistical Deformation Control

Each of the four components of a forming system—material, lubricant, tooling, and press—can be tracked using the SPC techniques described above. Typical measurements could include:
- Material thickness, coil/blank dimensions, and properties.
- Lubricant composition, viscosity, and application thickness.
- Tooling pressures, surface treatment, and dimensional accuracy.
- Press speed, stroke, and ram pressures.

Many of these measurements are charted in an attempt to reduce process variability and to improve product quality.

However, the components of forming systems are complex, interactive, and synergistic; reliable models are not available for predicting the output of the forming system based solely on the system inputs. Therefore, monitoring of the final output of the system is required. Dimensional checking of the final product can be easily accomplished, but monitoring forming severity is more difficult.

Numbers representing the percentage of scrap or the percentage of breakage are traditionally recorded to represent the status of the forming system. These numbers are inadequate measures of forming severity. For example, many stamping processes result in high levels of strain but not breakage. Therefore, the current behavior—no breakage—gives no indication that breakage may be imminent; some measure of performance must be sought that permits a broader range of conditions. Once breakage begins, the stamping process is out of control. General global straining ceases as the tear develops and opens; other forming modes become active. In addition, the percentage of breakage averages the forming severity over a large number of stampings instead of determining the forming severity at a preselected location in each individual stamping. For these cases, percentage of breakage does not accurately define the various levels of severity.

One means of evaluating forming severity used in many sheet metal press shops is circle grid analysis and forming limit diagrams. The actual amount of deformation that the sheet has experienced is determined from the deformed circles (Fig. 2-29). The forming limit diagram shows the maximum amount of deformation a stamping can undergo before failure. Forming severity can be defined as the maximum allowable deformation minus the actual deformation. This forms the basis for monitoring and controlling stamping performance.

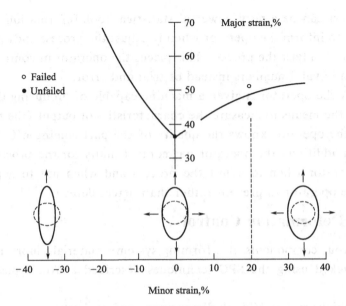

Fig. 2-29 Forming limit diagram showing strain states where forming is safe (below curve) and where stampings will begin to fail from localized necking during forming (above curve)

The process of pregridding the blank before deformation and measuring the deformed circles presents logistical problems if it is used for routine analyses of a large number of stampings over an extended period of time. These problems include removing blanks from the material lifts for pregridding, the time required for gridding, careful reapplication of lubrication to duplicate production levels, reinsertion of blanks into the production cycle without stopping production, proper lighting for grid reading, the time required for accurate reading, and disposal of gridded blanks after analysis. Therefore, only one or two stampings are commonly gridded to provide a single analysis (with respect to time) of the severity of the stamping. No information can be deduced about the change of the forming system with time, nor can the single stamping be characterized with respect to the dynamic changes of the system.

Dynamic changes, however, can be analyzed with statistical process control. A critical variable is measured at specified intervals and plotted as a function of time to generate a control chart. From this control chart, using SPC analysis techniques, the current status of the system can be identified relative to its historical performance. The dynamic variability of the system can be defined, and determinations can be made as to whether the system is in control, out of control, or changing.

Statistical deformation control (SDC) combines the best features of circle grid analysis, forming limit diagrams, and statistical process control. The deformation severity of the stamping under investigation becomes the critical variable that is tracked by statistical process control. To simplify the press shop procedures further, the amount of deformation experienced by the stamping is defined by the ratio of final thickness t_f to initial thickness t_0. The thickness ratio is determined from ultrasonic measurements of sheet metal thickness in the most critical zone of the stamping. The ultrasonic measurements are rapid, the blanks do not have to be pregridded, and the stampings are not damaged by a grid and therefore need not be scrapped after the measurement is made.

● **Vocabulary**

breakage　　*n.* 破坏；破损；裂口；破损量
statistical　　*adj.* 统计的；统计学的
synergistic　　*adj.* 协同的；协作的，协同作用的
disruption　　*n.* 破坏，毁坏；分裂，破裂
monitoring　　*n.* 监视，监控；检验　　*v.* 监视

imminent *adj.* 即将来临的；迫近的
preselected　　*adj.* 预选的　　*v.* 预选；预先决定
logistical　　*adj.* 后勤方面的；运筹的，逻辑的
ultrasonic　　*adj.* 超声的；超音速的　　*n.* 超声波

● **Questions**

1. What are the benefits of statistical process control?
2. What categories are devided of statistical techniques?

Part III
Welding

Part II

Welding

Unit 1
Energy Sources Used for Fusion Welding

Welding and Joining processes are essential for the development of virtually every manufactured product. However, these processes often appear to consume greater fractions of the product cost and to create more of the production difficulties than might be expected. There are a number of reasons that explain this situation.

First, welding and joining are multifaceted, both in terms of process variations (such as fastening, adhesive bonding, soldering, brazing, arc welding, diffusion bonding, and resistance welding) and in the disciplines needed for problem solving (such as mechanics, materials science, physics, chemistry, and electronics). An engineer with unusually broad and deep training is required to bring these disciplines together and to apply them effectively to a variety of processes.

Second, welding or joining difficulties usually occur far into the manufacturing process, where the relative value of scrapped parts is high.

Third, a very large percentage of product failures occur at joints because they are usually located at the highest stress points of an assembly and are therefore the weakest parts of that assembly. Careful attention to the joining processes can produce great rewards in manufacturing economy and product reliability.

● **Energy-Source Intensity**

One distinguishing feature of all fusion welding processes is the intensity of the heat source used to melt the liquid. Virtually every concentrated heat source has been applied to the welding process. However, many of the characteristics of each type of heat source are determined by its intensity. For example, when considering a planar heat source diffusing into a very thick slab, the surface temperature will be a function of both the surface power density and the time.

Fig. 3-1 shows how this temperature will vary on steel with power densities that range from 400 to $8000 W/cm^2$. At the lower value, it takes 2min to melt the surface. If that heat source were a point on the flat surface, then the heat flow would be divergent and might not melt the steel. Rather, the solid metal would be able to conduct away the heat as fast as it was being introduced. It is generally found that heat-source power densities of approximately $1000 W/cm^2$ are necessary to melt most metals.

At the other end of the power-density spectrum, heat intensities of $106 W/cm^2$ or $107 W/cm^2$ will vaporize most metals within a few microsecond. At levels above these values, all of the solid that interacts with the heat source will be vaporized, and no fusion welding can occur. Thus, the heat sources for all fusion welding processes should have power densities between approximately 0.001 and $1 MW/cm^2$. This power-density spectrum is shown in

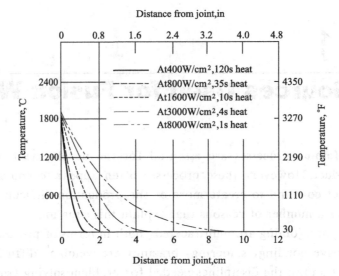

Fig. 3-1 Temperature distribution after a specific heating time in a thick steel plate heated uniformly on one surface as a function of applied heat intensity; initial temperature of plate is 25°C

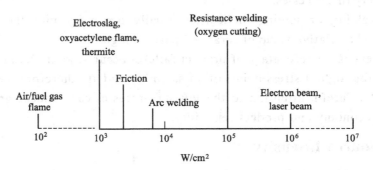

Fig. 3-2 Spectrum of practical heat intensities used fou fusion welding

Fig. 3-2, along with the points at which common joining processes are employed.

The fact that power density is inversely related to the interaction time of the heat source on the material is evident in Fig. 3-1. Because this represents a transient heat conduction problem, one can expect the heat to diffuse into the steel to a depth that increases as the square root of time, that is, from the Einstein equation:

$$x \sim \sqrt{at} \tag{3-1}$$

where x is the distance that the heat diffuses into the solid, in centimeters; a is the thermal diffusivity of the solid, in cm^2/s; and t is the time in seconds.

For the planar heat source on a steel surface, as represented by Fig. 3-1, the time in seconds to produce melting on the surface, t_m, is given by:

$$t_m = (5000/HI)^2 \tag{3-2}$$

where HI is the net heat intensity (in W/cm^2) transferred to the workpiece.

Eq (3-2) provides a rough estimate of the time required to produce melting, and is based upon the thermal diffusivity of steel. Materials with higher thermal diffusivities—or the use of a local point heat source rather than a planar heat source—will increase the time to produce melting by a factor of up to two to five times. On the other hand, thin materials tend to heat more quickly.

If the time to melting is considered to be a characteristic interaction time, then the graph shown in Fig. 3-3 can be generated. Heat sources with power densities that are of the order of $1000 W/cm^2$, such as oxyacetylene flames or electro-slag welding, require interaction times of 25s with steel, whereas laser and electron beams, at $1MW/cm^2$, need interaction times on the order of only $25\mu s$. If this interaction time is divided into the heat-source diameter, then a maximum travel speed, is obtained for the welding process.

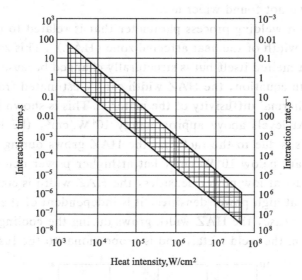

Fig. 3-3 Typical weld pool-heat source interaction times as fusion of heat-source intensity

The reason why welders begin their training with the oxyacetylene process should be clear: it is inherently slow and does not require rapid response time in order to control the size of the weld puddle. Greater skill is needed to control the more-rapid fluctuations in arc processes. The weld pool created by the high-heat-intensity processes, such as laser-beam and electron-beam welding, cannot be humanly controlled and must therefore be automated. This need to automate leads to increased capital costs. On an approximate basis, the W/cm^2 of a process can be substituted with the dollar cost of the capital equipment.

For constant total power, a decrease in the spot size will produce a squared increase in the heat intensity. This is one of the reasons why the spot size decreases with increasing heat intensity. It is easier to make the spot smaller than it is to increase the power rating of the equipment. In addition, only a small volume of material usually needs to be melted. If the spot size were kept constant and the input power were squared in order to obtain higher densities, then the volume of fused metal would increase dramatically, with no beneficial effect.

However, a decreasing spot size, coupled with a decreased interaction time at higher power densities, compounds the problem of controlling the higher-heat-intensity process. A shorter interaction time means that the sensors and controllers necessary for automation must operate at higher frequencies. The smaller spot size means that the positioning of the heat source must be even more precise, that is, on the order of the heat-source diameter, d_H. The control frequency must be greater than the travel velocity divided by the diameter of the heat source. For processes that operate near the maximum travel velocity, this is the inverse of the process interaction time, t_I (Fig. 3-3).

Thus, not only must the high-heat-intensity processes be automated because of an inherently high travel speed, but the fixturing requirements become greater, and the control systems and sensors must have ever-higher frequency responses. These factors lead to increased costs, which is one reason that the very productive laser-beam and electron-beam welding processes have not found wider use.

Another important welding process parameter that is related to the power density of the heat source is the width of the heat-affected zone (HAZ). This zone is adjacent to the weld metal and is not melted itself but is structurally changed because of the heat of welding. Using the Einstein equation, the HAZ width can be estimated from the process interaction time and the thermal diffusivity of the material. This is shown in Fig. 3-4, with one slight modification. At levels above approximately $10^4 \, W/cm^2$, the HAZ width becomes roughly constant. This is due to the fact that the HAZ grows during the heating stage at power densities that are below $10^4 \, W/cm^2$, but at higher power densities it grows during the cooling cycle. Thus, at low power densities, the HAZ width is controlled by the interaction time, whereas at high power densities, it is independent of the heat-source interaction time. In the latter case, the HAZ width grows during the cooling cycle as the heat of fusion is removed from the weld metal, and is proportional to the fusion zone width.

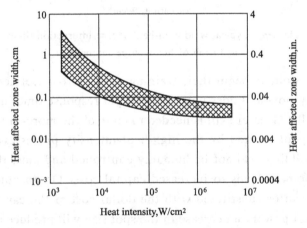

Fig. 3-4 Range of weld HAZ widths as function of heat-source intensity

The change of slope in Fig. 3-4 also represents the heat intensity at which the heat utilization efficiency of the process changes. At high heat intensities, nearly all of the heat is used to melt the material and little is wasted in preheating the surroundings. As heat intensity decreases, this efficiency is reduced. For arc welding, as little as half of the heat generated may enter the plate, and only 40% of this heat is used to fuse the metal. For oxyacetylene welding, the heat entering the metal may be 10% or less of the total heat, and the heat necessary to fuse the metal may be less than 2% of the total heat.

It should now be evident that all fusion welding processes can be characterized generally by heat-source intensity. The properties of any new heat source can be estimated readily from the figures in this article. Nonetheless, it is useful to more fully understand each of the common welding heat sources, such as flames, arcs, laser beams, electron beams, and electrical resistance.

● Vocabulary

joining   n. 连接；接缝；连接物
welding   adj. 焊接的   n. 焊接   v. 焊接；锻接
multifaceted   adj. 多层面的
fastening   n. 扣紧；固定；紧固
bonding   n. 黏合；压焊   adj. 结合的；黏结的
soldering   n. 焊接；焊料；焊接处；钎焊   adj. 用于焊接的   v. 焊接

brazing   n. 钎焊；铜焊；硬钎焊   v. 用锌铜合金钎接
fusion   n. 融合；熔化；熔接；融合物
spectrum   n. 光谱；频谱
oxyacetylene   adj. 氧乙炔的   n. 氧乙炔
welder   n. 焊接工；电焊机
spot   n. 斑点   vt. 弄脏   vi. 沾上污渍；满是斑点
adjacent   adj. 邻近的，接近的，毗连的

● Questions

1. Why do welding and joining processes appear to consume greater fractions of the product cost and to create more of the production difficulties than might be expected?

2. What are the welding process parameter that is related to the power density of the heat source?

3. Why do welders begin their training with the oxyacetylene process?

Unit 2
Heat Flow in Fusion Welding

During Fusion Welding, the thermal cycles produced by the moving heat source cause physical state changes, metallurgical phase transformation, and transient thermal stress and metal movement. After welding is completed, the finished product may contain physical discontinuities that are due to excessively rapid solidification, or adverse microstructures that are due to inappropriate cooling, or residual stress and distortion that are due to the existence of incompatible plastic strains.

In order to analyze these problems, this article presents an analysis of welding heat flow, focusing on the heat flow in the fusion welding process. The primary objective of welding heat flow modeling is to provide a mathematical tool for thermal data analysis, design iterations, or the systematic investigation of the thermal characteristics of any welding parameters. Exact comparisons with experimental measurements may not be feasible, unless some calibration through the experimental verification procedure is conducted.

Welding Thermal Process. A physical model of the welding system is shown in Fig. 3-5. The welding heat source moves at a constant speed along a straight path. The end result, after either initiating or terminating the heat source, is the formation of a transient thermal state in the weldment. At some point after heat-source initiation but before termination, the temperature distribution is stationary, or in thermal equilibrium, with respect to the moving coordinates. The origin of the moving coordinates coincides with the center of the heat source. The intense welding heat melts the metal and forms a molten pool. Some of the heat is conducted into the base metal and some is lost from either the arc column or the metal surface to the environment surrounding the plate. Three metallurgical zones are formed in the plate upon completion of the thermal cycle: the weld-metal (WM) zone, the heated-affected zone (HAZ), and the base-metal (BM) zone. The peak temperature and the subsequent cooling rates determine the HAZ structures, whereas the thermal gradients, the solidification rates, and the cooling rates at the liquid-solid pool boundary determine the solidification structure of the WM zone. The size and flow direction of the pool determines the amount of dilution and weld penetration. The material response in the temperature range near melting temperatures is primarily responsible for the metallurgical changes.

Two thermal states, quasi-stationary and transient, are associated with the welding process. The transient thermal response occurs during the source initiation and termination stages of welding, the latter of which is of greater metallurgical interest. Hot cracking usually begins in the transient zone, because of the nonequilibrium solidification of the base material. A crack that forms in the source-initiation stage may propagate along the weld if the solidification strains sufficiently multiply in the wake of the welding heat source. During source termination, the weld pool solidifies several times faster than the weld metal in the quasi-stationary state. Cracks usually appear in the weld crater and may propagate along the weld. Another dominant transient phenomenon occurs when a short repair weld is made to a weldment. Rapid cooling results in a brittle HAZ structure and either causes cracking problems or creates a site for fatigue-crack initiation.

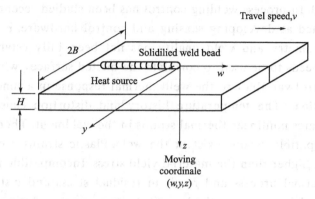

Fig. 3-5 Schematic of the welding thermal model

The quasi-stationary thermal state represents a steady thermal response of the weldment in respect to the moving heat source. The majority of the thermal expansion and shrinkage in the base material occurs during the quasi-stationary thermal cycles. Residual stress and weld distortion are the thermal stress and strain that remain in the weldment after completion of the thermal cycle.

Relation to Welding Engineering Problems. To model and analyze the thermal process, an understanding of thermally induced welding problems is important. A simplified modeling scheme, with adequate assumptions for specific problems, is possible for practical applications without using complex mathematical manipulations. The relationship between the thermal behavior of weldments and the metallurgy, control, and distortion associated with welding is summarized below.

Welding Metallurgy. As already noted, defective metallurgical structures in the HAZ and cracking in the WM usually occur under the transient thermal condition. Therefore, a transient thermal model is needed to analyze cracking and embrittlement problems.

To evaluate the various welding conditions for process qualification, the quasi-stationary thermal responses of the weld material need to be analyzed. The minimum required amount of welding heat input within the allowable welding speed range must be determined in order to avoid rapid solidification and cooling of the weldment Preheating may be necessary if the proper thermal conditions cannot be obtained under the specified welding procedure. A quasi-stationary thermal model is adequate for this type of analysis.

Hot cracking results from the combined effects of strain and metallurgy. The strain effect results from weld-metal displacement at near-melting temperatures, because of solidification shrinkage and weldment restraint. The metallurgical effect relates to the segregation of alloying elements and the formation of the eutectic during the high nonequilibrium solidification process. Using metallurgical theories, it is possible to determine the chemical segregation, the amounts and distributions of the eutectic, the magnitudes and directions of grain growth, and the weld-metal displacement at high temperatures. Using the heating and cooling rates, as well as the retention period predicted by modeling and analysis, hot-cracking tendencies can be determined. To analyze these tendencies, it is important to employ a more accurate numerical model that considers finite welding heat distribution, latent heat, and surface heat loss.

Welding Control. In-process welding control has been studied recently. Many of the investigations are aimed at developing sensing and control hardware. However, a link between weld-pool geometry and weld quality has not been fully established. A transient heat-flow analysis needs to be used to correlate the melted surface, which is considered to be the primary control variable, to the weld thermal response in a time domain.

Welding Distortion. The temperature history and distortion caused by the welding thermal process creates nonlinear thermal strains in the weldment. Thermal stresses are induced if any incompatible strains exist in the weld. Plastic strains are formed when the thermal stresses are higher than the material yield stress. Incompatible plastic strains accumulate over the thermal process and result in residual stress and distortion of the final weldment. The material response in the lower temperature range during the cooling cycle is responsible for the residual stresses and weldment distortion. For this type of analysis, the temperature field away from the welding heat source is needed for the modeling of the heating and cooling cycle during and after welding. A quasi-stationary thermal model with a concentrated moving heat source can predict, with reasonable accuracy, the temperature information for the subsequent stress and distortion analysis.

Literature Review. Many investigators have analytically, numerically, and experimentally studied welding heat-flow modeling and analysis. The majority of the studies were concerned with the quasi-stationary thermal state. Lance and Martin, Rosenthal and Schmerber and Rykalin independently obtained an analytical temperature solution for the quasi-stationary state using a point or line heat source moving along a straight line on a semi-infinite body. A solution for plates of finite thickness was later obtained by many investigators using the imaged heat source method. Tsai developed an analytical solution for a model that incorporated a welding heat source with a skewed Gaussian distribution and finite plate thickness.

With the advancement of computer technology and the development of numerical techniques like the finite-difference and finite-element methods, more exact welding thermal models were studied and additional phenomena were considered, including nonlinear thermal properties, finite heat-source distributions, latent heat, and various joint geometries. Tsai, Pavelic, Kou, Kogan, and Brody studied the simulation of the welding process using the finite-difference scheme. Hibbitt and Marcal, Friedman, and Paley made some progress in welding simulation using the finite-element method.

General Approach. The various modeling and analysis schemes summarized above can be used to investigate the thermal process of different welding applications. With adequate assumptions, analytical solutions for the simplified model can be used to analyze welding problems that show a linear response to the heat source if the solutions are properly calibrated by experimental tests. Numerical solutions that incorporate nonlinear thermal characteristics of weldments are usually required for investigating the weld-pool growth or solidification behavior. Numerical solutions can also be necessary for metallurgical studies in the weld HAZ if the rapid cooling phenomenon is significant under an adverse welding environment, such as welding under water.

Thermally related welding problems can be categorized as:
- Solidification rates in the weld pool.
- Cooling rates in the HAZ and its vicinity.
- Thermal strains in the general domain of the welding.

The domain of concern in the weld pool solidification is within the molten pool area, in which the arc (or other heat source) phenomena and the liquid stirring effect are significant. A convective heat-transfer model with a moving boundary at the melting temperature is needed to study the first category, and numerical schemes are usually required, as well.

The HAZ is always bounded on one side by the liquid-solid interface during welding. This inner-boundary condition is the solidus temperature of the material. The liquid weld pool might be eliminated from thermal modeling if the interface could be identified. A conduction heat-transfer model would be sufficient for the analysis of the HAZ. Numerical methods are often employed and very accurate results can be obtained.

The thermal strains caused by welding thermal cycles are caused by the nonlinear temperature distribution in the general domain of the weldment. Because the temperature in the material near the welding heat source is high, very little stress can be accumulated from the thermal strains. This is due to low rigidity, that is, small modulus of elasticity and low yield strength. The domain for thermal strain study is less sensitive to the arc and fluid-flow phenomena and needs only a relatively simple thermal model. Analytical solutions with minor manipulations often provide satisfactory results.

● **Vocabulary**

discontinuity　n. 不连续；中断；间断性；断绝
iteration　n. 迭代；反复；重复
calibration　n. 校准；刻度；标度
weldment　n. 焊件；焊成件；焊接装配
coordinate　n. 坐标　adj. 并列的；同等的　vt. 调整；整合
quasi-stationary　adj. 似稳定的，似稳态的
propagate　vt. 传播；传导

fatigue　n. 疲劳，疲乏　vt. 使疲劳　adj. 疲劳的
manipulation　n. 操纵；操作；处理
embrittlement　n. 脆化；脆裂；脆性
vicinity　n. 邻近，附近；近处
convective　adj. 对流的；传递性的
solidus　n. 固相线；固液相曲线
modulus　n. 系数；模数；模量

● **Questions**

1. What are the relationship between the thermal behavior of weldments and the metallurgy, control, and distortion associated with welding?
2. What does hot cracking result from?
3. Please talk about the thermally related welding problems.

Unit 3
Fluid Flow Phenomena During Welding

Molten Weld Pools are dynamic. Liquid in the weld pool in acted on by several strong forces, which can result in high-velocity fluid motion. Fluid flow velocities exceeding 1 m/s have been observed in gas tungsten arc (GTA) welds under ordinary welding conditions, and higher velocities have been measured in submerged arc welds. Fluid flow is important because it affects weld shape and is related to the formation of a variety of weld defects. Moving liquid transports heat and often dominates heat transport in the weld pool. Because heat transport by mass flow depends on the direction and speed of fluid motion, weld pool shape can differ dramatically from that predicted by conductive heat flow. Temperature gradients are also altered by fluid flow, which can affect weld microstructure. A number of defects in GTA welds have been attributed to fluid flow or changes in fluid flow, including lack of penetration, top bead roughness, humped beads, finger penetration, and undercutting. Instabilities in the liquid film around the keyhole in electron beam and laser welds are responsible for the uneven penetration (spiking) characteristic of these types of welds.

● Gas Tungsten Arc Welding

Most experimental and theoretical work on weld pool fluid flow and its effects has been directed toward GTAW. The motivation for much of this work was the observation of dramatically different weld pool shapes for GTA welds made using identical welding parameters on different heats of the same material with the same nominal composition. Early observations of variable weld shape (often referred to as variable penetration) were not only an intellectual puzzle but also an indication of a growing practical problem. Gas tungsten arc welding is commonly used for high-precision, high-quality automated welding applications, where reproducibility of weld shape or penetration is critical.

The possibility that fluid flow in the weld pool could alter weld shape has been recognized for many years. The forces driving fluid flow in GTA weld pools have also been long known. The four primary driving forces are surface tension gradients, electromagnetic or Lorentz forces, buoyancy forces, and aerodynamic drag forces caused by passage of the arc plasma over the weld pool surface.

Surface-Tension-Driven Fluid Flow Model. In 1982, Heiple and Roper proposed that surface tension gradients are commonly the dominant forces driving fluid flow in GTA welds and that these gradients could be drastically altered by very small concentrations of certain trace elements. Surface tension gradients exist on a weld pool surface because the surface tension is temperature dependent, and there are large temperature gradients on a weld pool surface. For pure metals and many alloys, the surface tension decreases as temperature increases; that is, the surface tension temperature coefficient is negative. For weld pools in such materials, the surface tension will be greatest on the coolest part of the pool surface at the edge and lowest on the hottest part under the arc near the center of the pool. Such a surface tension gradient produces outward surface fluid flow, as shown schematically in Fig. 3-6(a). This fluid flow pattern transfers heat efficiently from the hottest part of the weld pool (near the center) to the edge and produces a relatively wide and shallow weld.

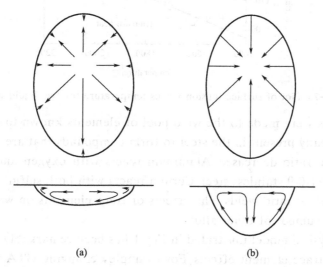

Fig. 3-6 Schematic showing surface fluid flow (top) and subsurface fluid flow (bottom) in the weld pool

Certain elements are surface active in molten metals; that is, they segregate to the surface of the solvent liquid metal and lower the magnitude of the surface tension, often drastically. Small concentrations of surface-active additions can also change the temperature dependence of the surface tension of the solvent metal or alloy so that, for a limited range of temperature above the melting point, the surface tension increases with increasing temperature. With a positive surface tension temperature coefficient, the surface tension will be highest near the center of the weld pool. Such a surface tension gradient will produce fluid flow inward along the surface of the weld pool and then down, as indicated schematically in Fig. 3-6(b). This fluid flow pattern transfers heat efficiently to the bottom of the weld pool and produces a relatively deep, narrow weld.

Experimental Observations. This physical model was developed and verified with a series of experiments in which stainless steel base metal was doped with low concentrations of various elements and the effect of the doping on weld pool shape measured. High-speed motion pictures of the weld pool surface suggested the fluid flow patterns indicated in Fig. 3-6. The addition of sulfur, oxygen, selenium, and tellurium to stainless steel in low concentrations (less than 150ppm) was shown to substantially increase GTA weld depth-to-width ratio (d/w). All these elements are known to be highly surface active in liquid iron. Measurements of the temperature dependence of the surface tension for steels with different GTA weld penetration characteristics produced an impressive correlation between a positive surface tension temperature coefficient arising from surface-active impurities and high d/w ratio welds (Fig. 3-7).

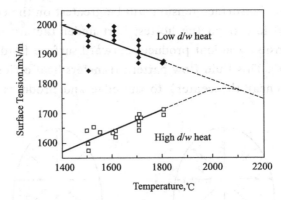

Fig. 3-7 Plot of surface tension versus temperature for two liquid steels

When additions were made to the weld pool of elements known to react with surface-active elements already present in the steel to form compounds that are not surface active, the GTA weld d/w ratio decreased. Aluminum reacts with oxygen and produced wider, shallower welds in 21-6-9 stainless steel. Cerium reacts with both sulfur and oxygen and also produced lower d/w ratio welds. The effects of trace elements on weld shape have also been observed in a number of other alloys.

The simple physical model illustrated in Fig. 1 has been remarkably successful in qualitatively explaining trace element effects. For example, changing GTA welding conditions alters the magnitude and distribution of arc energy input to the weld, which in turn changes temperature gradients on the weld pool surface. From Fig. 3-6, a change in welding conditions that makes the center of the weld hotter, such as increasing current, should drive the existing fluid flow pattern more strongly. As shown in Fig. 3-8, increasing current improves the d/w ratio of steel doped with surface-active elements and reduces it for high-purity base metal. If the center of the weld becomes so hot that there is a region where the temperature coefficient of the surface tension is no longer positive, then the fluid flow pattern necessary for deep penetration is disrupted and the d/w ratio decreases. This effect is seen at high currents in Fig. 3-8. Similar results have been obtained for other welding parameters. The surface temperature at which the change from positive to negative surface tension temperature coefficient occurs for stainless steel is estimated by extrapolation in Fig. 3-7 to be about 2050 °C. Detailed thermodynamic calculations of the temperature dependence of the surface tension of iron-sulfur alloys predict that the transition from positive to negative will occur at 2032 °C for the high-sulfur alloy in Fig. 3-7. Recent spectrographic weld pool temperature measurements and numerical simulations have indicated that this temperature can be exceeded in stainless steel GTA weld pools under normal welding conditions.

The surface-tension-driven fluid flow model should be applicable to non-arc processes, provided the energy input distribution is similar to a GTA arc. This condition is satisfied for conduction-mode electron beam and laser welds. Dramatic increases in weld d/w ratio in selenium-doped zones in stainless steel have been observed for both traveling laser and electron beam conduction-mode welds. The weld shape changes were similar to those ob-

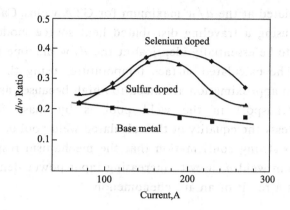

Fig. 3-8 Plot of weld d/w ratio versus weld current for the starting base metal as well as for zones doped with sulfur and selenium

served for GTA welds.

Conduction-mode electron beam welds can also be used to demonstrate that variations in weld shape with changes in welding parameters, as illustrated in Fig. 3-8, are not a result of some complex arc/weld pool interaction. One of the results of an investigation of the effect of changes in beam focus on weld shape in electron beam welds on low- and high-sulfur materials is shown in Fig. 3-9. The high-sulfur material exhibits a maximum in d/w ratio with increasing power density at a moderate power density away from sharp focus, which is analogous to that shown with increasing current in Fig. 3-8. Measurements of the electron beam power-density distribution verified that there were no anomalous changes in the beam, such as a beam width maximum, with increasing peak power density. The d/w ratio maximum away from sharp focus is therefore proposed to originate from exactly

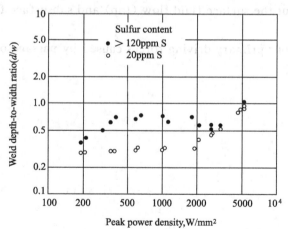

Fig. 3-9 Plot of electron beam weld pool ratio (d/w) versus electron beam power density for low-sulfur (20ppm) and high-sulfur (>120ppm) type 304L stainless steel

the same mechanism as for increasing current with GTA welds.

Measurements of electron beam power distribution were made as a function of beam focus and were used to calculate the beam power density at the d/w maximum. The power density was also calculated at the d/w maximum for GTA welds. Calculation of weld pool surface temperatures using a traveling distributed heat source model showed the central surface temperatures to be essentially identical at the d/w maxima for the electron beam and GTA processes. The calculated surface temperatures using the traveling distributed heat source conduction approximation are much too high because, as indicated previously, most of the heat transport in the weld pool is by mass flow rather than by conduction. Nevertheless, the equality of the calculated weld pool peak temperatures at the d/w maxima provides strong confirmation that the mechanism responsible for the presence of the maximum in weld d/w with increasing input power density is independent of heat source and is not a result of an arc phenomenon.

● **Vocabulary**

spiking   *n*. 尖峰形成；强化   *v*. 以大钉钉牢
fluid   *adj*. 流动的；不固定的   *n*. 流体；液体
submerged   *adj*. 水下的，在水中的   *v*. 潜入水中；使陷入
humped   *adj*. 有瘤的   *v*. 使隆起
undercutting   *n*. 根切；过度切割   *v*. 从下部切开
plasma   *n*. 等离子；等离子体
aerodynamic   *adj*. 空气动力学的，航空动力学的
gradient   *n*. 梯度；坡度   *adj*. 倾斜的；步行的
doping   *n*. 掺杂；（半导体）掺杂质
anomalous   *adj*. 异常的；不规则的；不恰当的
weld pool   焊池；熔池

● **Questions**

1. Please talk about the surface fluid flow (top) and subsurface fluid flow (bottom) in the weld pool.

2. What are the four primary driving forces caused by passage of the arc plasma over the weld pool surface?

Unit 4
Fundamentals of Weld Solidification

Of All Phase Transformations, few have been more widely observed and studied than the transformation of a liquid to a solid (that is, solidification). The process of solidification is the same in all cases, whether it is the freezing of water on a windshield or in a freezer, or the solidification of metal in a casting or in the weld that joins two solids.

The process is controlled by the free energy of the liquid phase, G_l, relative to that of the solid, G_s. This is depicted in Fig. 3-10, which shows the behavior of a pure (single component) material. Above the freezing temperature, T_f, the liquid phase has the lower free energy and is therefore stable, but below T_f, the solid is the stable phase. At T_f, both phases are in equilibrium, that is, $G_l = G_s$.

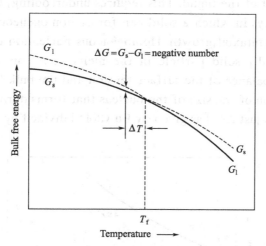

Fig. 3-10 Temperature dependence of bulk free energy of the liquid and solid phase in singlecomponent system

In the transition from one phase to another, the change in free energy, ΔG, is the difference in free energy of the product and the reactant. This free energy change can be expressed in terms of the enthalpy and the entropy changes, that is, for the transformation of a liquid to a solid during freezing:

$$\Delta G = G_s - G_l = (H_s - H_l) - T(S_s - S_l) = \Delta H - T\Delta S \tag{3-3}$$

At the freezing temperature, T_f, $\Delta G = G_s - G_l = 0$, because the free energy of the two phases is the same, and $\Delta H = T_f \Delta S$, It is necessary to cool below T_f for solidification, because at T_f both the solid and liquid phases are present and in equilibrium. Below T_f, ΔG is not equal to zero (Fig. 3-10 shows that $G_s < G_l$) and is given by Eq (3-3) with $T = T'$, where $T' < T_f$.

Because the ΔH and ΔS are not strong functions of temperatures, they can be assumed to be temperature independent. Therefore, at any temperature, $\Delta H = \Delta H_f$ and $\Delta S = \Delta S_f$, where ΔH_f and ΔS_f are the values of the enthalpy and the entropy changes for the equilibrium reactions at T_f (that is, the latent heat of fusion and the entropy change on fusion, respectively). Combining these enthalpy and entropy expressions, the fact that $\Delta H = T_f \Delta S$, and Eq (3-3), then at T', one obtains:

$$\Delta G = (\Delta H_f / T_f)(T_f - T) \tag{3-4}$$

where ΔH_f, the latent heat of fusion, is negative. Hence, in agreement with Fig. 3-10, ΔG is negative. The greater the amount of undercooling (supercooling) below $T_f(T_f - T')$, then the greater the thermodynamic driving force for solidification.

However, even when the conditions of Eq (3-4) are met, the liquid does not spontaneously transform to the solid below T_f. Rather, small amounts of solid nucleate and grow to produce complete solidification. Nucleation creates a new surface, that is, the surface between the solid and the liquid. The energy per unit are of this surface is the surface tension, γ, which is always positive. For solidification to occur, the increase in energy associated with the surface energy must be balanced by a greater decrease in the free energy of the solid relative to that of the liquid. This requires undercooling, as shown by Eq (3-4).

There are three ways in which a solid can form: homogeneous nucleation, heterogeneous nucleation, and epitaxial growth. Homogeneous nucleation occurs when there is no foreign body (mold wall, solid particle in the melt, etc.) on which to form the solid. Fig. 3-11 shows the balance of the surface tension and the bulk free energy per unit volume, ΔG_v, as a function of the size of the nucleus that forms during homogeneous nucleation. The ΔG_v, value is just ΔG [as given by Eq (3-4)] divided by the molar volume of the solid, V_s.

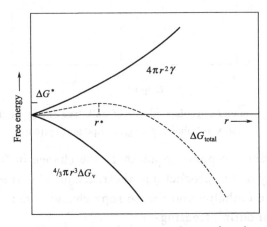

Fig. 3-11 Free energy of formation of a nucleus as function of its radius

For a spherical nucleus of radius greater than r_c, the volume free energy decrease outweighs the increase in energy that is due to the surface energy, and the nucleus is stable. At $r = r^*$, the net energy is a maximum, but if additional atoms are added to the nucleus, then the energy decreases. The value r^* is thus the radius at which the spherical nucleus is just stable, because as additional atoms are added, the energy is decreased. The value r^* is given by:

$$R^* = -2\gamma/\Delta G_v \qquad (3\text{-}5)$$

which is a positive number, because ΔG_v is negative. Substituting into Eq (3-4), one gets:

$$R^* = -2\gamma T_f V_s / \Delta H_f (T_f - T') \qquad (3\text{-}6)$$

The r^* is positive because ΔH_f is negative and, for undercooling, $(T_f - T')$ is positive. This equation is a general expression relating the radius of curvature of a surface and the degree of undercooling that is required for solidification of that surface. The greater the degree of undercooling, the smaller the radius of curvature that is stable. This equation will be considered again when nonplanar solidification is discussed.

Nucleation requires a thermal energy either equal to or greater than ΔG^* in order for a spherical nucleus of radius r^* to form. The ΔG^* value is the activation energy, which, as Fig. 3-11 shows, is a positive quantity. The greater the degree of undercooling, the more negative the free energy, the less positive the ΔG^* value, and the greater the rate of nucleation of the solid. For homogeneous nucleation, ΔG^* is given by:

$$\Delta G^* = (16/3)(\pi \gamma^3 T_f^2 V_s^2)/(\Delta H_f^2 \Delta T^2) \qquad (3\text{-}7)$$

where $\Delta T = T_f - T'$.

Heterogeneous nucleation develops when the solid forms on a foreign body. Now, the interaction of the nucleus and the foreign body must be considered. This interaction is defined in terms of the wetting angle between the nucleus and foreign body. The activation energy for heterogeneous nucleation is given by:

$$\Delta G^* = \frac{4\pi}{3} \times \frac{\gamma^3 T_f^2 V_s^2}{\Delta H_f^2 \Delta T^2} (2 - 3\cos\theta + \cos^3\theta) \qquad (3\text{-}8)$$

The angle is 180° if there is no wetting, and Eq (3-8) reduces to Eq (3-7), that is, with no wetting, there can only be homogeneous nucleation. With a wetting angle of 90°, ΔG^* is one half the value given by Eq (3-7). Instead of requiring a spherical nucleus of radius r^*, a hemispherical nucleus of the same radius is necessary, which requires one half the number of atoms and one half the activation energy. This is the sort of nucleation that develops in a casting, where the mold wall acts as the foreign body.

When the wetting angle is zero, Eq (3-8) shows that the activation energy is zero. This is the case for epitaxial growth on a substrate, where epitaxial derives from the Greek epi, upon, and taxis, to arrange, that is, to arrange upon. In effect, no new surface is being formed. Atoms are just being added to the substrate, thereby extending it. The important point is that no activation energy nor undercooling is required to add atoms onto an existing substrate. This is the situation that develops when a liquid solidifies on a substrate of the same material or one that is similar in composition and structure, as in the solidification of a weld.

● Comparison of Casting and Welding Solidification

A weld can be thought of as a miniature casting. The fundamentals of weld solidification are the same as those of a casting, but with different boundary conditions. These differences and their effects are described below.

First, by its very nature, a sound weld must attach to the metals being joined, whereas a casting must not adhere to the mold wall. To achieve this, the mold is treated to prevent adherence, whereas the joint to be welded is prepared to promote adherence. The practical result of this preparation is that there is generally excellent heat transfer through a weld joint, but relatively poor heat transfer through the mold, because oxides are often used as mold materials or for mold coatings.

Second, heat is continually being added to the weld pool as it travels, whereas no heat is added to a casting after the pour, except for possibly modest heating of the mold. The practical result of this and of the first consideration described above is that the temperature of the casting is relatively uniform. In contrast, a very large temperature gradient develops in a weld.

Third, solidification is developed at the mold wall of a casting by heterogeneous nucleation, whereas epitaxial growth develops at the weld fusion line. Thus, some supercooling is required for the casting, but only a vanishingly small degree of supercooling is required for the weld.

Fourth, the generally larger volume of a casting, relative to that of a weld, and the poorer heat transfer makes the cooling rate and the solidification rate much lower for castings than for welds.

Fifth, as a casting solidifies, the volume of the remaining liquid decreases. Thus, the shape of the molten pool is continually changing. In a weld, the weld pool shape is generally kept constant as it travels (if the heat input and section geometry are constant).

Sixth, because of the stirring action of the arc and the action of Marongoni surface tension gradient induced convection forces, there is good mixing of the molten weld pool. In contrast, there is comparatively little mixing of the molten material of a casting.

● Vocabulary

transformation　　n. 转化；转换；转变
windshield　　n. 挡风玻璃；防风罩
reactant　　n. 反应物；反应剂；成分
enthalpy　　n. 焓；热函；热含量
latent heat of fusion　熔化潜热；熔解潜热
undercooling　　n. 过冷；低冷却
　　vt. 使……过度冷却
supercooling　　n. 过冷　v. 使过冷
epitaxial　　adj. 外延的；取向附生的
outweigh　　vt. 比……重（在质量上）；超过；压过

curvature　　n. 弯曲，曲率，弧线
nonplanar　　adj. 非平面的；空间的（曲线的）
heterogeneous　　adj. 多相的；异种的；不均匀的；由不同成分形成的
wetting　　n. 变湿　v. 弄湿，润湿；浸润
hemispherical　　adj. 半球的；半球状的
miniature　　adj. 微型的，小规模的　n. 缩图；模型
vaporization　　n. 蒸发；汽化作用；喷雾器

● Questions

1. What are the ways in which a solid can form?
2. Please compare the differences of casting and welding solidification.

Unit 5
Shielded Metal Arc Welding

Shielded Metal Arc Welding (SMAW), commonly called stick, or covered electrode, welding, is a manual welding process whereby an arc is generated between a flux-covered consumable electrode and the workpiece. The process uses the decomposition of the flux covering to generate a shielding gas and to provide fluxing elements to protect the molten weld-metal droplets and the weld pool.

● **The SMAW Process**

The important features of the SMAW process are shown in Fig. 3-12. The arc is initiated by momentarily touching or "scratching" the electrode on the base metal. The resulting arc melts both the base metal and the tip of the welding electrode. The molten electrode metal/flux is transferred across the arc (by arc forces) to the base-metal pool, where it becomes the weld deposit covered by the protective, less-dense slag from the electrode covering.

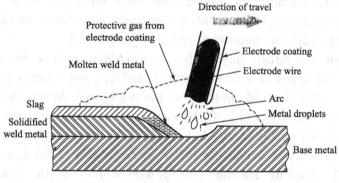

Fig. 3-12 SMAW process

Advantages and Limitations. The SMAW process is the most widely used welding process. It is the simplest, in terms of equipment requirements, but it is, perhaps, the most difficult in terms of welder training and skill-level requirements. Although welder skill level is a concern, most welders entering the field start as "stick welders" and develop the necessary skills through training and experience. The equipment investment is relatively small, and welding electrodes (except the very reactive metals, such as titanium, magnesium, and others) are available for virtually all manufacturing, construction, or maintenance applications. Shielded metal arc welding has the greatest flexibility of all the welding processes, because it can be used in all positions (flat, vertical, horizontal, and overhead), with virtually all base-metal thicknesses, and in areas of limited accessibility, which is a very important capability.

Because the SMAW process is basically a manual process, the skill level of the welder is of paramount importance in obtaining an acceptable weld. The welder duty cycle is generally low, because of the built-in work break, which occurs after each electrode is consumed and requires replacement. In addition to replacing the electrode when the arc is stopped (broken), the welder may "chip" or remove slag and clean it away from the starting and welding area with a wire brush to allow the proper deposition of the subsequent weld. This electrode replacement and cleaning operation occurs many times during the work day. This stopping, chipping, wire brushing, and electrode replacement prevents the welder from attaining an operator factor, or duty cycle, that is much greater than 25%.

Weld Quality. The quality of the weld depends on the design and accessibility of the joint, as well as on the electrode, the technique, and the skill of the welder. If joint details vary greatly from established design details, then a lower-quality weld can result. Other factors that also reduce quality are improper interbead cleaning, poor location of individual weld beads within the joint, and various problems with individual electrodes, including partially missing flux and core wires that are not centered within the flux covering. Overall, welds of excellent quality can be obtained with the SMAW process, as demonstrated by its use in joining submarine pressure hull sections and high-pressure oil/gas pipe lines.

The Base-Metal Thicknesses. that can be welded using the SMAW process generally range from 1.6 mm to an unlimited thickness. The thinner materials require a skilled welder, tight fitup, and the proper small-diameter welding electrode. Welding position also is important when determining the minimum plate thicknesses that can be welded. Flat-position butt welds and horizontal fillet welds are generally considered the easiest to weld. Out-of-position welding (vertical, overhead) requires greater skill.

Welding Circuit. The circuit diagram for the SMAW process is shown in Fig. 3-13. The equipment consists of a power source, electrode holder, and welding cables that connect the power source to the electrode holder and the workpiece. Alternating current (ac), or direct current, electrode negative (DCEN), or direct current, electrode positive (DCEP) can be used, depending on the electrode coating characteristics. The DCEN source is also called dc straight polarity, whereas the DCEP source is also called dc reverse polarity.

Equipment. The welding machine, or power source, is the crux of the SMAW process. Its primary purpose is to provide electrical power of the proper current and volt-

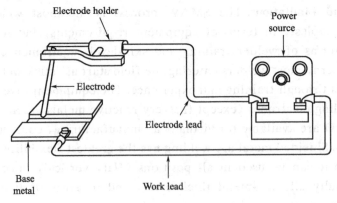

Fig. 3-13 Shielded metal arc circuit diagram

age to maintain a controllable and stable welding arc. Its output characteristics must be of the constant current (CC) type. SMAW electrodes operate within the range from 25 to 500A. The electrode producer should suggest a narrow optimum range for each size and type of electrode. Operating arc voltage varies between 15 and 35V.

The electrode holder, which is held by the welder, firmly grips the electrode and transmits the welding current to it. Electrode holders are available in several designs, such as the pincher type and the collet, or twist, type. Each style has its proponents and the selection is usually a personal preference. Electrode holders are designated by their current capacity. Selection factors, such as the current rating, duty cycle, maximum electrode size, and cable size. The most lightweight holder that will accommodate the required electrode size is usually desired.

All electrode holders should be fully insulated. Because they are used in proximity to the arc and are exposed to high heat, they will deteriorate rapidly. It is extremely important to maintain electrode holders to ensure that they retain their current-carrying efficiency, their insulating qualities, and their electrode gripping action. Manufacturers supply spare parts so that the holders can be rebuilt and maintained for safe and efficient operation.

Certain pieces of auxiliary equipment can be used with the SMAW process, such as low-voltage control circuits, which enable the relatively high open-circuit voltage to be cut off until the electrode touches the workpiece. Other items include remote-control switches for the contactors, remote-control current adjusting devices, and engine idling controllers for engine-driven power sources.

● Applications

Most manufacturing operations that require welding will strive to utilize the mechanized processes that offer greater productivity, higher quality, and, therefore, more cost-effective production. For these reasons, the SMAW process has been replaced where possible. However, the simplicity and ability of the SMAW process to achieve welds in areas of restricted accessibility means that it still finds considerable use in certain situations and applications. Heavy construction, such as shipbuilding, and welding "in the field" away from many support services that would provide shielding gas, cooling water, and other necessities, rely on the SMAW process to a great extent.

Although the SMAW process finds wide application for welding virtually all steels and many of the nonferrous alloys, it is primarily used to join steels. This family of materials includes low-carbon or mild steels, low-alloy steels, high-strength steels, quenched and tempered steels, high-alloy steels, stainless steels, and many of the cast irons. The SMAW process is also used to join nickel and its alloys and, to a lesser degree, copper and its alloys. It can be, but rarely is, used for welding aluminum.

In addition to joining metals, the SMAW process is frequently used for the protective surfacing of base metals. The surfacing deposit can be applied for the purpose of corrosion control or wear resistance (hard surfacing).

● Weld Schedules and Procedures

Welding schedules are tables of operating parameters that will provide high-quality welds under normal conditions. Strict welding schedules are not as important for the manual SMAW process as they are for semiautomatic and automatic welding for several reasons. First, in a manual welding process, the welder controls conditions by arc manipulation, which achieves better control than any of the other arc welding processes. The welder also directly controls the arc voltage and travel speed and, indirectly, the welding current.

Second, meter readings are rarely used in the SMAW process for the duplication of jobs. It is generally considered that the recommended welding current ranges for the different types of electrodes are sufficient for most operations. The settings provide a good starting point when first welding on a new application, although they are not necessarily the only welding settings that can be used under every condition. For example, for high-production work, the current settings could be increased considerably over those shown. Factors such as weld appearance, welding position, and welder skill also allow variations from the settings.

Welder Training. The SMAW process generally requires a high degree of welder skill to consistently produce quality welds. As a result, many training programs emphasize the SMAW process because of the arc manipulation skills developed by the welder. This acquired skill level makes the training on other processes much easier.

The exact content of a training program will vary, depending on the specific application of the process. The complexity of the parts to be welded and the governing codes or specifications involved also dictate the length of the training program. For example, because a pipe welder would need more skill than a tack welder, the length of his training program would be greater.

● **Vocabulary**

electrode   n. 电极；电焊条
flux   n. 焊剂；熔剂   vt. 使熔融；用焊剂处理
shielding   n. 屏蔽；防护   adj. 屏蔽的；防护的
slag   n. 炉渣；熔渣   vt. 使成渣；使变成熔渣
crux   n. 关键；难题；十字架形，坩埚
twist   vt. 扭歪   n. 扭曲   vi. 扭动；弯曲
weld deposit   焊缝熔敷；堆焊
collet   n. 夹头；筒夹   vt. 镶进底座；装筒夹或夹头
tempered   adj. 调节的；热处理的；回火的
chipping   n. 破片；碎屑
polarity   n. 极性；两极；对立
shielded metal arc welding   自动保护金属极电弧焊
butt weld   对接焊缝；对焊
fillet weld   角焊缝；角焊
electrode holder   焊钳；电极夹；焊条夹钳

● **Questions**

1. What is shielded metal arc welding?
2. Please tell the important features of the SMAW process.
3. What are the advantages and limitations of the SMAW process?

Unit 6
Gas-Metal Arc Welding

Gas-Metal Arc Welding (GMAW) is an arc welding process that joins metals together by heating them with an electric arc that is established between a consumable electrode (wire) and the workpiece. An externally supplied gas or gas mixture acts to shield the arc and molten weld pool.

The GMAW process can be operated in semi-automatic and automatic modes. All commercially important metals, such as carbon steel, high-strength low-alloy steel, stainless steel, aluminum, copper, and nickel alloys can be welded in all positions by this process if appropriate shielding gases, electrodes, and welding parameters are chosen.

● Process Fundamentals

Principles of Operation. In the GMAW process (Fig. 3-14), an arc is established between a continuously fed electrode of filler metal and the workpiece. After proper settings are made by the operator, the arc length is maintained at the set value, despite the reasonable changes that would be expected in the gun-to-work distance during normal operation. This automatic arc regulation is achieved in one of two ways. The most common method is to utilize a constant-speed (but adjustable) electrode feed unit with a variable-current (constant-voltage) power source. As the gun-to-work relationship changes, which instantaneously alters the arc length, the power source delivers either more current (if the arc length is decreased) or less current (if the arc length is increased). This change in current will cause a corresponding change in the electrode melt-off rate, thus maintaining the desired arc length.

The second method of arc regulation utilizes a constant-current power source and a variable-speed, voltage-sensing electrode feeder. In this case, as the arc length changes, there is a corresponding change in the voltage across the arc. As this voltage change is detected, the speed of the electrode feed unit will change to provide either more or less electrode per unit of time. This method of regulation is usually limited to larger electrodes with lower feed speeds.

Metal Transfer Mechanisms. The characteristics of the GMAW process are best described by reviewing the three basic means by which metal is transferred from the electrode to the work: short-circuiting transfer, globular transfer, or spray transfer. The type of transfer is determined by a number of factors, the most influential of which are:
- Magnitude and type of welding current.
- Electrode diameter.
- Electrode composition.
- Electrode extension beyond the contact tip or tube.

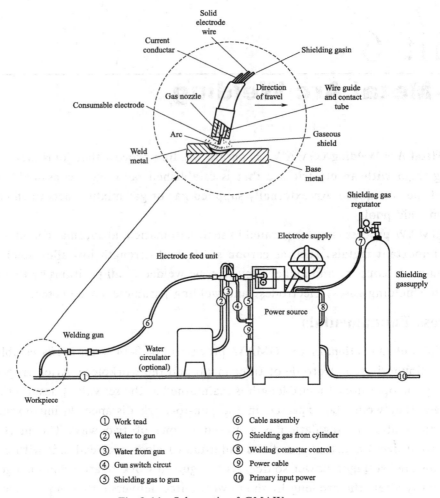

Fig. 3-14 Schematic of GMAW process

- Shielding gas.
- Power supply output.

Short-Circuiting Transfer encompasses the lowest range of welding currents and electrode diameters associated with the GMAW process. This type of transfer produces a small, fast-freezing weld pool that is generally suited for joining thin sections, for out-of-position welding, and for bridging of large root openings. Metal is transferred from the electrode to the workpiece only during a period when the electrode is in contact with the weld pool, and there is no metal transfer across the arc gap.

The electrode contacts the molten weld pool at a steady rate that can range from 20 to over 200 times per second. As the wire touches the weld metal, the current increases and the liquid metal at the wire tip is pinched off, initiating an arc. The rate of current increase must be high enough to heat the electrode and promote metal transfer, yet low enough to minimize spatter caused by violent separation of the molten drop. The rate of current increase is controlled by adjusting the power source inductance. The optimum setting depends on the electrical resistance of the welding circuit and the melting temperature of the electrode. When the arc is initiated, the wire melts at the tip as it is fed forward toward the next short circuit. The open-circuit voltage of the power source must be low enough so that the drop of molten metal cannot transfer until it contacts the weld metal.

Because metal transfer only occurs during short circuiting, the shielding gas has very little effect on the transfer itself. However, the gas does influence the operating characteristics of the arc and the base-metal penetration. The use of carbon dioxide generally produces high spatter levels, when compared with inert gases, but it allows deeper penetration when welding steels. To achieve a good compromise between spatter and penetration, mixtures of carbon dioxide and argon are often used. With nonferrous metals, argon-helium mixtures are used to achieve this compromise.

Globular Transfer. With a positive electrode, globular transfer takes place when the current density is relatively low, regardless of the type of shielding gas. However, the use of carbon dioxide or helium results in this type of transfer at all usable welding currents. Globular transfer is characterized by a drop size with a diameter that is greater than that of the electrode. This large drop is easily acted upon by gravity, which limits successful transfer to the flat position.

At average currents that are slightly higher than those used in short-circuiting transfer, axially directed globular transfer can be achieved in a substantially inert gas shield. However, if the arc length is too short, then the enlarging drop can short to the workpiece, become superheated, and disintegrate, producing considerable spatter. Therefore, the arc length must be long enough to ensure that the drop detaches before it contacts the weld pool. However, when higher voltage values are used, the weld is likely to be unacceptable, because of a lack of fusion, insufficient penetration, and excessive reinforcement. This limits the use of this transfer mode to very few production applications.

Carbon Dioxide shielding produces a randomly directed globular transfer when the welding current and voltage values are significantly higher than the range used for short-circuiting transfer. Although severe spatter conditions result when conventional techniques are used, carbon dioxide is still the most commonly used shielding gas for welding mild steel when the quality requirements are not too rigorous. The spatter problem is controlled by "burying" the arc below the weld/base-metal surface. The resulting arc forces are adequate enough to produce a depression that contains the spatter. This technique requires relatively high currents and results in very deep penetration. Good operator setup skills are required. However, poor wetting action can result in an excessive weld reinforcement.

Spray Transfer. A very stable, spatter-free "spray" transfer mode can be produced when argon-rich shielding is used. This type of transfer requires the use of direct current with the electrode positive and a current level that is above a critical value called the "transition current." Below this current level, transfer occurs in the globular mode at the rate of a few drops per second. At values above the transition current, transfer occurs in the form of very small drops that are formed and detached at the rate of hundreds per second and are accelerated axially across the arc gap.

The transition current is proportional to the electrode diameter, and, to a lesser extent, to the electrode extension. It also has a direct relationship to the filler metal melting temperature.

The spray transfer mode results in a highly directed stream of discrete drops that are accelerated by arc forces to velocities that overcome the effects of gravity. This enables the process to be used in any position, under certain conditions. Because the drops are separated, short circuits do not occur, and the spatter level is negligible, if not totally eliminated.

Another characteristic of spray transfer is the "finger" penetration pattern that it produces directly below the electrode tip. Although the penetration can be deep, it can be affected by magnetic fields that must be controlled to ensure that it is always located at the center of the weld penetration profile. Otherwise, a lack of fusion and an irregular bead surface profile can result.

The spray transfer mode can be used to weld almost any metal or alloy, because of the inert characteristics of the argon shield. Sometimes, thickness can be a factor, because of the relatively high current levels required. The resultant arc forces can cut through, rather than weld, thin sheets. In addition, high deposition rates can result in a weld pool size that cannot be supported by surface tension in the vertical and overhead positions. However, the thickness and position limitations of spray transfer have been largely overcome by specially designed power supplies. These machines produce carefully controlled current outputs that "pulse" the welding current from levels below the transition current to levels above it.

Fig. 3-15 shows the two levels of current provided by these machines. One is a constant, low-background current that sustains the arc without providing enough energy to cause the formation of drops on the wire tip. The other is a superimposed pulsing current with an amplitude that is greater than the transition current necessary for spray transfer. During this pulse, one or more drops are formed and transferred. The frequency and amplitude of the pulses control the energy level of the arc and, therefore, the rate at which the wire melts. By reducing the arc energy and the wire melting rate, it is possible to retain many of the desirable features of spray transfer while joining sheet metals and welding thick metals in all positions.

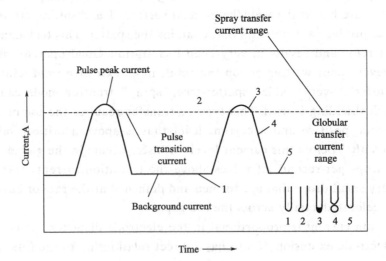

Fig. 3-15 Characteristic current waveform for a "pulsing" power supply

Vocabulary

feeder   n. 送料机；给料机
globular   adj. 球状的；球形的；球的
transfer   n. 转让；转移；传递   vi. 转让
spray   vt. 喷射   vi. 喷
encompass   vt. 包含；包围，环绕；完成
bridging   n. 桥接；桥连   v. 架桥
arc gap   弧隙；弧长
gap   n. 间隙；缺口   vt. 使成缺口
spatter   n. 溅；喷溅   vt. 溅；洒
filler metal   填充金属；焊料，焊丝

circuiting   n. 电路，回路   vt. 绕回……环行
disintegrate   vt. 使分解；使碎裂   vi. 瓦解；碎裂
discrete   adj. 离散的，不连续的   n. 分立元件；独立部件
superimposed   adj. 叠加的；重叠的
amplitude   n. 振幅；幅度；波幅
pulsing   adj. 脉冲的   n. 脉动

Questions

1. What is gas-metal arc welding?
2. Please talk about the fundamentals of GMAW process.
3. Please talk about the characteristics of the GMAW process.

Unit 7

Gas-Tungsten Arc Welding

  Gas-Tungsten Arc Welding（GTAW）, also known as HeliArc, tungsten inert gas (TIG), and tungsten arc welding, was developed in the late 1930s when a need to weld magnesium became apparent. Russell Meredith developed a welding process using the inert gas helium and a tungsten electrode to fuse magnesium. This joining method replaced riveting as a method of building aircraft with aluminum and magnesium components. The Heli-Arc welding has continued to this day with many refinements and name changes, but with no change in the fundamentals demonstrated by Meredith.

  The melting temperature necessary to weld materials in the GTAW process is obtained by maintaining an arc between a tungsten alloy electrode and the workpiece (Fig. 3-16). Weld pool temperatures can approach 2500℃. An inert gas sustains the arc and protects the molten metal from atmospheric contamination. The inert gas is normally argon, helium, or a mixture of helium and argon.

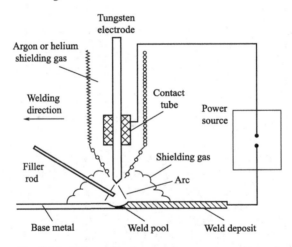

Fig. 3-16 Schematic showing key components and parameters of the GTAW process

● Applications

  Gas-tungsten arc welding is used extensively for welding stainless steel, aluminum, magnesium, copper, and reactive materials (for example, titanium and tantalum). The process can also be used to join carbon and alloy steels. In carbon steels, it is primarily used for root-pass welding with the application of consumable inserts or open-root techniques on pipe. The materials welded range from a few thousandths of an inch to several inches in thickness.

● **Advantages and Limitations**

Advantages of GTAW include:
- Produces high-quality, low-distortion welds.
- Free of the spatter associated with other methods.
- Can be used with or without filler wire.
- Can be used with a range of power supplies.
- Welds almost all metals, including dissimilar ones.
- Gives precise control of welding heat.

The GTAW process is applicable when the highest weld quality is required. It can be used to weld almost all types of metals. The operator has excellent control of heat input, and vision is not limited by fumes or smoke from the process.

Limitations of GTAW include:
- Produces lower deposition rates than consumable electrode arc welding processes.
- Requires slightly more dexterity and welder coordination than gas metal arc welding or shielded metal arc welding for manual welding.
- Less economical than consumable electrode arc welding for thick sections greater than 9.5 mm.
- Problematic in drafty environments because of difficulty in shielding the weld zone properly.

Power supplies for GTAW are usually the constant-current type with a drooping (negative) volt-ampere (V-A) curve. Saturable reactors and thyristor-controlled units are the most common. Advances in the electronics industry have readily been accepted in the welding community, resulting in sophisticated, lightweight power supplies. Transistorized direct current (dc) power supplies are becoming common, and the newer rectifier-inverter supplies are very compact and versatile.

The inverter supplies can be switched from constant current to constant voltage for GMAW, resulting in a very versatile piece of equipment. The inverter-controlled power supplies are more stable and have faster response times than conventional silicon-controlled rectifier (SCR) power supplies.

Torch Construction. The welding torch holds the tungsten electrode that conducts the current to the arc, and it provides a means of shielding the arc and molten metal. The major components of a typical welding torch are shown in Fig. 3-17.

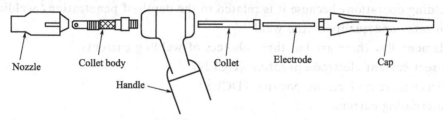

Fig. 3-17 Schematic showing exploded view of key components components comprising a GTAW manual torch

Welding torches rated at less than 200A are normally gas-cooled (that is, the shielding gas flows around the conductor cable, providing the necessary cooling). Water-cooled torches are used for continuous operation or at higher welding currents and are common for mechanized or automatic welding. The cooling water may be supplied to the torch from a recirculating tank that uses a radiator or chiller to cool the water.

Electrodes. The nonconsumable electrodes used in GTAW are composed of tungsten or alloys of tungsten. The most common electrode is a 2% ThO_2-W alloy. This material has excellent operating characteristics and good stability. Thoria is radioactive, so care must be taken when sharpening electrodes not to inhale metal dust. The grindings are considered hazardous waste in some states, and disposal may be subject to environmental regulations. Lanthaniated (EWLa-1) and yttriated tungsten electrodes have the best starting characteristics in that an arc can be started and maintained at a lower voltage. Ceriated tungsten (EWCe-2) is only slightly better than the thoriated tungsten with respect to arc starting and melt-off rate. Any of the aforementioned electrodes produce acceptable welds. The easy starting of the lanthaniated electrode is a result of the lower work function which allows it to emit electrodes readily at a lower voltage.

Wire Feed Systems are made from a number of components and vary from simple to complex. The basic system consists of a means of gripping the wire sufficiently to pull it from the spool and push it through the guide tube to the point of welding. Electronic switches and controls are necessary for the electric drive motor. The wire will be fed into the leading edge for cold wire feeds and into the trailing edge for hot wire feeds.

Cables, Hoses, and Gas Regulators are necessary to deliver the process consumable of electricity, water, and inert gas to the welding torch.

Arc Oscillation is used in both manual and mechanized welding. The benefits in manual welding are basic to the control of the weld when adapting to changes in the weld joint and gap. In mechanized welding, the oscillation is typically produced by moving the entire welding torch mechanically or by moving the arc plasma with the aid of an externally applied magnetic field. Oscillation allows the welding heat to be placed at precise locations. This is advantageous when welding irregularly shaped parts. The number of welding passes and total heat input can be decreased when arc oscillation is used, because it reduces the cost as well as the weld shrinkage and upsetting.

● Process Parameters

Welding Current. Current is one of the most important operating conditions to control in any welding operation, because it is related to the depth of penetration, welding speed, deposition rate, and quality of the weld.

Fundamentally, there are but three choices of welding current:
- Direct current electrode negative (DCEN).
- Direct current electrode positive (DCEP).
- Alternating current.

Alternating current is characterized as reversing the polarity of the work and electrode at 60Hz. The rapidly changing polarity gives a cathodic cleaning action that is beneficial for oxide removal when welding aluminum and magnesium. The alternating currents result in electrode heating during the DCEP portion of each cycle. This necessitates the use of larger-diameter electrodes, normally made of pure tungsten. Variable polarity welding allows the frequency of polarity switching to be preset. This can produce the cleaning effects to ac welding and the high efficiency of dc welding. Direct current electrode negative is most often used in the GTAW process. This results in maximum application of heat to the work and maximum melting of the workpiece.

Pulsed versus Nonpulsed Current. Nonpulsed or continuous current is the standard for GTAW. However, there are several advantages to using pulsed current. Pulsing produces the maximum amount of penetration while minimizing the total heat applied to the part. Pulsing also aids in timing the motion necessary in manual welding and allows the weld pool to cool between pulses.

Microwelding refers to a class of weldments that are made at welding currents from 1 to 20A. In most cases, the welding is used for electronic applications, bellows, wires, and other components where heat input must be precisely controlled.

Shielding Gases. The original GTAW process used helium as the shielding gas for welding magnesium and aluminum. Today, argon is the predominant shielding gas.

Argon is the least expensive of the inert gases used for shielding gas-tungsten arc welds, which is only partially responsible for its widespread use. Argon has a low ionization potential (2.52×10^{-18}J, or 15.7eV), making it easier to form an arc plasma than with other shielding gases. Argon is approximately 1.4 times heavier than air, so it displaces air, resulting in excellent shielding of the molten weld pool.

Gas Purity. Most materials can be welded using a welding grade torch gas with a purity of 99.995% or 50ppm impurities. However, some reactive materials (for example, titanium, molybdenum, and tantalum) require that the contaminant level be less than 50ppm, which may require certified purity or the use of gas filters and purifiers.

Filler Metals. The thickness of the part to be welded will determine the need for filler metal additions. Material thinner than 3.2mm can be successfully welded without filler metal additions. Filler metal, when needed, can be added manually in straight length or automatically from a roll or coil. The filler metal is normally added cold; hot wire can be used for automatic applications. A welding insert is preplaced filler material of several possible configurations to aid in root-pass welding.

● **Vocabulary**

riveting   n. 铆接；铆接加工   v. 用铆钉固定
dissimilar   adj. 不同的；相异的
deposition   n. 沉积物；沉积
problematic   adj. 问题的；有疑问的；不确定的
thyristor   n. 半导体闸流管
saturable   adj. 可饱和的；能浸透的
transistorized   adj. 晶体管化的；装有晶体管的
rectifier   n. 整流器；改正者，矫正者

recirculating   adj. 再循环的；回路的   v. 再循环
sharpening   n. 削尖；锐化   v. 加强；使尖锐
dust   n. 灰尘；尘埃；粉尘
grinding   n. 研磨；磨削；磨光
hazardous   adj. 有危险的；冒险的；碰运气的
oscillation   n. 振荡；振动；摆动
cathodic   adj. 阴极的；负极的
microwelding   微型焊接；微件焊接

● Questions

1. What are the advantages and limitations of the GTAW process?
2. Please tell the applications of GTAW process?
3. What are the fundamental choices of welding current?

Unit 8
Plasma Arc Welding

Plasma Arc Welding (PAW) can be defined as a gas-shielded arc welding process where the coalescence of metals is achieved via the heat transferred by an arc that is created between a tungsten electrode and a workpiece. The arc is constricted by a copper alloy nozzle orifice to form a highly collimated arc column (Fig. 3-18). The plasma is formed through the ionization of a portion of the plasma (orifice) gas. The process can be operated with or without a filler wire addition.

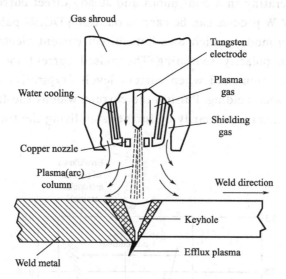

Fig. 3-18 plasma arc welding process, showing constriction of the arc by a copper nozzle and a keyhole through the plate

Principles of Operation. Once the equipment is set up and the welding sequence is initiated, the plasma and shielding gases are switched on. A pilot arc is then struck between a tungsten alloy electrode and the copper alloy nozzle within the torch (nontransferred arc mode), usually by applying a high-frequency open-circuit voltage. When the torch is brought in close proximity to the workpiece or when the selected welding current is initiated, the arc is transferred from the electrode to the workpiece through the orifice in the copper alloy nozzle (transferred arc mode), at which point a weld pool is formed (Fig. 3-18).

The PAW process can be used in two distinct operating modes, often described as the melt-in mode and the keyhole mode.

The Melt-in-Mode refers to a weld pool similar to that which typically forms in the gas-tungsten arc welding (GTAW) process, where a bowl-shaped portion of the workpiece material that is under the arc is melted.

In the Keyhole Mode, the arc fully penetrates the workpiece material, forming a nominally concentric hole, or keyhole, through the thickness. The molten weld metal flows around the arc and resolidifies behind the keyhole as the torch traverses the workpiece.

Current and Operating Modes. The PAW process uses three current modes: microplasma (melt-in mode), medium-current plasma (melt-in mode), and keyhole plasma (keyhole mode). This categorization is primarily based on the level of welding current. The microplasma mode is usually defined in the current range from 0.1 to 15A. The medium-current plasma mode ranges from 15 to 100A. The keyhole plasma mode is above 100A. There is a certain degree of overlap between these current ranges. For example, keyholing can be achieved at 70A on a 2mm sheet. Equipment is available for welding currents up to 500A, although a 300A maximum is typical. Microplasma and medium-current melt-in modes are used for material up to 3mm thick, whereas the keyhole plasma mode is used for greater thicknesses and higher travel speeds.

In addition to operating in a continuous and steady direct current electrode negative (DCEN) mode, the PAW process can be carried out using DCEN pulsed current, as well as in the variable polarity mode, which uses both direct current electrode positive (DCEP) and electrode negative polarity switching. The pulsed current mode (both DCEN and DCEN/DCEP) is most often used when current levels (typically, above 100A) are employed for keyhole plasma welding. Pulsing the current widens the tolerance region of acceptance welding parameters, primarily by further stabilizing the formation of the keyhole itself (Fig. 3-19).

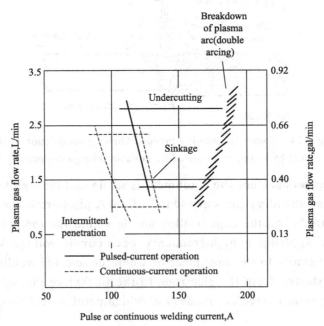

Fig. 3-19 Tolerance to variation in welding current and plasma gas flow rate in pulsed and continuous current keyhole welding; boundaries show the welding parameter combinations at which specific defects are likely to occur

The electrode positive component of the variable polarity plasma arc (VPPA) welding process promotes cathode etching of the tenacious surface oxide film when welding aluminum alloys, allowing good flow characteristics and consistent bead shape. Pulsing times are typically 20ms for the electrode negative component and 3ms for the electrode positive polarity. The VPPA welding process is used very effectively in specialized aerospace applications.

The PAW process is generally applied when the high penetration of the keyhole welding mode can be exploited to minimize the number of welding passes and, hence, welding time. The time saved can reduce the direct labor element of the welding operation. At the other end of the scale, the microplasma operating mode is used to weld small, thin-section components (as low as 0.025mm, or 1mil, thick), where the high arc constriction and low welding current can be beneficial in controlling heat input and distortion.

Advantages and Disadvantages. The advantages of the PAW process are primarily intrinsic to the keyhole mode of operation, because greater thicknesses of metal can be penetrated in a single pass, compared with other processes, such as GTAW. This greater amount of penetration allows a reduced amount of joint preparation. In some materials, for example, a square-grooved butt joint preparation can be used for thicknesses up to 12mm. The process can produce high weld integrity (similar to GTAW) while minimizing weld passes and, hence, welding times and labor costs. The columnar shape of the arc results in a greater tolerance to variations in torch standoff distance, when compared with the conical arc shape of a GTAW arc. The tungsten electrode used in the PAW process is protected from contamination by the constricting nozzle (Fig. 3-18). The longer arc length allows better viewing of the weld pool, which is important in manual welding.

Disadvantages include the greater capital equipment cost, when compared with its main rival, the GTAW process. Although high arc constriction achieves higher penetration, it also reduces the tolerance of the process to joint gaps and misalignment, when compared with the broader, conical arc of the GTAW process. The greater complexity of the PAW torch design and the greater number of parts requires more scheduled maintenance. The accurate set-back of the electrode tip, with respect to the nozzle orifice, is required to maintain consistent results. However, this task is facilitated by a general-purpose tool designed for nozzle removal and replacement and for electrode set-back adjustment.

● Applications

Material Types. The PAW process is commonly used to weld stainless steels in a wide range of thicknesses. The process can also be used with carbon and alloy steels, aluminum alloys, titanium alloys, copper and nickel alloys, and more specialized materials, such as zirconium and tantalum. The thicknesses that can be welded in a single pass range from 0.025mm for microplasma applications to 12.5mm (0.5in) for the VPPA welding of aluminum. Direct-current pulsing can be used on most materials.

The PAW process is often carried out in an autogenous mode, that is, without filler wire. When edge beveling is used, a filler wire is required to complete the joint. A filler wire can also be used with the keyhole mode of operation to avoid undercut at high welding speeds. Wire composition depends on that of the parent materials in the joint. The same continuous-wound wire that is used in GTAW operations is suitable.

The Industries that use the PAW process can be categorized as those that weld thin-section sheet using microplasma or medium-current plasma welding and those that weld plate using keyhole plasma welding.

A wide range of small devices and assemblies made from thin stainless steel sheet, including bellows assemblies and associated fittings, are welded using the microplasma operating mode. The narrow weld bead that can be produced provides sheet-metal fabrications with a good cosmetic appearance. Furthermore, the high welding speed that can be achieved, coupled with the good tolerance to stand-off variations resulting from the columnar nature of the arc, makes the process attractive for high-volume production work.

Microplasma, as well as medium-current plasma modes, can be used to spot weld guide wires and lamp filaments, as well as in other applications that require highly repetitive autogenous welds. This type of application allows a user to limit the number of high-frequency arc starts that would be required with tungsten-inert gas welding.

Keyhole plasma welding is extensively used to weld stainless steel pipe and tankage. The process is applied to individual strakes from plate to make stainless steel vessels in the food and chemical processing industries. Circumferential welding of strakes also can be used to create these products. Longitudinal seam welds in stainless steel pipe with wall thickness of 3mm are ideally suited to keyhole plasma welding, because joint preparation is minimized and single-pass welding can be consistently achieved without the use of weld-backing devices. Pipes with wall thickness above 5 to 6mm employ the keyhole mode of operation for the root pass. Depending on the material type and wall thickness, melt-mode PAW, GTAW, gas-metal arc welding (GMAW), or submerged arc welding (SAW) are used to complete the joint. High-alloy composition piping is similarly manufactured.

The manufacturing of stainless steel tube from strip was one of the first applications of the PAW process. Because the process can reliably produce full-penetration welds without the use of backing, it is extensively used on tube mills, because a lack of access precludes welding from the inside.

● **Vocabulary**

coalescence   n. 合并；联合；接合
orifice   n. 孔口；孔板；注孔
nozzle   n. 喷嘴；管口；排气口
collimated   adj. 平行的；照准的   v. 使平行；瞄准
ionization   n. 离子化；电离作用
traverses   n. 穿过；横贯；摇臂
microplasma   n. 微等离子体；微等离子区

stabilizing   n. 稳定化；稳定化处理；消除内应力处理
etching   n. 腐蚀；侵蚀；表面蚀刻
distortion   n. 变形；畸变；扭曲
misalignment   n. 不重合；未对准
autogenous   adj. 自生的；自发的
fabrication   n. 制造，制作；加工
filament   n. 灯丝；细丝；细线；单纤维

● **Questions**

1. Please tell the principles of operation of plasma arc welding process.
2. What are the advantages and disadvantages of the PAW process?
3. Please tell the applications of the PAW process?

Unit 9
Electron-Beam Welding

Electron-Beam Welding (EBW) is a high-energy density fusion process that is accomplished by bombarding the joint to be welded with an intense (strongly focused) beam of electrons that have been accelerated up to velocities 0.3 to 0.7 times the speed of light at 25 to 200kV, respectively. The instantaneous conversion of the kinetic energy of these electrons into thermal energy as they impact and penetrate into the workpiece on which they are impinging causes the weld-seam interface surfaces to melt and produces the weld-joint coalescence desired. Electron-beam welding is used to weld any metal that can be arc welded; weld quality in most metals is equal to or superior to that produced by gas-tungsten arc welding (GTAW).

Because the total kinetic energy of the electrons can be concentrated onto a small area on the workpiece, power densities as high as 10^8W/cm^2 can be obtained. That is higher than is possible with any other known continuous beam, including laser beams. The high-power density plus the extremely small intrinsic penetration of electrons in a solid workpiece results in almost instantaneous local melting and vaporization of the workpiece material. That characteristic distinguishes EBW from other welding methods in which the rate of melting is limited by thermal conduction.

● **Principles of Operation**

Basically, the electron beam is formed (under high-vacuum conditions) by employing a triodestyle electron gun consisting of a cathode, a heated source (emitter) of electrons that is maintained at some high negative potential; a grid cup, a specially shaped electrode that can be negatively biased with respect to the hot cathode emitter (filament); and an anode, a ground potential electrode through which the electron flow passes in the form of a collimated beam. The hot cathode emitter (filament) is made from a high-emission material, such as tungsten or tantalum. This emitter material, usually available in wire, ribbon, or sheet form, is fabricated into the desired shape for being either directly or indirectly heated to the required emitting temperature of about 2500℃.

Electrons emitted from the surface of the filament are accelerated to a high velocity and shaped into a collimated beam by the electrostatic field geometry generated from the cathode/grid/anode configuration employed, thus producing a steady stream of electrons that flows through an aperture in the ground plane anode. By varying the negative potential difference between the grid and cathode, this flow of electrons can be altered easily in a precisely controlled manner.

Diode-style electron guns are also employed, but not to the extent that triode-style electron guns are. In a diode gun, the specially shaped electrode (grid cup) is maintained at the same voltage as the emitter, thus making the diode gun a two-element (cathode and anode) device. With this design, the flow of electrons from a diode gun cannot be adjusted by simply varying a grid voltage, as is done with triode guns, and beam current adjustments are usually accomplished by varying the operating temperature of the cathode emitter instead.

Once the electrons exit the anode, they receive the maximum energy input allowable from the operating voltage being applied to the gun. Electrons then pass down through the electron beam column assembly and into the field of an electromagnetic focusing coil (a magnetic lens). This focusing lens reduces the diameter of the electron beam, as it continues in its passage, and focuses the stream of electrons down to a much smaller beam cross section in the plane of the workpiece. This reduction in beam diameter increases the energy density, producing a very small, high-intensity beam spot at the workpiece. In addition, an electromagnetic deflection coil (positioned below the magnetic lens) can be employed to "bend" the beam, thus providing the flexibility to move the focused beam spot. Fig. 3-20 illustrates the main elements of the electron beam welding head. As described above and shown in Fig. 3-20, electrons are emitted from the cathode and are accelerated to high speed by the voltage between cathode and anode.

The "gun" portion of an electron gun/column assembly generally is isolated from the welding chamber through the use of valves when desired. The gun may be maintained in a vacuum on the order of 13mPa when the welding chamber is vented to atmosphere (for access reasons). This level of vacuum in the gun region is needed to maintain gun component cleanliness, prevent filament oxidation, and impede gun arcing (high-pressure short circuiting between electrodes at different voltages). During welding, this same degree of vacuum is required in both the gun column and welding chamber areas to minimize scattering of beam electrons by excitation collisions with residual air molecules as they traverse the distance from the gun to the workpiece. This type of interaction tends to produce a broader beam spot and a resulting decrease in energy density. Generally, electron guns are operated with applied voltages that vary from 30 to 200kV, and they employ beam currents that range from 0.5 to 1500mA. Electron-beam welding equipment with power levels up to 30kW is common, and several units with power levels of up to 200kW are commercially available.

Typically, high-vacuum EBW beams can be focused down to spot sizes in the range of 0.25 to 1.3mm in diameter, with a power density of about $10^7 W/cm^2$. This high level of beam spot intensity generates temperatures of approximately 14,000°C and is sufficient to vaporize almost any material, forming a vapor hole that penetrates deep into the workpiece. When this vapor hole is advanced along a weld joint, the weld is produced by three effects that occur simultaneously: (1) the material at the leading edge of the vapor hole melts; (2) this molten material flows around the sides of the vapor hole to the trailing edge; and (3) this continuous flow of molten material fills in the trailing edge of the advancing vapor hole and solidifies as the vapor hole moves forward to produce a continuous weld.

Originally, EBW generally was performed only under high-vacuum conditions; because an ambient vacuum environment was required to generate the beam, welding the part within the same clean atmosphere was considered beneficial. However, as the demand for greater part production increased, it was found that the weld chamber vacuum level need not be as high as that needed for the gun region; ultimately, the need for any type of vacuum surrounding the workpiece was totally eliminated for some applications.

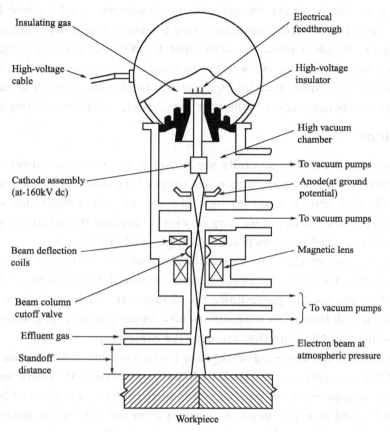

Fig. 3-20   Schematic showing primary components of an electron-beam welding head

● Advantages

One of the prime advantages of EBW is the ability to make welds that are deeper and narrower than arc welds, with a total heat input that is much lower than that required in arc welding. This ability to achieve a high weld depth-to-width ratio eliminates the need for multiple-pass welds, as is required in arc welding. The lower heat input results in a narrow workpiece heat-affected zone (HAZ) and noticeably fewer thermal effects on the workpiece.

In EBW, a high-purity vacuum environment can be used for welding, which results in freedom from impurities such as oxides and nitrides. The ability to employ higher weld speeds, due to the high melting rates associated with the concentrated heat source, reduces the time required to accomplish welding, thereby resulting in an increased productivity and higher energy efficiency for the process. Total energy conversion efficiency of EBW is approximately 65%, which is slightly higher than so-called conventional welding processes and much higher than other types of high-energy-density welding processes, such as laser-beam welding (EBW).

These characteristics: (1) minimize distortion and shrinkage during welding; (2) facilitate welding of most hardened or work-strengthened metals, frequently without significant deterioration of mechanical properties in the weld joint; (3) facilitate welding in close proximity to heat-sensitive components or attachments; (4) allow hermetic seal welding of evacuated enclosures, while retaining a vacuum inside the component; and (5) permit welding of refractory metals, reactive metals, and combinations of many dissimilar metals that are not joinable by arc welding processes. The ability to project the electron beam a distance of over 510mm under high-vacuum conditions, as well as the low end of medium-vacuum conditions, allows otherwise inaccessible welds to be completed.

● Limitations

Equipment costs for EBW generally are higher than those for conventional welding processes. However, when compared to other types of high-energy density welding (such as LBW), production costs are not as high. The cost of joint preparation and tooling is more than that encountered in arc welding processes, because the relatively small electron beam spot size that is used requires precise joint gap and position.

The available vacuum chamber capacities are limited; workpiece size is limited, to some degree, by the size of the vacuum chamber employed. Consequently, the production rate is affected by the need to pump down the chamber for each production load. Because the electron beam is deflected by magnetic fields, nonmagnetic or degaussed metals must be used for tooling and fixturing that are near the beam path.

Although most of the above advantages and disadvantages generally are applicable to all modes of EBW, several do not specifically apply to EBW-NV. Nonvacuum EBW does not offer the advantage of a high-purity environment (unless some form of inert-gas shielding is provided), and it is not subject to vacuum chamber limitations. Because welding is not done within the confines of a vacuum environment, the maximum practical "standoff", the working distance between the bottom of the electron beam column and the top of the workpiece, currently used on EBW-NV systems is limited to approximately 35mm.

● Vocabulary

bombarding n. 炮击；碰撞；撞击
conversion n. 转换；转化；转变
impinging n. 冲击；碰撞 v. 冲击，撞击
triode n. 三极管；三极真空管
emitter n. 发射器，发射体，发射管
anode n. 阳极，正极
electrostatic adj. 静电的；静电学的

aperture n. 孔，穴；孔径
diode n. 二极管；二极体
electromagnetic adj. 电磁的 n. 电磁式；电磁场
valve n. 阀；阀门；真空管 vt. 装阀于
vacuum n. 真空 adj. 真空的；利用真空的

● Questions

1. What is the concept of electron-beam welding?
2. What are the primary components of an electron-beam welding head?

Unit 10
Plasma-MIG Welding

Plasma-MIG Welding can be defined as a combination of plasma arc welding (PAW) and gas-metal arc welding (GMAW) within a single torch, where a filler wire is fed through the plasma nozzle orifice. The process can be used for both welding and surfacing.

The Principles of Operation, in terms of equipment, are illustrated in Fig. 3-21. Separate power supplies are used for the PAW and the GMAW elements of the equipment. An arc is struck between the tungsten electrode and the workpiece in a similar fashion to that of a PAW system. The filler wire can be fed to the plasma arc, either with or without the GMAW arc established. Without power supplied to the filler wire, the system can be operated as a PAW system with concentric feed of filler wire.

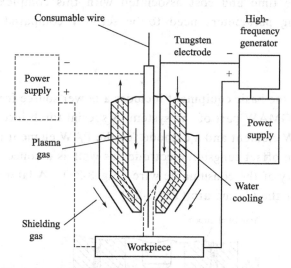

Fig. 3-21 Schematic of plasma-MIG welding equipment

Current and Operating Modes. The equipment can be operated either with a single power source, effectively as a PAW system with concentric filler wire feed, or with two power sources, for the plasma-MIG operation.

The polarity of the tungsten electrode is direct current, electrode negative (DCEN), as is that of the GMAW part of the system. The heat of the plasma arc is sufficient to achieve good metal transfer stability for the GMAW element, despite the fact that when this process is used separately, it is almost always used in a direct-current, electrode positive (DCEP) mode. The filler wire is heated by the constricted plasma arc, as well as by the cathode heating of its own arc, and by resistance heating along the wire extension. Therefore, the melting and deposition rates of the wire are higher than the rates achieved by heating with either arc alone.

Metal transfer is governed not only by plasma streaming, but also by arc forces between the wire tip and the workpiece. Because the metal droplets are totally enclosed by the plasma stream, spray transfer takes place even though the GMAW element operates on negative polarity.

Advantages and Disadvantages. The advantages of the plasma-MIG process include deposition rates and joint completion rates that are higher than those of the conventional GMAW process. The independent control of the plasma arc and current to the filler wire leads to more control of metal deposition. This capability can yield improved productivity and good flexibility for controlling heat input and arc characteristics in both welding and surfacing operations. Good control of dilution is achieved by running the system without any power applied to the filler wire. Metal transfer stability is increased, compared to that of the conventional GMAW process, and results in lower spatter levels. The cleaning action of the plasma arc results in lower porosity in aluminum alloys, compared to that of the conventional GMAW process.

Disadvantages include the capital cost of two power sources (although there are systems that are designed to operate with one), the greater complexity of the torch, and the increased maintenance time and cost associated with this complexity. With two power sources, more welding parameters need to be set up, compared to the conventional GMAW process.

● Equipment

As noted earlier, the basic equipment includes a power source for the plasma arc and a power source for the GMAW part of the system. A special torch incorporating both a contact tip for the GMAW element and a cathode for the PAW element is required. The initial design incorporated an offset tungsten electrode, as well as a concentric conduit and contact tip for the delivery of the consumable wire (Fig. 3-21). A later design incorporated a concentric cathode for the plasma arc (Fig. 3-22).

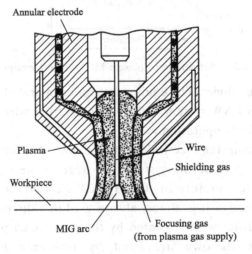

Fig. 3-22 Schematic of modern plasma-MIG torch with annular paw electrode and additional gas stream

The plasma-MIG torch can be readily fitted to existing welding equipment such as side beams and welding carriages, to replace the GMAW process in mechanized welding operations.

Power Sources. A constant-current power source with a high-frequency circuit to initiate the pilot arc is used for the plasma arc component of the system. The power source for the GMAW component can be used as a constant-voltage or a constant-current rectifier. Power sources have welding currents that typically range from 40 to 200A for the plasma arc and from 60 to 300A for the GMAW element at 100% duty cycle. However, equipment with welding currents up to 800A is available and can be used for surfacing applications.

Welding Torches. A special torch with a concentric cathode for the plasma arc and a concentric conduit and contact tip for the delivery of the consumable wire is required (Fig. 3-22). A water-cooled copper alloy nozzle is used to constrict the arc and to form a collimated plasma jet that exits the nozzle orifice. A plasma orifice gas and a focusing gas from the same supply are used; the latter is delivered via channels between the plasma welding electrode and the constricting nozzle. The focusing gas results in greater arc constriction and arc stability and prolongs the life of the constricting nozzle by creating a boundary gas layer between the nozzle orifice and the plasma arc.

Shielding Gases. Three shielding gases are utilized: one for the plasma (orifice) gas, one to provide additional arc constriction and arc stability, and one for supplementary shielding. The plasma gas and the focusing gas are usually argon, because an inert gas is required to prevent oxidation of the PAW electrode. The supplementary shielding gas can be argon, argon-oxygen, argon-carbon dioxide, or argon-hydrogen, depending on the nature of the workpiece being welded or, in the case of a surfacing operation, on the material being deposited. Argon is used when welding aluminum alloys, whereas argon-oxygen and argon-carbon dioxide are used when welding steels. Argon-hydrogen is used when welding stainless steels or when surfacing with them.

● Procedure

Process Operating Procedure. The plasma arc is ignited using a pilot arc in a fashion similar to that of a PAW system. The main arc is transferred from the electrode to the workpiece and the plasma jet passes through the nozzle orifice. The system can be operated in this way, with the concentric cold wire being fed through the axis of the torch. A higher melting rate is achieved when power is applied to the wire through the contact tip and when both arcs are run simultaneously. The higher energy imparted to the wire by the plasma arc results in an increased wire deposition rate. In this operating mode, deposition rates higher than those typical of the GMAW process can be achieved.

Inspection and Weld Quality Control. Inspection requirements are similar to those of other arc welding or surfacing operations. Visual, ultrasonic, and radiographic inspection techniques are most appropriate. The dual action of the GMAW and plasma arcs results in weld quality that is sometimes higher than that achieved by the GMAW process alone. This is particularly true for aluminum alloys, because the cleaning action of the plasma arc often results in reduced porosity.

Quality control requires monitoring the welding parameters for both power sources, as well as monitoring the wire feed. In addition, the condition of the nozzle orifice (that is, the wear and concentricity of the orifice) should be monitored.

Troubleshooting. The relatively complex nature of the welding torch involves increased maintenance time. Erosion of the copper alloy nozzle orifice will cause a change in the arc shape and will affect the weld profile. Therefore, the nozzle should be checked periodically.

● Applications

Material Types. The plasma-MIG process is suitable for welding a wide variety of materials. The high heat energy supplied by the plasma and gas-metal arcs makes the process suitable for high-melting-point materials, such as tungsten and molybdenum. The most common application is welding aluminum sheet and plate. Wear-resistant steels are used with the process in hardfacing applications. Austenitic stainless steels, as well as nickel alloys, are used in cladding applications. Both solid and flux-cored wires can be employed for welding and surfacing, although most applications involve solid wires.

Industries. The plasma-MIG welding process has been used for the deposition of corrosion-resisting stainless steel and nickel-base alloys in the offshore industry, for the general fabrication of silos and tank trailers made from aluminum alloys, and for hardfacing applications in the excavation equipment industry, as well as the dredging and offshore industries.

Typical Components and Joints. The plasma-MIG process is suitable for welding of joints and for surfacing operations. The wide range of heat inputs available by choosing how to apply current to the consumable electrode provides additional flexibility for surfacing operations, compared to the range of heat inputs available with an external wire feed using the GTAW/PAW or the conventional GMAW process.

Single-V butt joints are commonly used for the plasma-MIG welding of plate. A full-penetration weld can be made in a single pass on a 9.5 mm thick mild steel plate when operating the plasma and gas-metal arcs simultaneously. This compares to three passes when just the PAW process is used. One would expect the same joint to require two or three passes for the conventional GMAW process.

● Vocabulary

constricted   *adj.* 收缩的   *v.* 使……收缩
streaming   *n.* 流；串流   *v.* 流动
droplet   *n.* 小滴，微滴；液滴
dilution   *n.* 稀释，冲淡；稀释法
parameter   *n.* 参数；系数；参量
constant-current   直流
pilot arc   导引电弧；维持电弧
ignite   *vt.* 点燃；使燃烧   *vi.* 点火；燃烧
radiographic   *adj.* 射线照相术的
erosion   *n.* 侵蚀，腐蚀

dual   *adj.* 双的；双重的   *n.* 双数；双数词
troubleshooting   *n.* 发现并修理故障   *v.* 检修
hardfacing   *n.* 耐磨堆焊；表面耐磨堆焊
cladding   *n.* 包层；电镀；喷镀；覆盖层
surfacing   *n.* 表面堆焊；堆焊
excavation   *n.* 挖掘，发掘
butt   *n.* 截头；对接
flux-cored wire   药芯焊丝

● **Questions**

1. What shielding gases are utilized in plasma-MIG welding?
2. Please talk about the principles of plasma-MIG welding.

Unit 11

Friction Welding

Friction Welding (FRW), in its simplest form, involves two axially aligned parts. While one part is rotated, the other stationary part is advanced to make pressure contact. Axial force then increases to generate the frictional heat necessary for welding at the abutting surfaces in order to form a solid-state joint. Friction welding can be divided into two major process variations, depending on the manner by which rotational energy is converted into frictional heat. The first process, direct-drive, or continuous-drive, FRW, has been used commercially since the 1940s. It requires constant energy from a source for any desired duration. The second process, inertia-drive FRW, which was developed in the early 1960s, uses the kinetic energy stored in a rotating flywheel.

● **Direct-Drive Friction Welding**

Fig. 3-23 shows the layout of a direct-drive FRW system. The spindle is first driven to a predetermined constant speed, and the two parts are brought together under a preset axial force. Both rotation and force are maintained for a specific period determined either by a time or a distance, so that the frictional heat will raise temperatures at the abutting surfaces enough to render the material plastic and suitable for welding. (However, direct-drive friction welds are almost never made using a single level of axial load. The vast majority of welds are made using a minimum of two axial force levels. The second axial load is basically added to the beginning of the weld cycle to yield a preheating phase. In fact, direct-drive friction welds using three axial loads are more commonly applied than those using a single load.) The spindle is then disengaged from the driving unit, and a brake is applied to bring the spindle to rest. At the same time, axial force either remains unchanged or is raised to complete the weld.

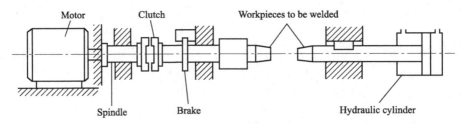

Fig. 3-23 Schematic showing relation of workpieces to key components of a direct-drive FRW system

● **Inertia-Drive Friction Welding**

In inertia-drive FRW (Fig. 3-24), a flywheel and the rotating part are mounted in a spindle, which is driven to the desired speed. The drive source is then disengaged, and the two parts make contact under a preset axial force. The free-rotating flywheel decelerates under either the same applied force or later under a larger force. Meanwhile, kinetic energy stored in the flywheel and spindle is converted to frictional heat at the abutting surfaces. The weld is complete when the flywheel comes to a stop. A subsequent higher forging force may be used after the flywheel has stopped.

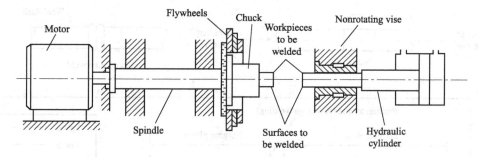

Fig. 3-24 Schematic showing relation of workpieces to key components of an inertia-drive FRW system

● Welding Parameters

Direct-Drive FRW Variables. Three parameters control the character of a weld in direct-drive FRW: rotational speed, duration of rotation, and axial force. During welding, there is not only an axial shortening of the part length, often called axial displacement or upset, but also a resisting torque of friction to rotation, which also undergoes change. Fig. 3-25 shows the change in various events occurring throughout the whole process. Based on the shape of the friction torque curve, it is convenient to divide direct-drive FRW into three phases:

- Phase 1: Initial friction (that is, bread-in or first friction) phase.
- Phase 2: Heating (that is, friction) phase.
- Phase 3: Forging (that is, upsetting) phase.

In phase 1, the torque rises rapidly after the start of the process. It then peaks and drops before leveling off when phase 1 ends. The rapid rise and gradual fall of torque is associated with the interlocking and breaking of asperities and subsequent softening of the material at the faying surfaces by frictional heating.

Friction torque remains somewhat constant in phase 2, indicating that the process reaches a balance of effects between strain hardening and thermal softening. Both the faying surfaces and material immediately behind are by then sufficiently heated to permit the two parts to be forged together.

Forging takes place in phase 3, which starts at the time of declutching and braking. Spindle rotation is immediately retarded, and the deceleration depends on braking time. Because the brake force itself can be set, braking time can also be a variable. Deceleration varies in the welding of different materials. However, the torque may not rise at all but drops abruptly at the onset of phase 3 if braking is sudden. This brings the rotating spindle to rest almost instantly, and the larger force is applied after spindle rotation stops. In this case, there is no torsional forge, and forging is brought about by upsetting.

Axial force in phase 3 is usually increased to effect forging. The friction torque again rises after the onset of this phase, reaching another peak before sharply falling off to zero. This peak varies with deceleration and applied axial force. Under some circumstances, this final peak can be omitted by delaying the onset of the forging force.

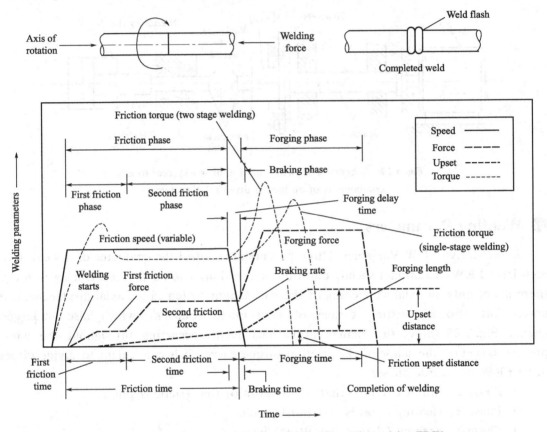

Fig. 3-25 Plot of welding parameters versus time for a direct-drive FRW system

This is done only at or after the stoppage of spindle rotation by braking. In this case, forging is carried out by upsetting without torsional forging. Although two-stage welding is applied more frequently in direct-drive friction welding, onstage welding is sometimes used, especially in research work.

When the axial force remains unchanged, slower deceleration (longer braking time by reduced braking) leads to higher peak. If the axial force is increased in phase 3, braking time is shortened, but the peak still rises because of the larger applied force. Rising friction torque in phase 3, characteristic of FRW, contributes to torsional forge, which is more effective than conventional forge by upsetting. Phase 3 ends shortly after spindle rotation stops. This period of forging or upsetting time can also be considered a fourth welding parameter.

Inertia-Drive FRW Variables. There are three welding parameters in inertia-drive FRW: flywheel mass (expressed by moment of inertia), rotational speed, and axial force. The events described for direct-drive FRW also occur in inertiadrive FRW. Except for rotational speed, the curves shown in Fig. 3-26 are similar to those shown in Fig. 3-25. The process can also be divided into three phases based on the shape of the friction-torque curve. Unlike direct-drive FRW, duration of rotation and forging time in phase 3 are not predetermined but controlled by the three welding parameters.

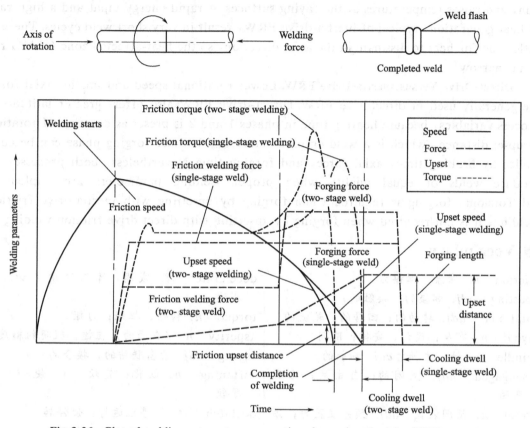

Fig. 3-26 Plot of welding parameters versus time for an inertia-drive FRW system

If axial force differs in phases 2 and 3, the process is called two-stage welding, and the forces, called heating force and forging force, respectively, are both included as a welding parameter of axial force. On the other hand, when the force remains constant throughout the process, it is called one-stage welding. The second friction-torque peak in two-stage welding is generally higher than that in one-stage welding because of the larger axial force applied in phase 3.

In two-stage welding, the larger axial forging force is applied when the flywheel rotational speed decreases to a fraction of the initial value—for example, 0.1 to 0.5. Friction torque again rises to a second peak, which as in direct-drive FRW, is higher than in one-stage welding. This phase is prolonged beyond cessation of the flywheel rotation. This extra time, called dwell time, is used for cooling of the joint to avoid debonding by the release of stored strain energy. Although dwell times can range from 0 to 30s, 1 to 2s is typical.

The kinetic energy used for inertia-drive FRW depends on the product of the flywheel moment of inertia and the square of rotational speed. The frictional heat generated at the faying surfaces, however, is determined by the rate of change of this energy (or the energy delivery rate), which is influenced by the moment of inertia of the flywheel and the axial force. For a given kinetic energy input and a given axial force, a smaller flywheel (with smaller moment of inertia) delivers the energy at the faying surfaces faster than a larger flywheel (with larger moment of inertia). For a given energy input using the same flywheel, a larger axial force increases flywheel deceleration rates, intensifies heat generation, and raises temperatures at the faying surfaces. A rapid energy input and a high rate of heat generation, typical of inertia-drive FRW, result in very short weld cycles. There is little time for heat to dissipate in the axial direction, so the heat-affected zone (HAZ) remains narrow.

Direct-Drive Versus Inertia-Drive FRW. Lower rotational speed and smaller axial force are generally used in directdrive FRW. Direct-drive FRW also offers greater latitude in process variables, because heating time in phases 1 and 2 is preset as duration of rotation or upset distance, which is a welding parameter, and because forging phase can be controlled by braking time, axial force, and forging time. Nevertheless, both processes do produce welds of equal quality when proper welding parameters are implemented. Torsional forging is required when forging by upsetting with inertia-drive friction welding; it is not required when forging by upsetting with direct-drive friction welding.

● Vocabulary

friction   *n.* 摩擦，摩擦力
abutting   *adj.* 邻接的；接触的；
rotational   *adj.* 转动的；回转的；轮流的
layout   *n.* 布局；设计；安排；陈列
spindle   *n.* 轴；主轴   *adj.* 细长的
disengaged   *adj.* 空闲的；自由的；已脱离的
preset   *n.* 预调装置   *adj.* 预先装置的；预先调整的
dwell   *v.* 保压；停歇；暂停

decelerate   *vi.* 减速，降低速度   *vt.* 使减速
torque   *n.* 转矩，扭矩；力矩
asperity   *n.* （表面的）粗糙；微观粗糙度
faying   *adj.* 紧密联结的；接合的
softening   *n.* 软化；变软   *v.* 使……变柔软
declutch   *vt.* 使停止运行；使停转
stoppage   *n.* 停止；故障；中断

● Questions

1. How many phases do direct-drive FRW include? What are they?
2. What parameters can control the character of a weld in direct-drive FRW?

Unit 12
Brazing Processes

● **Torch Brazing**

Torch Brazing (TB) utilizes a fuel gas flame as the heat source for the brazing process. The fuel gas is mixed with either air or oxygen to produce a flame, which is applied to the workpiece until the assembly reaches the proper brazing temperature. Then, preplaced filler metal will be melted or hand-fed wire can be introduced.

Advantages and Limitations. Torch brazing is used with various base metals and on many different sizes of assemblies. The process offers many advantages, including:
• Flexibility, in that one torch with multiple tips can be used to braze a variety of assemblies.
• Low capital equipment cost (manual torch brazing).
• Entire assembly does not have to be heated; small joints on large assemblies can be heated locally.
• Automation is possible in many cases.
• Most base metals and combinations of base metals can be torch brazed if a suitable flux is available.

Although the process provides versatile, low-cost heating for brazing, its limitations include:
• Oxidation/discoloration can occur on surfaces of the assembly not covered with flux, because process is conducted in air.
• Flux residues need to be removed after brazing.
• Highly reactive materials, such as titanium and zirconium, cannot be torch brazed, because no flux is available.
• Large assemblies can be difficult to heat, because of the localized nature of flame heating.

Applications. Torch brazing is commonly used on copper, brass, and other copper alloys, as well as steel, stainless steel, aluminum, carbides, and various heat-resistant materials. Most combinations of these materials can also be torch brazed. It is necessary to use flux with these materials, except when a phosphorus brazing alloy is used to braze pure copper parts. In this case, the phosphorus acts as the flux. The low-temperature silver-base and silver/copper/phosphorus filler metals are commonly used with torch brazing. Various other copper-base and gold-base filler metals can also be used with this process.

● **Techniques**

The key to torch brazing, as in all methods of heating, is to heat evenly the components to be brazed. This may require directing the torch primarily on a large, rather than small, component. Because the filler metal will flow to the hottest portion of an assembly, the flame should be applied in such a way as to flow the filler metal in the required direction.

When preplaced (preform or paste) filler metal is used in torch brazing, the operator need only know where and how much heat to apply. When the operator is also responsible for the filler metal, he must not apply it until the assembly has reached brazing temperatures. This may require practice and experience. Torch brazing is a skill that can be attained relatively quickly with the proper training.

● Furnace Brazing

Furnace Brazing is a mass production process for joining the components of small assemblies with a metallurgical bond, using a nonferrous filler metal as the bonding material and a furnace as the heat source. Furnace brazing technology was initiated in the 1920s and was first used commercially circa 1930, primarily to provide a brazing process that did not require a chemical flux, thereby eliminating the flux entrapment problem. Currently, furnace brazing is widely applied in a variety of industries. The essentially automatic nature of the process and its use of unskilled labor account for its popularity.

Process Advantages. There are at least five advantages to using the furnace brazing process:

- It is a method in which many variables can be easily controlled to ensure repeatability of the process and guarantee a high-quality joint. Brazing temperature and process duration, as well as heating and cooling rates, can be controlled and monitored. in addition, the brazing atmosphere can be easily regulated.
- When all the brazing procedures are well established, relatively unskilled operators can carry out everyday manufacturing operations.
- The absence of flux entrapment allows more flexibility in joint design. the postbraze cleaning of the brazed part and the furnace are unnecessary.
- Because a whole assembly is heated, distortion of the parts can be minimized or eliminated. in some cases, heat treatment of the part can be incorporated into the brazing cycle.
- More than one joint per workpiece can be brazed in a brazing cycle. Several different assemblies requiring the same brazing conditions can also be brazed simultaneously.

Industrial Applications. The furnace brazing process is employed in many industries because of its high quality and reproducibility. The vacuum device, jet engine, and automotive industries represent three examples. In the vacuum device industry, a vacuum tube with an envelope of alumina ceramic is used, the nature of which requires that the whole assembly be heated. The control of heating and cooling rates is very important to the prevention of alumina ceramic cracking.

Other applications of furnace brazing can be found in the jet engine industry, where the quality of the brazed joint and the dimensional control of the brazed assembly are critical. Vacuum furnace brazing is the most common system used in the production of jet engine components.

The automotive industry makes extensive use of the continuous belt furnace because it is easily automated and is a costeffective, high-production joining process for components made of carbon steel, stainless steel, and aluminum.

● Induction Brazing

Induction Brazing (IB) is a process that joins metal components to form an assembly by selectively heating the joint area to the brazing temperature with electrical energy transmitted from an inductor that has been energized by a heating generator. It is classified as a brazing process because joints are made at elevated temperatures, using copper alloys that often contain silver.

Heating results from resistance to the flow of induced current in the assembly components. It occurs when the electrically conductive components are placed in the electromagnetic field created by rapidly alternating current flow in the inductor. With proper coil design, heating occurs rapidly at the joint area, providing localized brazing temperatures. Response to the electromagnetic field depends on the frequency of the alternating current and the nature of the materials being heated, as well as on the shape of the component parts and coil design. Nonmagnetic materials with low electrical resistance such as copper and brass take longer to heat than magnetic, higher resistivity, ferrous materials such as steel.

Process Applications. Induction brazing is used where relatively high-strength heat-resistant joints are required between components parts. The strength of the joint depends on the joint design, the brazing alloy, the strength of the components being joined, and the clearance between the components. A clearance of 0.038 to 0.050mm is recommended. Induction brazing has been used extensively in the production of consumer and industrial products, structural assemblies, electric and electronic products, mining equipment, machine and hand tools, military and ordnance equipment, and aerospace components.

Advantages. Induction brazing features rapid heating that produces joints in seconds because each joint area is exposed to the electromagnetic field of the specific coil involved. Uniform and reliable joints can be produced piece after piece with smooth joint fillets, eliminating the need for finishing operations. Because a suitable induction coil can provide heat simultaneously at several locations in an assembly, a number of joints can be made in a single heating operation. Induction brazing provides control of the heat pattern and rapid heating, which serve to localize the heated zone, thereby preventing or minimizing deterioration of properties in previously heat-treated or cold-worked materials, and, if desired, permitting sequential brazing of nearby joints using alloys with decreasing melting temperatures.

Induction brazing uses predetermined amounts of brazing alloys in the form of rings, strip, or powder; thus, the possibility of excessive material use is avoided, lowering joining alloy costs. Rapid heating minimizes oxidation and discoloration in most instances, even without the use of a controlled atmosphere.

● Resistance Brazing

Resistance Brazing (RB) is a resistance joining process. The workpieces are heated locally, and the filler metal that is preplaced between the workpieces is melted by the heat generated from resistance to the flow of electric current through the electrodes and the work. In the usual application of RB, the heating current is passed through the joint itself. Equipment is the same as that used for resistance welding, and the pressure needed for establishing electrical contact across the joint is ordinarily applied through the electrodes. The electrode pressure is also the usual means for providing the tight fit needed for capillary behavior in the joint. The heat for resistance brazing can be generated mainly in the workpieces themselves, in the electrodes, or in both, depending on the electrical resistivity and dimensions.

Resistance brazing is used for many applications involving small workpieces, for small joints that are part of very large equipment, or for low-volume production runs because it provides:

- Very rapid and highly localized heating.
- Flameless, clean operation.
- Precise brazing that is easy to control.
- High-quality joints without extensive operator training.
- Equipment cost savings (one transformer and a pair of electrodes can be used for a wide variety of joint designs).
- Easy portability in some of its equipment.

However, RB is impractical for:

- Joint areas that exceed approximately $1300 mm^2$.
- Workpieces that are large or heavy.
- Workpieces that have variable thickness or complex contours.

● Vocabulary

flame n. 火焰；光辉 v. 焚烧；泛红
brazing n. 钎焊；铜焊；硬钎焊 v. 用锌铜合金钎接
hand-fed 人工进料
discoloration n. 变色；污点
repeatability n. 重复性；可重复性；再现性
cracking n. 破裂；开裂，裂缝 v. 破裂
ceramic adj. 陶瓷的；陶器的 n. 陶瓷；陶瓷制品
costeffective adj. 成本效益的
elevated adj. 提高的 v. 提高；抬起
conductive adj. 传导的；传导性的；导电的
localized adj. 局部的；地区的；小范围的
nonmagnetic adj. 无磁性的 n. 非磁性物

ordnance n. 军火；大炮；军械署
fillet n. 圆角；嵌边；倒圆角
deterioration n. 恶化；退化；变质
resistance n. 阻力；电阻；抵抗；反抗；抵抗力
capillary n. 毛细管；毛细管现象 adj. 毛细管的
impractical adj. 不切实际的，不现实的；不能实行的
resistance brazing 电阻钎焊；电阻硬焊
torch brazing 吹管硬焊；火焰钎焊
furnace brazing 炉内钎焊；炉热硬焊；炉内铜焊
induction brazing 感应钎焊，高频钎焊
alternating current 交流电

● Questions

Please give some kinds of brazing processes and talk about their characteristics and application respectively.

Unit 13

Soldering Welding

● Torch Soldering

Torch Soldering (TS) utilizes a fuel gas flame as the heat source in the soldering process. The fuel gas is mixed with either air or oxygen to produce the flame, which is applied to the materials to be soldered until the assembly reaches the proper soldering temperature. Solder filler metal, which melts at temperatures below 450℃, is added to the assembly to bond it. Successful torch soldering is accomplished when parts are clean and fit together closely, and when oxides are not excessive.

Torch soldering is used in numerous industries that utilize a variety of base metals. It is most often used to produce a leaktight assembly with some degree of mechanical strength. This process does have several advantages when compared with other metal-joining methods.

These advantages include:
- Relatively low temperatures, which result in minimal distortion and heat discoloration of the soldered assembly.
- Flexibility, such that one torch can be used to solder a variety of assemblies.
- Relatively inexpensive capital equipment cost.
- Ability to solder most base metals and basemetal combinations with an appropriate flux.
- Local heating of small joints on large assemblies, which precludes the need to heat the entire assembly.
- Process automation, in many cases.

The limitations of the process are that:
- A flux is needed because the process is accomplished in air, and this flux often must be removed in order to prevent part corrosion.
- Highly reactive materials, such as titanium and many refractory metals, cannot be soldered, because no suitable fluxes are available.
- Soldered joints do not normally exceed the strength of the parts being soldered, that is, the process produces relatively weak joints, when compared with brazed and welded assemblies.

Applications. Torch soldering is used extensively on copper, brass, and other copper alloys. Steel, stainless steel, aluminum, gold, and other metals, as well as many combinations of these, also can be soldered by this process.

The plumbing industry utilizes this process extensively on residential copper tubing for water lines, primarily because of its flexibility and ease of use. Soldered copper water lines provide leak-tight joints with the requisite strength. Torch heating is also used for liquid and gas conduit in industrial processing applications.

This process is also used by many other industries in assembly processes, such as the soldering of jewelry, aluminum heat exchangers, radiators, and pressure-sensing devices. Tube-to-fitting types of assemblies also are commonly torch soldered, as are butt and lap joints.

Basic Heating Techniques. The key to torch soldering, as in all methods of heating, is to equally heat the components that need to be soldered. This may require directing the torch to a larger mass component of an assembly. Because the filler metal will flow to the hottest portion of an assembly, the flame should be applied so that the filler metal will flow in the intended direction. Also, movement of the torch is required to avoid overheating or burning the assembly.

● Dip Soldering

Dip Soldering (DS) is accomplished by submerging parts to be joined into a molten solder bath. The molten bath can be any suitable filler metal, but the selection is usually confined to the lower melting point elements. The most common dip soldering operations use zinc-aluminum and tin-lead solders.

The molten bath can be heated by electricity or gas. The bath container is made from ceramic materials or a metal that is nonreactive to the filler metal used for dipping. The dip baths, which can range in size from very small to large, are used in a wide range of industries.

The process of dip soldering is simple to carry out. The joint areas are cleaned and then coated with an appropriate flux. The parts are then lowered into the molten filler metal and joining takes place by capillary attraction into the joints. The solder does not wet surfaces that are not coated with flux. Jigs and fixtures are normally essential to hold components at proper clearances for joining purposes and to maintain overall dimensions of the finished product. They should not be wetted by the solder. Furthermore, any substrates that must be submerged should be able to tolerate the solder temperature.

The molten bath supplies both the heat for raising the temperature of the part and the filler metal to make the joints. It is therefore important that the dip soldering pot capacity be large enough to allow heating of the part and joining without significantly reducing the temperature of the molten filler metal. For some applications, soldering pots are designed for specific production rates.

An advantage of the dip soldering process is the wide range of part sizes, shapes, and thicknesses that can be accommodated by the same apparatus and still result in satisfactory joints. Larger parts require a preheating operation in order to reduce thermal shock when the part enters the dip pot. The preheat also allows quicker attainment of equilibrium between the molten metal in the pot and the part being joined. Atmosphere protection of the dip soldering pot is necessary when the filler metal has oxidation tendencies. Surface oxides on the workpieces must be removed prior to dip soldering, because they can interfere with a proper joining operation.

Applications. Dip soldering is used in job shops, as well as high-rate production situations. Therefore, the parts joined by dip soldering vary from individually designed products to mass-produced items. Dip soldering is ideal for the production of prototype engineered products, which are often made for test purposes. The process also can be used to join limited-production items for the automotive, aircraft, consumer, electronic, and other industries. High-production products are typically heat exchangers for automotive use, high-volume telecommunications equipment, and appliances.

Joints produced by dip soldering techniques are usually sleeve, lap, or T-joints that fill by capillary attraction. The parts to be joined are assembled with gaps appropriate to the particular filler metal surface tension and viscosity characteristics. The joint/fixture design must accommodate thermal expansion that is due to heating the entire substrate or part. Joint gaps also depend on the reactions of the molten filler metal with the material to be joined. For example, aluminum filler metals (or those with zinc, tin-zinc, or zinc-aluminum alloys) react more quickly with aluminum than a tin-lead solder will with copper and therefore require larger gaps for joining.

● Resistance Soldering

Resistance Soldering (RS) is a soldering process in which the heat needed to melt the solder is developed by the resistance of the material when a large electrical current is supplied. Resistance soldering can be applied to electrically conductive materials that allow the passage of electric current. The process can be used for selective spot soldering of small components, for the soldering of closely placed parts on an assembly, or for heat restriction when necessary.

When the current is applied, rapid local heating occurs, melting the solder. This molten solder wets the surface. As a result, the resistance in the material falls and the current increases, tripping a control. The heat rapidly dissipates into the surrounding area, and the solder quickly solidifies.

Process Applications. The RS process can be used in all soldering operations and with all solderable metals. The only limitations are the thickness and the design of the parts to be soldered. Resistance soldering is used to join steels (for example, carbon, low alloy, and stainless) and nonferrous alloys (for example, aluminum and aluminum alloys, nickel and nickel alloys, and copper and copper alloys) up to 3.2mm in thickness.

The RS process is suitable where:
- An open flame constitutes a potential hazard in the workplace.
- The heat needed for soldering must be confined to a specific area.
- The oxidation attributed to heating of the solder must be minimized.
- The components to be joined are inaccessible with a conventional soldering iron.
- The bead produced can be adapted to automated processing/mass production methods.

Resistance Soldering Practice. The RS process requires preassembly of the workpiece components. Because the workpiece and the solder are integral parts of the current loop, care must be taken to ensure that the current path is not blocked by any foreign or nonmetallic substance. Hence, the preassembled workpiece requires a clean, deburred surface and the proper solder alloys (preform or in paste form). The use of wire solder and flux is not recommended because of the rapidity of heating and the potential hazard of electrical shock.

The preassembled workpieces are positioned in a grounded jig or clamp, and the movable electrode is brought in contact with the workpiece to complete the circuit. When the power is turned on, the operator waits for signs that the solder is starting to flow and then immediately turns the power off. When using automatic soldering equipment, the duration of the current flow is monitored by sensors that determine the length of the "on" cycle. As the workpiece cools, the solder solidifies, and the workpiece is removed from the jig. The next assembly can then be placed in the jig. A properly designed movable electrode head allows multiple solder connections to be produced in a single operation.

● **Laser Soldering**

Industrial Lasers are able to deliver large amounts of heat with great precision and without contact, making them ideal for applications that have either a destructive nature, such as cutting or drilling, or a constructive nature, such as soldering or annealing.

The use of focused energy generated by either a CO_2 or a neodymium-doped yttrium-aluminum-garnet laser continues to gain acceptance as a process for a number of operations requiring high-temperature injection with speed and precision. For example, in the electronics field, component soldering can be carried out one joint at a time with highly reliable results. Laser soldering uses the well-focused, highly controlled beam to deliver energy to a desired location for a precisely measured length of time.

Advantages of laser soldering are that it is a noncontact procedure; it avoids thermal stress by localizing heat input and confining it to the solder joint area; it reduces intermetallic compound formation, due to rapid joint formation which results in a more ductile joint; and it involves a fine grain size (due to rapid cooling), resulting in better fatigue properties. Disadvantages include low output rates, high power requirements, and high capital requirements.

● **Vocabulary**

soldering　n. 焊接；焊料；焊接处
　adj. 用于焊接的　v. 焊接
leaktigh　adj. 不漏的；密封的
preclude　vt. 排除；妨碍；阻止
refractory　adj. 难治的；难熔的　n. 耐火物质
conduit　n. 导管；导线管；导水管
overheating　n. 过热；超温；过载
jig　n. 夹具；定位模具；钻模
apparatus　n. 装置，设备；仪器

deburred　vt. 倒角；清理毛刺；去毛刺；去毛边
clamp　vt. 夹紧，固定住　n. 夹钳，夹具
drilling　n. 钻孔；钻削　v. 钻孔
annealing　n. 热处理；低温退火；磨炼
　v. 退火
noncontact　n. 无触头，无触点
intermetallic　adj. 金属间（化合）的
　n. 金属间化合物

● **Questions**

1. Please compare the four soldering processes mentioned in this article?
2. What is the process of dip soldering?
3. Please tell the advantages of laser soldering.

Unit 14
Inspection of Welding

Welded Joints in any component or structure require thorough inspection. The role of nondestructive evaluation (NDE) in the inspection of welds is very important, and the technology has become highly developed as a result. This article describes the applications, methods, and limitations of NDE.

Nondestructive evaluation comprises a range of test methods for detecting discontinuities in a material, component, or structure, without causing damage. Therefore, the principal advantages of nondestructive tests, as opposed to alternative destructive proof tests, are that a 100% inspection can be performed at manufacture and that monitoring of the structure or component can continue while it is in service. The principal disadvantage of NDE is that the measurements obtained are only indirectly related to the presence and severity of the flaws, and much subjective interpretation is necessary.

Any discussion of NDE requires a clear definition of the term "defect". A defect is a discontinuity that creates a substantial risk of failure in a component or structure during its service life. Although the aim of NDE is to detect defects, it provides evidence of flaws, as well. The significance of these flaws and whether or not they are actually defects must then be determined.

There are five principal test methods: penetrant testing, magnetic-particle testing, eddy-current testing, radiographic testing, and ultrasonic testing. Although visual inspection is not strictly a test method, it does have an important role in NDE procedures and is often the only inspection method used.

● Applications

A useful distinction can be made between those NDE methods that are applied to welds during manufacturing and those that are applied to welds as part of plant and machinery maintenance. Although the same methods and techniques can be applied in both areas, there are important differences in inspection goals and, therefore, in test procedures.

In manufacturing, NDE is one of a series of quality-control techniques. The integration of these techniques into the manufacturing process is an important management subject. The first step is to decide at what stage or stages the NDE is to be carried out. Components that are brought in-house can be inspected prior to welding. An ultrasonic examination of a parent plate, for example, will show areas that contain laminations. Although these laminations may not be defects in themselves, lamellar tears could result where they occur near the weld in a specific orientation.

During the welding of thick sections, the magnetic-particle testing (MPT) of the root-pass and hot pass, in an attempt to find cracks before filling the weld groove, could save on repair costs. Using dry powder techniques, MPT can be carried out while surfaces are still hot.

Attempts have been made to incorporate NDE techniques with continuous monitoring of the weld process. Eddy-current testing, for example, has been used on small-bore induction-welded tube to provide feedback to control the welding process. However, total automation with real-time evaluation of test results is still not generally available, except in very simple applications, where results can be evaluated with simple go/no-go acceptance criteria.

Nondestructive evaluation is usually conducted at the end of a manufacturing process. In that capacity, it functions as part of the specification requirements and thus provides a safeguard against sending defective components or structures to customers. Unfortunately, conducting NDE after welding has been completed is not satisfactory. The necessity of repairs has given NDE a negative image in the manufacturing process.

● NDE Methods

A variety of NDE methods are briefly described below, along with some of the operating problems that can be encountered.

Visual Inspection, although not itself a test method, is the most common NDE method and, arguably, the most important. Indeed, a thorough visual examination is a prerequisite of successful NDE. Much can be inferred from the surface of the weld, including information about its internal condition, although a good weld surface does not necessarily indicate a defect-free weld.

Penetrant Testing. Penetrants provide a method of enhancing the visibility of flaws. A strongly colored, or fluorescent, liquid is applied liberally to the test surface and left to infiltrate surface-breaking cavities and cracks. The surface contact time is typically about 15 min. The excess liquid is then wiped from the surface, using some solvent, and a fine white developer powder is applied, usually as an aerosol in a volatile solvent. As the solvent evaporates, the penetrant liquid that is trapped in the flaws is drawn into the dry developer powder by a reverse-capillary action. For a cavity, this process may take no more than 1 s, but for a fine hairline crack, it may be necessary to wait more than 1 h for a visible indication.

The several penetrant types that exist can be distinguished on the basis of color, method of removal, and the form of the developer. Red penetrants, which are the most commonly used, require good daylight viewing conditions and a white background to improve contrast. Fluorescent penetrants are used when high sensitivity to fine flaws on relatively smooth surfaces is needed. They require black-light viewing conditions.

Although it is the most common NDE method, penetrant testing is widely misused. The test surfaces are often inadequately cleaned, the penetrant contact time with the surface is too short, or the excess penetrant is removed carelessly from flaws, as well as from the surface. In addition, because the method only detects flaws that are open to the surface, abrasive cleaning methods may peen over fine, surface-breaking cracks. This problem can arise when penetrants are used to chase fine hairline cracks or incomplete fusion with grinding.

Magnetic Particle Testing is the preferred method for detecting surface-breaking and, under certain circumstances, near-surface flaws in situations where a test material can be magnetized.

This method depends on the flaw disrupting the magnetic flux generated along the surface of the weld by a permanent magnet or electromagnets, or by electric-current-carrying electrodes and cables. Flux leakage from the surface creates magnetic poles, which attract the magnetic particles, creating a clearly visible image of the flaw. The method is particularly sensitive to the detection of cracks, where, like penetrants, the particles identify flaws with well-defined features. However, the flux leakage may be absent altogether, if the crack runs parallel with the magnetic field. It is therefore vital that the inspection surface be magnetized in two directions at right angles to each other.

Eddy-Current Testing techniques have been used widely in automated tube-testing systems and material sorting, as well as in the inspection of aircraft components and structures. For the testing of welds, there is a growing interest in using eddy-current testing as an alternative to MPT and penetrant testing, because the method is able to detect cracks beneath a thick layer of paint.

Like MPT, eddy-current testing relies on the flaw disrupting the energizing field, which is electrical, circular, and induced by a small coil carrying high-frequency alternating current. Therefore, the orientation of vertical planar flaws is not important, but the coil has to be scanned intensively over the test surface to ensure coverage. Laminar flaws are not detectable.

Radiographic Testing, in the past, has formed the basis of weld inspection for internal flaws. However, it is an expensive method, and increasing restrictions on the use of ionizing radiation has led to a shift toward alternative ultrasonic testing techniques.

The radiographic technique uses radiation, either as X-rays or gamma rays, to penetrate the weld to create a latent image on radiographic film. The test piece absorbs radiation, but when flaws are present, less is absorbed than the amount absorbed by the parent material, which produces a localized darkening of the film. If the radiation source is sufficiently far from the object, then the image of the flaw will be sharp. Cavities with a through thickness of the order of only 1% of wall thickness can be discerned.

Ultrasonic Testing receives more attention in the literature than any other NDE method, because of its use in critical applications, such as in the nuclear industry, and because it requires the highest level of skill. Like sonar, the method relies on propagating pulses of sound through a medium and then picking up reflected echoes. However, because the sound is of an ultrasonic frequency, the pulses are propagated along a narrow beam in a fixed direction, typically at refraction angles of 0, 45°, 60°, or 70° from the probe placed on the surface. To achieve coverage, the beam must therefore be scanned in a tight raster fashion over the test surface.

● Evaluation of Test Results

The evaluation of test results and the setting of accept/reject criteria for weld flaws are the subjects of much current debate. This is because of the empirical way in which the criteria were derived in the past. As new developments in defect assessment, such as fracture mechanics, set the trend toward more sophisticated methods of evaluating NDE results, the discrepancies in current practice become more apparent. This is particularly true of ultrasonic testing.

In general, the accept/reject criteria used in national standards draw a distinction between rounded and elongated flaws, as well as volumetric and planar ones. With NDE methods that produce an image of the flaw, this is a simple task. An elongated flaw is usually defined as one in which the length is more than three times the width.

Flaws rarely occur in isolation, and their distribution and proximity to each other are important characteristics. Porosity may be isolated, clustered, or aligned. If it is aligned, then it is more significant than if it were random, because there is likely to be incomplete fusion.

The NDE methods that produce signals from the flaw are the most difficult to evaluate. In ultrasonic tests, the simplest method of evaluation is to use echo amplitude and length criteria only. This can lead to planar flaws being undersized, if they are poorly oriented in the ultrasound beam. It is therefore important, in an ultrasonic test, to first characterize the flaw and, in particular, to distinguish planar flaws from volumetric ones. The identification of planar flaws such as cracks and incomplete fusion primarily depends on the skill of the test operator, who considers the signal location, shape, response to probe movement, and relative amplitude from different sides of the weld and with different probe beam angles.

Volumetric flaws, on the other hand, can be evaluated in terms of signal amplitude and length. In some specifications, for example, if the signal amplitude exceeds the DAC set-off 3mm diameter holes, and the dB-drop length of the flaw exceeds the wall thickness of the weld, then the flaw is rejected as a defect.

The accept/reject criteria are usually set by a fabrication or manufacturing standard. In the past, these standards have been application specific.

● Vocabulary

nondestructive　*adj.* 无损的；非破坏性的
evaluation　*n.* 评价；评估；估价
discontinuity　*n.* 不连续；中断；间断性
flaw　*n.* 瑕疵，裂纹；缺陷　*vt.* 使破裂，使有缺陷
eddy-current　*n.* 涡流
acoustic　*adj.* 声学的；声的；声音的
maintenance　*n.* 维护，维修；保养
groove　*n.* 凹槽，槽；坡口　*vt.* 开槽于
feedback　*n.* 反馈；回馈
defective　*adj.* 有缺陷的；有缺点的　*n.* 次品

fluorescent　*adj.* 荧光的；萤光的；发亮的　*n.* 荧光；日光灯
infiltrate　*vt.* 使渗入，使浸润　*n.* 渗透；渗入；浸透
solvent　*adj.* 有溶解力的　*n.* 溶剂；溶解
abrasive　*adj.* 粗糙的；有研磨作用的　*n.* 研磨料；耐磨性
energizing　*v.* 活化；通电
validation　*n.* 确认；批准；校验
isolation　*n.* 隔离；隔离性；孤立；绝缘
undersized　比一般小的；尺寸过小的

Unit 14 Inspection of Welding

● **Questions**

1. What are the five principal test methods in nondestructive evaluation?
2. What are the useful distinctions between those NDE methods that are applied to welds during manufacturing?

Unit 15

Repair Welding

Repair and Maintenance of parts and components is a multibillion dollar industry. Repair welding can be carried out as a logical procedure that ensures the production of a usable and safe component or it can be approached haphazardly. The latter approach results in poor-quality workmanship and can lead to failed parts, large warranty claims, and dissatisfied customers.

It is to the advantage of the individual welder, job shop owner, end user, and others who depend on the weld repair industry to approach each repair with a thorough knowledge of component history in terms of:
- Component function.
- Material composition.
- Component surface or through hardness.
- Part originally cast, fabricated, or welded.

Repair welding can fall into one of three general categories: repair of weld defects, repair of failed parts, and repair of worn parts. This article describes the repair of weld defects and structural failures.

Requirements and repair techniques discussed in this article apply to arc and oxyfuel welding processes. Materials can be any that are usually joined successfully using arc or oxyfuel welding processes. Generally, the repair welding procedures will apply whether the structure is built under code construction specifications or not. Many construction codes require that a written procedure be prepared prior to any repair welding. Code or contractual requirements supersede any statements made in this article.

If the component to be repaired was originally a welded fabrication, then data and information on the original process are important to a successful repair. If access to this information is not practical, then an analysis of the base material, including previous weld deposits, becomes mandatory. If dimensions require close tolerances or if flatness is critical, then benchmarks that will aid the repair without causing excessive and expensive damage to the workpiece must be established.

Understanding the basics of each group of metals covered in this article helps to ensure a successful repair. All references and sources of information should be exhausted before any job commences. Excellent sources include filler-metal manufacturers and manufacturers of bar, plate, forgings, and castings. Either of these producers can supply key information on the weldability of the workpiece alloys.

Depending on the specific application, all of the common welding processes can be used for repair welding:
- Shielded metal arc welding (SMAW).

- Gas-metal arc welding (GMAW).
- Gas-tungsten arc welding (GTAW).
- Submerged arc welding (SAW).
- Plasma arc welding (PAW).

For the highest-quality welds, the GTAW and PAW processes find the widest application. For long runs or when a large amount of weld metal must be deposited and mechanization is feasible, the SAW process or, to a lesser extent, the GMAW process, is utilized. For general repairs, the SMAW process still enjoys the widest range of applications for outof-position welding and for short runs, especially when time is critical and when readily portable equipment is utilized. Electrodes are easily transported in sealed 4.5kg containers.

● Preliminary Assessment

Before attempting a repair, three factors must first be considered: material weldability, nature of the failure that prompted the repair, and involvement of any code requirements.

● Base Metal Weldability

If the item to be repaired was not welded previously, then a special investigation may be necessary to determine weldability. Original documents and drawings are helpful in determining the specifications or description of the base metal. Some tests that can determine degree of weldability include the spark test, chemical analysis test, and simulated weld tests.

The spark test determines the approximate base metal chemistry for carbon steels. Full chemical analysis using drillings can accurately determine chemistry, but not necessarily the heat treatment history of the base metal. Simulated weld tests can determine some practical approaches to repair welding, but seldom give any absolute requirements. These tests require samples of some of the base metal from the workpiece to be repaired.

● Nature of Failure

When designing and producing a successful repair, it is often necessary to assess the reasons that a repair is required. Failures can be grouped into four major categories:
- Base-metal defects.
- Base-metal strength deficiencies.
- Failures introduced during fabrication.
- Defects caused by abrasion, cavitation, corrosion, or erosion.

Base-Metal Defects. During or subsequent to fabrication, defects in the base metal may be detected. Defects can include pits, stringers, slivers, and a variety of internal discontinuities, the latter of which may be discovered when sawing through the base metal or subjecting the base metal to nondestructive testing (NDT).

Base-Metal Strength Deficiencies. Weld repair alone may not adequately repair a structure that has been overloaded. Reduction of load and additional reinforcing may be necessary. The loading and member arrangement should be thoroughly investigated. Repair of a crack or other structural discontinuity may involve repairing the crack as a weld repair and adding reinforcing plates or members to the workpiece by welding.

Weld Failure if Fabricated. Repair may be required on weld joints that have failed structurally or have undergone nondestructive evaluation (NDE), but do not meet soundness criteria. In these cases, it is usually prudent to prepare the joint for rewelding with procedures similar to the original welding operations.

Defects Caused by Abrasion, Cavitation, Corrosion, and Erosion. Buildup of the workpiece to repair surface damage that is due to abrasion, cavitation, corrosion, or erosion can be carried out as a weld repair. These conditions may or may not be associated with an original weld. The same weldability problems associated with structural repairs are encountered with the defects induced by these conditions.

● Codes and Standards

Repairs may be governed by welding or construction standards. Some codes address repair welding requirements as a specific subject and others simply require welding qualification that would apply to both new and repair welding.

● Welding Process Selection

When selecting a welding process for a specific application, several factors that affect productivity and weld quality must be balanced. Selection can be difficult because each process has a number of conflicting advantages and limitations in specific situations.

Productivity is usually not an important consideration on most repair jobs. Each process can be ranked in terms of its deposition rate in kilograms (pounds) of weld metal deposited per hour. However, there are other factors that must be considered, as a minimum, before selecting a welding process:

- Base-metal type.
- Joint design and thickness.
- Welding position.
- Environmental conditions.
- Equipment availability.

Base-Metal Type. Some processes are better suited for use with certain base materials. The maximum heat input must be limited on certain types of materials, such as heat-treated materials that have been quenched, tempered, and age hardened, as well as other heat-treated or cold-worked materials. Processes that derive their advantage from high productivity and high heat input may be unsuitable for these applications.

Joint Design and Thickness. As section thickness increases, welding productivity becomes more important, which should be reflected in the process selection. The length of the weld must also be considered, because a higher-productivity process may not realize this advantage, particularly if the operator must frequently stop the process in order to set up the next pass, as would be necessary with a small repair. Because some processes require more access to the joint root to avoid fusion defects, the selection of some processes may also require a joint design change.

Welding Position. The weld joint position is very important in terms of process selection, because many processes are limited to only a few positions. Whenever possible, the joint should be in the flat (1G) position, because the highest productivity and weld quality are attained when welding is accomplished in this position. Because most field repair work is done on large weldments that cannot be repositioned and because access to the joint is limited, the use of high-productivity processes and filler materials is also limited.

Environmental Conditions. Wind and rain are the two conditions that typically affect field welding. It takes very little wind to disturb the gas shield that is critical for high-quality GMAW and GTAW processes. This restricts their use outside of sheltered containments. The SMAW and FCAW processes can also be affected by wind, but to a lesser degree. Because no process ever tolerates direct exposure to rain, the proper placement of tarps, dams, or other temporary containments is in order.

Availability of Equipment. Most large welding shops have access to the welding equipment required for the processes discussed. However, there are occasions when new equipment must be evaluated to determine if its increased productivity or versatility would offset the capital expense of its initial cost and training.

● Base-Metal Preparation

Methods of preparing base metal for repair welding may vary, depending on the specific metal to be welded. Generally, all coatings in the vicinity of the repair weld should be removed. Coatings can cause defective welds and can become surface contaminants when heated to the temperatures required for welding.

Where cracks are to be excavated and the part rewelded, a welding groove should be prepared. Most base metals can be cut or grooved using air-carbon arc cutting (CAC-A).

● Vocabulary

workmanship n. 手艺，工艺；技巧
defect n. 缺点，缺陷；过失
weldability n. 焊接性；可焊性；焊接能力
cavitation n. 空化；汽蚀；穴蚀；气穴现象
pit n. 凹陷 vt. 使凹下 vi. 凹陷；起凹点
stringer n. 纵梁，纵桁
sliver n. 裂片 vt. 使成薄片；使裂成小片

sawing n. 锯切；锯削 v. 锯开；锯断
fabricated adj. 焊接的；组合的，装配式的
prudent adj. 谨慎的；精明的；节俭的
reposition vt. 使复位；改变……的位置 n. 复位；重新定位
containment n. 包含；牵制；容量；密闭度
oxyfuel 氧化燃料
benchmark n. 基准；标准检查程序

● Questions

1. What general categories can repair welding be fallen into?
2. What factors should be considered before attempting a repair welding?

Unit 16

Characterization and Modeling of the Heat Source

The Heat That is Supplied to The Workpiece, which then is transferred within the workpiece to produce melting, forms the basis of every welding process. The heat-transfer process, or thermal cycle, in the weldment has many consequences, including the complex metallurgical changes that take place in the fusion zone, where the metal is liquefied and subsequently solidified, and in the adjacent heat-affected zone, where material is heated to temperatures that are below the melting point, but are sufficiently high to produce changes in the microstructure and in mechanical properties.

The description of the input-energy source is basic to any numerical modeling formulation designed to predict the outcome of the welding process. Both the magnitude and distribution of the source are fundamental and unique to each joining process, and the resultant output of any numerical model is therefore affected by the initial description of the heat source. An understanding of both the physics and the mathematical simulation of these sources is essential for characterizing the heat source. This article briefly reviews the physical phenomena that influence the input-energy distribution and discusses several simplified and detailed heat-source models that have been used in the modeling of arc welding, high-energy-density welding, and resistance welding processes.

● Simplified Modeling of the Heat Source

Analytical modeling of the welding heat source is generally complex, because of the nature of energy transfer to the workpiece, whether the source of that energy is an arc, a high-energy-density beam of electrons or laser light, or joule heating. For numerical modeling purposes, heat input to the weldment is usually applied as a distribution of surface flux, a distribution of heat generated internally, or a combination of both. Many analytical treatments, however, have sought to simplify the characterization of the heat source by assuming that the effective thermal energy supplied by the heat source is deposited in such a narrow band of material that it may be idealized mathematically as a point or a line source, depending on the geometry of the weldment. Heat input idealizations of this sort lend themselves to the derivation of closed-form welding temperature solutions and the avoidance of developing numerical finite-element or finite-difference models to calculate temperatures. These solutions are valid only for simple geometries and in regions removed from the fusion and heat-affected zones, where details of the distribution of heat input from the source and accurate representations of the thermal energy transferred from the weld bead to the rest of the weld joint are not important.

The fundamental simplified heat-source model is developed for a flat plate of infinite extent bounded by the planes $z = 0$ and $z = h$. Heat is input at a point that is either stationary or is moving at uniform speed, v, in the x direction on the surface $z = 0$, so that at any time, t, the point source is located at $x = vt$ (Fig. 3-27). If the end effects that result from the initiation or termination of the heat source or the finite dimensions of the weldment are neglected, then the resulting temperature distribution associated with the moving source is stationary with respect to a moving coordinate system, the origin of which coincides with the point of application of the heat source. This class of temperature response is termed "quasi-stationary".

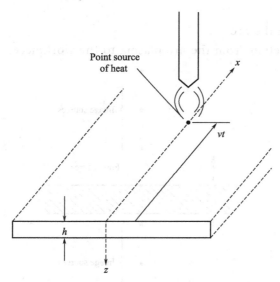

Fig. 3-27 Moving point source in infinite plate

In general, for either a stationary or a moving point source, heat is conducted through the plate without hindrance until the insulating effect of the ideally adiabatic surface at $z = h$ is felt. For a sufficiently thick plate, the temperature rise at $z = h$ is so small that the solution for an infinitely thick plate, which is associated with a single source of heat, is applicable. For a moderately thick plate, the temperature rise at $z = h$ from the infinitely thick plate point source solution is large enough to result in nonzero heat flow at $z = h$. An image source of the same strength applied at $z = 2h$ ensures that the surface zh is adiabatic. However, the image source produces nonzero heat flow at $z = 0$, and another image source applied at $z = -2h$ is now required to satisfy conditions at $z = 0$.

Carrying this imposition of image point sources of heat along ad infinitum (Fig. 3-28), an infinite distribution of image sources superposed with the original source at $z = 0$ yields the desired adiabatic conditions at both the $z = 0$ and $z = h$ surfaces. The temperature solution for this series of image sources is in the form of an infinite series, which converges more rapidly for thicker plates. The solution for the moderately thick plate applies to thin plates as well, but convergence of the infinite series would be extremely slow. As an alternative, the heat source can be applied as a line source distributed uniformly through the thickness. This approach eliminates any variation of the temperature distribution through the thickness, and is often used model high-energy-density welding processes that result in the formation of a keyhole, as will be discussed later.

Arc Welding

Gas-tungsten arc welding (GTAW) is the most frequently modeled arc-welding process in which the heat source is a nonconsumable electrode. In the direct current electrode negative GTAW process, the pieces of material are joined together by energy that is transferred to the workpiece by four primary mechanisms:

- Kinetic energy of the electrons that constitute the arc current.
- Heat of condensation of the electrons (work function) penetrating the solid work surface.
- Radiation from the arc.
- Thermal conduction from the arc plasma to the workpiece.

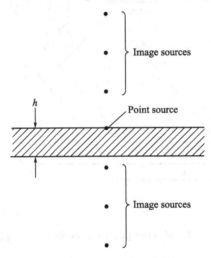

Fig. 3-28 Superposition of image sources in finite-thickness plate

Because of the complicated nature in which energy is transferred from the arc, heat input to the weldment can be modeled by one of the point- or line-source approaches. If none of these treatments is appropriate for the particular application, then a more realistic approach is to input the energy by a distribution of surface flux, a distribution of heat generated internally, or a combination of the two. If an internal heat distribution is confined to a thin layer of material adjacent to the heated surface, then the choice of heat-input model is immaterial. The magnitude of heat input to the workpiece is expressed simply as the product of what has traditionally been defined as the arc power (that is, the product of the voltage drop across the arc and the arc current) and a factor called the arc efficiency, which accounts for energy losses from the arc.

Estimates of arc efficiency can be made by correlating computed temperatures with thermocouple readings from test welds, making calorimeter measurements for a specific set of welding conditions, or utilizing some other observable response to the welding thermal cycle. Because the voltage used is usually determined from measurements at some point within the power supply, estimates need to be made to account for losses within the electrode and other parts of the system. Changes in welding process variables, such as shielding gas, electrode configuration, arc gap, and minor element additions to the arc, all affect arc efficiency, as does the material that is being welded.

● High-Energy-Density Welding

In modeling the heat source for high-energy-density welding, one first needs to determine the type of welding process being formulated. Depending on the weld parameters, high-energy-density welding can simulate either a conduction-mode weld process or a keyhole weld process. If a strict conduction-mode weld process is being modeled, then the energy density will be low enough to prevent intense vaporization of the material. All of the energy of the beam is deposited directly on the surface of the weldment as a heat flux, similar to that discussed in terms of the GTAW process. The major difference between this mode of welding and that of arc welding is in the magnitude and distribution of the heat source. In laser-beam welding, the input-energy distribution is very dependent on the operational mode of the laser system.

Fig. 3-29 shows several shapes of the source distribution that can be present at any one time. The fundamental transverse electromagnetic mode, TEM_{00} (a Gaussian distribution), is often selected as the heat-input description for conduction welding. It is also assumed to be the source distribution for electron-beam welding. The exact determination of the Gaussian width parameter, r', depends on the optics of the laser-or electron-beam welding system. In many cases, a point source on the surface is an excellent approximation. In laser-beam welding, if the energy is delivered via a fiber-optic system, then the output source distribution is often described as a truncated Gaussian source distribution of specified width. However, the beam exiting a fiber-optic system has been examined, and the output-energy distribution is reported to depend on the incident angle of the beam into the fiber. A variety of output configurations can be obtained as a function of the angle.

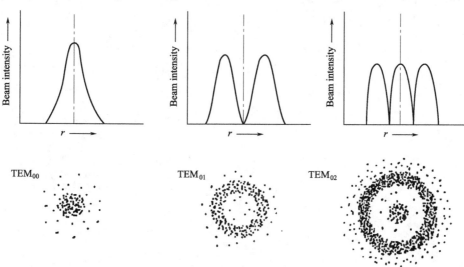

Fig. 3-29 Appearance of laser beam for three different transverse electromagnetic modes (tem)

Some laser systems, such as the multikilowatt carbon-dioxide laser, operate with the TEM_{01} as the dominant mode. This donut shape (Fig. 3-29) has been used very effectively for specific welding operations. Other laser systems may display a combination of these modes (for example, TEM$_{02}$), as well as higher-order modes. Beam analyzers are currently being employed to measure the precise distribution of the laser input energy to the weldment.

● **Vocabulary**

outcome   n. 结果，结局；输出
joining   n. 连接；接缝；连接物
resultant   n. 合力；合成；结果   adj. 结果的；合成的
modeling   n. 建模，造型   adj. 制造模型的
joule   n. 焦耳
hindrance   n. 障碍；妨碍；阻碍物
adiabatic   adj. 绝热的；隔热的

nonzero   adj. 非零的
convergence   n. 收敛；会聚，集合
condensation   n. 冷凝；凝结；压缩
calorimeter   n. 热量计；量热器
optics   n. 光学；光学器件
truncated   adj. 切去顶端的   v. 缩短；截断；截去……的顶端
incident   adj. 入射的；附带的

● **Questions**

1. How to simplify the modeling of the heat source in analytical treatment?
2. What approaches can be used to model the heat input to the weldment in arc welding?
3. What is the major difference between this mode of welding and that of arc welding?

References

[1] ASM Handbook, 9th ed., ASM International, 1992.
[2] R. J. Gettens. The Freer Chinese Bronzes, Vol II, Technical Studies. Washington, DC, 1969, 79.
[3] Steel Castings Handbook, 5th ed., 1980.
[4] Iron Castings Handbook, 3rd ed., 1981, p 38.
[5] 张军. 材料专业英语译写教程 [M]. 北京：化学工业出版社, 2003.
[6] J. K. Lee and H. I. Aaronson. in Lectures on the Theory of Phase Transformations, H. I. Aaronson, Ed., The Metallurgical Society, 1975.
[7] J. H. Hollomon and D. Turnbull. Prog. Met. Phys. 1953, 4.
[8] J. H. Perepezko. Mater. Sci. Eng., 1984, 65.
[9] D. Turnbull. The Liquid State and the Liquid-Solid Transition, Trans. AIME, 1961, 221.
[10] W. Kurz and D. J. Fisher. Fundamentals of Solidification. Trans. Tech. Publications, 1984.
[11] M. A. Eshelman, V. Seetharaman, and R. Trivedi. Cellular Spacings—I. Steady State Growth, Acta Metall., 1988, 36.
[12] M. C. Flemings. Solidification Processing. McGraw-Hill, 1974.
[13] J. D. Verhoeven. Fundamentals of Physical Metallurgy. John Wiley & Sons, 1975.
[14] J. D. Hunt. Primary Dendrite Spacing in Solidification and Casting of Metals. Book 192, The Metals Society, 1979.
[15] S. C. Huang and M. E. Glicksman. Fundamentals of Dendritic Solidification, Acta Metall., 1981, 29.
[16] T. Altan, S. I. Oh, and H. L. Gegel. Metal Forming: Fundamentals and Applications, American Society for Metals, 1983.
[17] K. Lange, Ed. Machine Tools for Metal Forming, and Forging. in Handbook of Metal Forming, McGraw-Hill, 1985.
[18] H. Lippmann. Engineering Plasticity: Theory of Metal Forming Processes. Springer Verlag, 1977, 2.
[19] E. Erman et al. "Physical Modeling of Upsetting Process in Open-Die Press Forging", Paper presented at the 116th TMS/AIME Annual Meeting, Denver, CO, The Metallurgical Society, 1987.
[20] G. Rau. A Die Forging Press With a New Drive, Met. Form., 1967.
[21] Engineers Handbook, Vol 1 and 2, VEB Fachbuchverlag, 1965 (in German).
[22] The Forming of Galvanized Sheet Steels: Guidelines for Automotive Applications, American Iron and Steel Institute, 1986.
[23] Tool and Manufacturing Engineers Handbook, Volume 2, Forming, Society of Manufacturing Engineers, 1984.
[24] A. J. Medland and P. Burnett. CAD/CAM In Practice. John Wiley & Sons, 1986.
[25] H. O. McCormick. CAD/CAM for Automotive Die Design. Society of Manufacturing Engineers, 1977.
[26] Statistical Quality Control Handbook, Western Electric Company, 1977.
[27] J. F. Siekirk. Process Variable Effects on Sheet Metal Quality, J. Appl. Metalwork., 1986, 4 (3).
[28] N. M. Wang and S. Tang, Ed.. Computer Modeling of Sheet Metal Forming Processes: Theory, Verification, and Application. The Metallurgical Society, 1986.
[29] H. R. Daniels. Mechanical Press Handbook. 3rd ed.. Cahners Publishing, 1969.
[30] N. S. Boulton and H. E. Lance-martin. Residual stresses in arc welded plates. Proc. Inst. Mech. Eng., 1986, 33.
[31] D. Rosenthal and R. Schmerber. Thermal study of arc welding, Weld. J., Vol 17, 1983.
[32] P. G. Kogan. The temperature field in the weld zone, Ave. Svarka, Vol 4, 1979.
[33] J. H. Devletion and W. E. Wood. Vol 6, Metals Handbook, 9th ed., American Society for Metals, 1983.
[34] W. Kurz and D. J. Fisher. Fundamentals of Solidification, 3rd ed.. Trans Tech, 1989.
[35] P. Burgardt and R. D. Campbell. Chemistry Effects on Stainless Steel Weld Penetration. Ferrous Alloy Weldments, Trans Tech Publications, Switzerland, 1992.
[36] K. C. Mills and B. J. Keene. Factors Affecting Variable Weld Penetration. Int. mater. Review, 1990, 35.
[37] H. B. Cary. Modern Welding Technology. 2nd ed.. Prentice-hall, 1989.
[38] "Specification for Carbon Steel Electrodes for Flux Cored Arc Welding", AWS, 1979.
[39] K. J. Pfahl. Automatic Contour Welding of Tube and Pipe, Tube Pipe Q., 1992, 3.
[40] Brazing Handbook, 4th ed., American Welding Society, 1991.

[41] R. Skipp. Soldering Handbook. BSP Professional Books, 1988.
[42] M. J. Donachie, ed.. Titanium: A Technical Guide, ASM International, 1988.
[43] C. L. Tsai, O. A. Jammal, J. C. Papritan, and D. W. Dickinson. Modeling of Resistance Spot Weld Nugget Growth, Weld. J. RES. Suppl. , FEB 1992.
[44] H. S. Carslaw and J. C. Jaeger. Conduction of Heat in Solids. Clarendon Press, London, 1959.